ACKNOWLEDGMENTS

Words from the Soul draws from my fifteen years' experience with "spiritual emergence" as Director of the Kundalini Clinic (founded by Lee Sannella in 1977 as the first transpersonally oriented counseling service in the United States) and another eleven years working in school, geriatrics, psychiatric crisis, juvenile probation, developmentally disabled, mediation, and correctional settings, and teaching and supervising trainees at the graduate level. As well, I draw from twenty-five years of personal *kundalini yoga* experience and close instruction with several "full-time" (ten hours per day for thirty years) *yogis*, and from the intimate experience of assisting in the translation of commentaries on the *Hathayogapradipika* with one of them.

I thank S. Kripalvanand, S. Vinit-muni, S. Rajarsri-muni, and Baba Hari Dass, and others for rare *yogic* teachings. For academic and writing support I acknowledge G. Feuerstein, M. Vich, K. Hoeller, M. Foucault, M. Jordan, A. Bodin, the Association for Transpersonal Psychology, and the Kundalini Research Network. For clinical input I thank K. Bradford, H. Streitfeld, M. Kahn, J. Rosberg, the staff and clients at Gateway Institute, Blue Oak Counseling, and the Kundalini Clinic, and my students at John F. Kennedy University (and for a research grant in 1995), Rosebridge Institute, and the California Institute of Integral Studies. I thank S. Sheats for combining *anahata-nada* with fusion-jazz forms in the ensemble, *Sushumna*, the ten years with the Orinda Chanting Mandal, and one year with Cantor Rubin for training in *nigune*. I thank my editors, R. Mann, Susan Geraghty, Kay Bolton, and referees at State University of New York Press for their input and belief in this project.

WORDS FROM THE SOUL

SUNY Series in Transpersonal and Humanistic Psychology
Richard D. Mann, Editor

WORDS FROM THE SOUL

Time, East/West Spirituality, and Psychotherapeutic Narrative

STUART SOVATSKY

State University
of New York
Press

Pages 102–103: 25 lines (p. 114) from *Leaves of Grass* by Walt Whitman (New York: Signet, 1958).

Pages 149 and 167: 12 lines (pp. 168, 147) from *Speaking of Siva* translated by A. K. Ramanujan (Penguin Classics, 1973) copyright © A. K. Ramanujan, 1973. Reproduced by permission of Penguin Books, Ltd.

Page 35: First 5 lines from "The First Elegy," from *Duino Elegies* by Rainer Maria Rilke, translated by David Young. Translation copyright © 1978 by W. W. Norton & Company, Inc. Reprinted by permission of W. W. Norton & Company, Inc.

Pages 24 and 31–32: 21 lines (pp. 12 and 85) from *Knots* by R. D. Laing. Copyright © 1970 by R. D. Laing. Reprinted by permission of Pantheon Books, a division of Random House, Inc.

Page 153: 5 lines (p. 122) from *The Essential Rumi*, translated by C. Barks with J. Moyne (San Francisco: Harper, 1996). Copyright © 1996. Reproduced by permission of Coleman Barks.

Published by
State University of New York Press, Albany

© 1998 State University of New York

All rights reserved

Production by Susan Geraghty
Marketing by Fran Keneston

Printed in the United States of America

No part of this book may be used or reproduced in any manner whatsoever without written permission. No part of this book may be stored in a retrieval system or transmitted in any form or by any means including electronic, electrostatic, magnetic tape, mechanical, photocopying, recording, or otherwise without the prior permission in writing of the publisher.

For information, address State University of New York Press, State University Plaza, Albany, N.Y., 12246

Library of Congress Cataloging-in-Publication Data

Sovatsky, Stuart, 1949–
    Words from the soul : time, east/west spirituality, and psychotherapeutic narrative / Stuart Sovatsky.
        p.   cm. — (SUNY series in transpersonal and humanistic psychology)
    Includes bibliographical references and index.
    ISBN 0-7914-3949-6 (hardcover : alk. paper). — ISBN 0-7914-3950-X (pbk. : alk. paper)
    1. Transpersonal psychology. I. Title. II. Series.
BF204.7.S68 1998
150.19′8—dc21   97-47049
                                                                                                 CIP

10 9 8 7 6 5 4 3 2 1

CONTENTS

Acknowledgments	*vii*
Introduction: Toward a Spiritual Psychotherapy	*1*
Chapter 1 Questioning Words—Reviving Time	11
Chapter 2 Revenge against Impermanence: Temporal-Spiritual Psychopathology	111
Chapter 3 Maturation of the Ensouled Body: Kundalini Yoga and the Far Reaches of Human Development	141
Chapter 4 Spiritual Emergence: Toward a Spirituality-Inclusive Psychopathology	179
Notes	*199*
Glossary of Yogic Terms	*209*
Bibliography	*213*
Index	*227*

INTRODUCTION

Toward a Spiritual Psychotherapy

Thank you—I forgive you—I wish—You're so wonderful!—How unfortunately tragic!—Wow, can this last forever? Gratitude, forgiveness, longing, praise-love, compassion, and awe of the Eternal. Known in the Judeo-Christian traditions as soteriological or "redemptive-healing" sentiments and central to all world religions, these affects comprise a spiritual path of expressive feelings that is purported to extend from the utterly mundane to the most ecstatic and saintly of heights. But what makes them special or redeeming? And redeeming into *what*? And most practically, how might we tap their greater potencies, specifically within the contemporary "paths of redemptive expression" of psychotherapy?

A facile answer is that these are the sentiments of "the soul" while various degrees of hopelessness, cynicism, or vengefulness ("psychopathology") are in need of redeeming. That is, they are the essence of conscientious life at heart capable of prevailing over various personal difficulties. And when I focus on the dramatic ardour of forgiveness and apology overcoming resentment and vengeance, or hope and longing overcoming despair, I become convinced that these sentiments are something remarkable. I erase the ironic quotation marks and wonder: If this (which I call a) longing or forgiving feeling *is* of the *soul*, then by traditional lore, it is a hint of inexhaustible goodness, even immortality. I feel drawn into a vast and mysterious spiritual context where extraordinary powers are purported to dwell.

Here, perhaps, is the beginning of a soul psychology with possibilities that clinical insight or catharses themselves might be *for* the *sake of*. For when I next thank (instead of bypass expressing any gratitude), feel compassion (instead of disregard or pity), apologize (instead of falsely defending myself), or forgive (instead of blaming) someone, I feel a warm glow. I sense that I have done *something significant*, perhaps even noble. So, *are these* feelings the beginning of a spiritual *path* through life's uncertain way?—that is, a maturational progression leading *to* the greatest of human possibilities? How can these (merely?) polite sentiments unfold *that* far?

When I recall certain experiences of *kundalini* yoga (my own or others' I have researched), I am compelled to believe that the core sentiment is awe—a soothing, ecstatic, daunting awe of the vast Eternal, awe of one another, or of something profound. Seemingly derived from the physical yoga practices, I consider the body—its glands, nerves, energies, and, particularly, the spinal channel *sushumna* ("path where Eternal Grace flows")—to be the anatomical substrate of this maturational path. I consider the body to be more than mere flesh, much more. The other sentiments seem almost *designed* to honor perfectly any poignant beauties or to true wisely any troubling situation back toward time as Grace and in such a way as to mature us in the very process. Indeed, even the most horrific problems seem, tragically, only to be the ever-compounding consequences of under- or misapplied soteriological truings, a spiritual twist to Hannah Arendt's austere observation that mere sustained "thoughtlessness" is what underlies even holocaust-scale evils.

At weddings, births, funerals, and other momentous events this awe arises, most certainly. Grudges are dropped, hopes soar, sublimity arises—at least temporarily. And, in considering more subtle shades of awe, I recall the poignant longing of a frankly psychotic client who, in a moment of cogency, asks of the fates, "I just want to fight traffic with everybody else to get home to the wife and kids." Even in a homeward-bound traffic jam a sense of the shared flow of life impermanent can breed hope in someone bereft and longing.

But when I skeptically wonder: *If* these simple sentiments are so potent, why do historical horrors loom so heavily? I begin to scoff and now consider the above as mere self-talk, as moralistic superego "shoulds" that verify no such thing as "a true course" or an "immortal soul." In the face of war, abuse, and severe psychopathology, my previous "wisdom" feels embarrassingly naive. With modest problems, the sentiments might work fine enough, but certainly not in these extreme situations. But, if situations become so extreme through a sustained lack of soteriological concern, perhaps such a retracing of our steps *is* the spiritual path to their resolution and to our own fullest maturation.

Thus, when I have noticed or brought praise, forgiveness, and the like, into my clinical work in a wide range of situations, undeniable momentary progress would invariably occur—and then wither impermanently away. But instead of faulting these sentiments and giving up on them in favor of more complex analyses, I accepted impermanence as our given condition. I let in the fact or sense that all passes and shared this observation with my clients as our common condition, a condition whose demand on us to merely persevere was exactly what matured us and, to a great degree, regardless of previous deprivations. I questioned the psychoanalytic scoff that such impermanent results indicated "shallowness." Indeed, I esteemed impermanence as ontological, as profound, as entering (finally!) into the problematics of "real time" that is elusive, happening, and takes arduous attentive and linguistic "keeping up with" to stay in it. And this deep "it," so-called presence—what goes on in *its* depths?

Glimmers of eyes, quavers of voice, sheer sharing of time—in such fleeting subtleties a kind of subatomic world of myriad, soteriological possibilities emerged. For, in this (more real?) fleeting time, a preciousness prompts cultivating what is *most* hoped for. Thus, I would see (or merely imagine?) nasceant ideal outcomes spark within intense client struggles and in various ways would fan their glow into a flicker and then a flame.

With humor, persuasion, or emotional confrontations, I would doggedly guide embittered couples into looking at each other a few seconds longer to see an innuendo of hope or a nuance of apologetic shame that their own shyness or vengefulness would have averted them from seeing. Tears of anguished appreciation would quake when, a moment ago, divorce loomed. I repeated my praises in various ways until skeptical or shy clients finally believed me. "Oh, so this is what 'getting a need met' is like! *This* letting-it-in is what I want more of in my life!" After another and another thanking, praising, or confrontive apologizing moments of optimism would quaver; hopefulness and confidence would arise. Clients would take new actions in their lives and progress impermanently. By ministering to this reformulated "superego as soul," the ego would take heart and grow inspired.

The constant flickerings of soteriological or soul sentiments revealed ironic emotionalities such as "longings negatively stated" hidden in the verbiage of angry complaints. "Grief and hope" was another frequent oscillation. Conventional psychopathologies appeared as permutations of hopeless cynicism, vengeance, and highly compromising sadomasochistic—as in the hot pleasures of "Fuck-you's!" and "I'm outta here's!"—emotionalities.

Trapped in adaptive self-justifications at some colder distance from the soteriological sentiments, these anguished pleasures would grow into mockeries of the soul sentiments. Righteousness, humility, guilt, and shame devolved from their spiritual modes into demeaned contortions of self-righteous blaming and humiliating oneself and others. Here, the religious penitents and Jobs of yore emerged clothed in the half-lurid, off-the-rack language of pop psychology ("original pain," "shame based") instead of the hair shirt. Yet, the noble struggles with hope, forgiveness, and awe of the impermanent continued.

I also began to see that the conventional clinical vocabulary of the same few emotion descriptors (anger, sadness, pain, fear), the common diagnostic terms (anxiety, depression, psychosis, personality disorder), analytic terms (unconscious intention, resistance, transference/countertransference, superego, id, ego, abandonment anxiety) and pop psychology terms (codependency, caretaking, inner child) was unable to grasp the more mutable, hopeful, and interactive aspects of what I saw occuring in this so fleeting temporality. Indeed, the overuse of these terms was revealing undesired iatrogenic effects that various critics of psychotherapy also saw.

Thus, in pursuing this more spiritually oriented psychotherapy, we must also turn a critical ear toward the prevailing psychoanalytically derived therapies and their popularizations, even their spiritually oriented ones. We will need to break a kind of spell that these theories have cast, leaving therapists and clients to believe them without question as if someone, somewhere, did actually prove them when such has never been the case. Of course, this is what psychoanalysis claimed as well: to break "unconscious" guilt-inducing spells cast by religion or others that had become symptomatic and limiting. But now as the pendulum of diminishing returns swings again, it is any limitations or iatrogenics within these therapies that we must uncover.

To do so requires special efforts equal to the binding power of the psychoanalytic "spell" that operates at subtle levels of assumption. Otherwise there would be no spell to these theories, which many others have shown is simply not the case: all "talking cures"—psychoanalytic or soteriological—are systems of educative persuasion, belief, faith, and ethically pragmatic results. Thus, it is important to state the matter clearly and to delineate the assumptions of any talking cure: *what* words and narrative practices each puts its faith *in*. And the more deterministic or invariant any treatise depicts its own assumptions, (mere) observations, or (contrived) methods, the more watchful we might need to be.

And tapping greater degrees of spiritual powers requires the arduous efforts of breaking through cynicisms or any leveling, normative concerns that might make us doubt that we could ever be heroic and certainly not saintly. Furthermore, from the soteriological perspective and inverse to the psychoanalytic-medical model, we will see our spiritual *progress* in these very attainments, not merely our injuries, as fomenting some of the greatest developmental difficulties. And "the past" is less than useful in explaining these difficulties of awakening—but awakening into *what*?

Thus, transpersonalists have coined the term *spiritual emergency*, now softened to the euphemism of *spiritual emergence*, to refer to difficulties resulting *from* enlightening experiences (with their own resistances to progress) and even noted rudimentarily in the DSM-IV. Instead of being a rarified phenomenon, I am suggesting we view all psychopathology as spiritual emergence: the maturing struggle to apologize, forgive, know gratitude, and awaken a little more to the vast, eternal impermanence in which our daily lives take place. Through such maturation, the (now overly focused upon) "ego" develops, not through a "restoration from woundedness," but characterologically, via this deepened soul-superego. To borrow from the Yiddish: Through the soulful sentiments and in acceptance and forgiveness of suffering one becomes not a self or an ego, but a *mensch*—a soulful person, who has overcome herself and her sorrow.

To accomplish the difficult task of breaking word spells, I draw from Wittgenstein's linguistic "perspicuity" (what he himself called a method of "psychotherapy," Russell noted positively as "mystical" and Sontag called a "spiritual practice"), a contribution that broke certain spells in Western philosophy and changed its very course. And like the spell-breaking zen *koan*, reading Wittgenstein's writings takes the very effort necessary to develop a liberating, perspicuous way of describing and perceiving things—a way that Wittgenstein too claimed leads to a deep silence (quiet awe). Without this effort (or texts that require it), we are in danger of performing the mere rewordings known as "cognitive reframing" or what is known in the street vernacular as bullshitting oneself or others with psychobabble.

There are two tasks in which such perspicuous efforts will be called for in reading this text:

1. *To grasp when terms such as* anger, pain, need, *or* abandonment *are unwittingly and iatrogenically misused within the "talking cure."* Here I am arguing for a deconstruction of jargon and an expansion of a psychological vocabulary that has otherwise gone maudlin, if not sadomasochistic. For example, we will find that the concept of a *need to be met* is often used when there is hardly any credible sense of necessity to the (so-called) need beyond one's willful entoned demand. Here the effects of the absence of various soteriological sentiment terms from the clinical vocabulary is crucial too.

2. *To continually revive the sense of time passage from the stultifying effects of reading printed texts, of certain narrative/rhetorical structures, and, most blatantly, through the psychoanalytic hallmark preoccupation with an etiological, overly deterministic developmental past.* Even the popular existential/spiritual phrase "being (fully) present" can disguise the profound awe of impermanence with a conclusive, almost cliched, and too-easy mundaneity. Thus, to point toward this more elusive-to-the-word "deep present," I will employ various grammatic, poetic, and typographic devices.

To keep vivid the sense of time as a flow of impermanence, I will at times use convoluted or run-on sentences and strings of hyphenated emotion descriptors to help convey the continuous, even incessant, flux of emotional, attitudinal, and behavioral changes that can be underrepresented in simpler sentence structures. For it is within various shifting ambiguities, fleeting ironies, or subtle innuendos that some degree of engageable hope might be discerned when, a split second ago, conventional therapies would have us see/name only a repeating pattern of "unmet needs" from the past or a kind of pain, projection, or anxiety. In such syntactic complexity, the power of a too-coherent narrative with its trapped protagonist can give way. The pondersome length of some sentences aims to *engender* the soaring-deepening state their words depict.

Where parentheticals and further bracketed parentheticals appear, read it as a kind of hypertext. Imagine looking through a zoom microscope into the interstitial layers of words, emotions, situations, which can zoom in and out, again and again. For in those nested subtleties we can hear how commonly used words or ambiguous metaphors slightly misconstrued derail the therapeutic project toward iatrogenia, ending up giving therapy a bad name.

I employ an aphoristic, brief paragraph format in chapter 1 to simulate a stitched-together (Wittgensteinesque) patchwork of neighboring observations that float near one another, not chaotic, but also not forged to some structural undergirding logic into an airtight system. When they appear, see unannounced thematic shifts woven through the text as shows of freedom. It is *a kind of* seeing, feeling, acting, and time sense that might show itself through the aesthetic of this format. A "living" kind that a long-paragraph-built text, built as if from a predetermined blueprint, can too much lull. For, as Wittgenstein mused, languages are "forms of *life.*"

Where flash-forwards in the first chapter appear introducing material on kundalini yoga from chapter 3, imagine looking into a telescope that brings developmental eventualities rare and distant into seeming and perhaps shocking proximity to what is near at hand. For, according to the kundalini developmental anatomy, we are all at each moment physically and spiritually maturing toward those inherent possibilities of, let us say, evolutionary or teleological proportions. The whole of adulthood emerges as developmentally potent as psychoanalytic childhood, thus lightening the hermeneutic burden conventional therapy has placed upon "the formative years" to explain adult difficulties.

And, like certain famed astronomical observations, the yogic phenomena portend a remapping of our most core assumptions regarding identity, the role of language, and the body—beginning with the transformative "spinal puberty" of kundalini awakening itself. Something of "the absolute" comes into view, as unfashionable as that possibility may be in a postmodern age of sheer relativity. The messiah? She is us, someday, and a little bit everyday, for she is humanity seen, finally, with reverence.

Yet, on the grittier side of such ultimate possibilities as kundalini awakening, we hear that the liberal agenda of social services has "failed." As my work maintains, it is in part the psychoanalytically derived methods used in such "soft service" programs that have run aground. As Hillman, Lasch, Kaminer, and others assert, the therapeutic cult of hyperindividualism distanced many from contemporary social causes and from their own resilience. Yet, the failure of the soteriological sentiments to inspire us beyond a three-strikes punitive mentality is also telling. Curiously, by drawing more deeply from these most traditional of virtues in constructing a revised therapeutic map, the noble hopes of liberalism might move effectively forward.

For, much of analytic psychology arose because the soteriological sentiments had not been abstracted from sectarian religions into a universal "spiritual psychology," nor seen as just as endogenous to us as anger, sorrow, or desire (maybe even more endogenous), and taken far enough into resolving human problems with the careful skill necessary to obtain undeniable success. Further, the Judeo-Christain emphasis upon the sentiments of guilt and forgiveness and suffering and compassion over the centuries has bequested us a soteriology skewed away from joy and sensual delight. In comparison to kundalini yoga, Western religions have underexplored the soteriological potencies of the body, also contributing to a sense that the sentiments are not truly endogenous, and perhaps not even "spiritual."

Thus, the soulful powers were separated conceptually from "the self," externalized (as cultural rules), despiritualized (as compromised products of "sublimation") and misrepresented as being mere "introjected superego controls" that "repress" the "truth of instinctive life." But, as humans are seen as essentially spiritually developing bodily beings, the superego returns to the ground of our consciousness as "soul," and its sentiments as hormonally endogenous. A soteriological psychology serves as a map to their ever-maturing, hormonal emotionalities and radiances. Thus, the centrist slogan of "family values" is given a way to foster its ideals of cohesiveness and mutual respect, whether in gay or single-parent, nuclear-straight, or blended families.

Of course, psychoanalysis has come a long way since Freud. Contemporary interest in spirituality, "the present," mutuality, and in the *intersubjective field* (the jargonized term for a more two-way therapeutic relating), is consistent with various aspects of a soteriological psychology, as is the shift from drive theories to social-affect theories. Should "the present" be seen as an inexplicable, awesome impermanence, even greater interest in the soteriological sentiments might arise. For the present might be more than potential space. And should the body be granted more of a role in adult psychological development, then interest in kundalini yoga could also quicken. Indeed, based on recent research findings, it already has.

And perhaps there are better words (or *yogas*) somewhere, someday, that can do with even greater precision and efficacy what medications do expeditiously yet with undeniable compromise for those who, at this time in the state of the art, are seen as requiring them. Call it "spiritual emergence" or whatever, some get relief at this time only with medications. Yet better methods might very well be found in the simplest of immediacies taken to a high level of thoughtful sensitivity again and again and again.

OVERVIEW

In chapter 1, *Questioning Words, Reviving Time*, I critique prevailing past-oriented psychotherapies and the linguistic devices that protect them from scrutiny and obscure their possible side effects. I also offer a more temporally balanced, past-present-future psychotherapy based in such spiritual sentiments as past-rectifying apology, forgiveness, missing, forebearance, and gratitude; the poignantly fleeting impermanent present (the "living spirit"); and future-oriented faith, uncertainty, awe, dread, longing, devotion, and the advanced maturational stages of kundalini yoga. I posit an inexhaustible yet nonomnipotently hopeful soul as the fundamental human essence, and time passage itself as the primordial soteriological power. A perspicuous attunement to the impermanent flickerings of soul hopefulness is presented as the therapist's primary task. I address how this soteriological therapy can avoid various pitfalls that might be concerns of the conventionalist.

Chapter 2, *Revenge against Impermanence: Temporal-Spiritual Psychopathology*, I consider the resistance to the passage of impermanence that Nietzsche described as "the spirit of revenge" and difficulties with the ominous powers of apology and forgiveness as fundamental "spiritual psychopathologies" and trace these difficulties to their antitemporal depths in the suicidal narrative and its linguistic subtleties.

In chapter 3, *The Ensouled Body: Kundalini Yoga and the Far Reaches of Human Development*, I ground this soteriological psychology in a "spiritual neurophysiology" as described in kundalini yoga. I address the difficulties of fathoming the *yogic body* faced by transpersonal psychology, which has focused primarily on Eastern theories of consciousness. I introduce the concept of *postgenital puberties* to depict the full impact of kundalini awakening on identity, physiology, and emotionality.

In chapter 4, *Spiritual Emergence: Toward a Spirituality-Inclusive Psychopathology*, I discuss "spiritual emergence," the "transcendence or psychosis" diagnostic debate, and the innovative opportunities of the *DSM-IV*, including the V Code for "Religious Issues."

CHAPTER 1

Questioning Words—Reviving Time

> "There is another solution as well" means: there is something else that I am prepared to call a "solution."
> —Wittgenstein, *Philosophical Investigations*, p. 140

INTRODUCTION

In this chapter, I reconsider from a philosophical/spiritual perspective many elements of psychotherapy that, unfortunately, have become known among therapists, clinical instructors, supervisors, interns, and many clients as "the basics." This includes:

1. Ubiquitous and priviledged past referencing and transference interpretations and etiological explorations (and the kind of "time," "lifestories," and "identities" this creates, and the other times, lifestories, and identities it eclipses);
2. The "rule of abstinence" regarding client gratification and therapist self-disclosure and other verbal proscriptions (and the kind of clinical/human relationship this rule creates or models and others it aborts);
3. A singular reliance on empathy (and the emotional realm this reliance fosters and other realms that it withers);
4. A select (limited) vocabulary of emotion descriptors, pathologies, and therapeutic metaphors (and the Wittgensteinian "forms of life" created or avoided by this vocabulary).

I have said "unfortunately" in that such ensconcing terminology squelches innovation and scrutiny of these concepts and practices—mainly those of psychoanalysis, object relations, self-psychology, and their popularizations, including recovery psychology and self-help. Although "basic" only to these theories, they are often used as pseudo-proven criteria against which innovation is assessed or even allowed. "First learn 'the basics,' then you can branch out," is the guidance given to trainees, as if these basics are any more than unverified psychoanalytic persuasions that will become tools of persuasion with their clients. As Bouveresse notes in *Wittgenstein Reads Freud*:

> The mistake of psycho-analysis is . . . not necessarily to use persuasion the way it does, but rather to refuse to recognize that this is essentially what it is doing and to underestimate the considerable dangers this use involves. (Bouveresse 1995, p. 125)

And, as Wittgenstein noted after years of detailed, "disciple-like" study of psychoanalysis:

> The enormous influence of psychoanalysis in Europe and America [is] harmful—[and] "it will take a long time before we lose our subservience to it." To learn from Freud you have to be critical; and psychoanalysis generally prevents this. (Wittgenstein 1967, Rhees's notes in *Wittgenstein Lectures and Conversations*, p. 41)

For example, how basic concepts of *individuation* or *client-centered inquiry* are widely understood dictates that therapists accept a client's praise with "I wonder why you feel a need to praise me?" Thus unfolds "the therapeutic process" with the predictable self-pathologizing answers: "Why? It's because I've always taken care of other people." Or, "I'm afraid if I don't, you won't like me." Or, "If I don't you'll abandon me." It *sounds* centered on the client's process (real inner world), but in myriad ways the characteristically intoned question already carries with it the therapist's whole theory—now well known to many therapy consumers as pointing to certain "right" answers that must not be denied. And since there is obvious goodness in empathy, concern for the individual, and so forth, it takes perspicuity to grasp when unwitting iatrogenic side effects have devolved. Consider by contrast the unfolding of soteriological basic responses to deepen gratitude and appreciation, basics that conventional therapy might not at first appreciate.

CLIENT. "You've really helped me a lot."

THERAPIST. "Thank you, and you deserve to know how nourishing your praise is to me and I believe to anyone you might give it to.

CLIENT. "Well, I didn't know my appreciation could be nourishing to you, so that makes me feel that I must be, well, nourishing. But as soon as I say so, I feel embarrassed.

THERAPIST. You have become shy. There is a glow about you from taking my appreciation to heart.

CLIENT. I feel both good and uncomfortable.

THERAPIST. Receiving, as great as it is, is challenging. We can only feel appreciated as much as we let it in, and others get to know how nourishing they are mainly to the degree that we receive their appreciations. So, I want to receive your appreciation for your sake and mine, and as a model for all our relationships.

Supplementing analytic "thinking" with evermore skillful "thanking" ("meditative *danken*" is to replace "calculative *denken*" as foundational consciousness, as Heidegger mused regarding closure in the long reign of reason in Western cultures) in the therapeutic project is part of exactly what I am proposing. The results of permutations of this simple method taken to ever subtler and more precise levels, I am prepared to say, exceed what might be expected.

But read psychoanalytically, the therapist appears to be intellectualizing; and shouldn't he have explored his client's discomfort instead of giving a sermon? Must be his countertransference and narcissistic needs taking over. On the other hand, can we ever climb out of such suspicious analytic narratives onto more innocent ground? What would a therapeutics of giving and receiving look like?

Indeed, it is common for the therapized to make life imitate therapy such that "processing" (analyzing in ever-expanding contexts [dreams, original pain, family history, addictionological, and enneagram or other characterological analyses] *how* they go awry) displaces at home the same giving and receiving that it displaced in therapy. As Crews (1993) noted, psychoanalysis is "the method least likely to be 'over when it's over.'"

Individual clients analyze and reexperience their childhoods for years while being taught to see and describe their current problems as symptomatic of mere "repeating patterns" and "issues." The analytic joy of identifying a pattern from childhood eclipses the tremulous joy of the unique and fleeting present, a joy whose first glimmer is so challenging to feel that without another sort of therapy to help us move into its flux, we back into far less satisfying past-tense narratives. And most times, the conventional therapist and her theories have helped us to do so, unknowingly missing the very present she so much seeks.

Paraphrasing John Lennon, "Life is something that happens when we're busy analyzing yesterday's conversation." The transpersonalist's retrospective concern with in utero, neonatal and, of course, past-life experiences can preoccupy therapist and client even longer. And even granting the mystery of reincarnation, I have yet to hear of a transpersonal interest in the possibilities of future lives.

This overbearing augering into an etiologicial past presses so much upon some clients that the question of therapist-induced false memories has arisen and naggingly persists. Capping the matter, we learn from nontherapist historians that, in his zeal, Freud practiced such induction as his very method from the beginning. Thus, over the past one hundred years, wielding the basics has become an end in itself, a dogma and, at times, an iatrogen. As James Hillman's 1993 book title scoffed, *We've Had One Hundred Years of Psychotherapy and the World Is Worse Than Ever.*

Following its singular etiological trajectory, conventional therapy comes to overusing its own limited terminology leading its popularizers into diagnostic hypergeneralizations and bizarre etiological asssessments. We see this in A. W. Shaef's wild claim that everyone is "codependent" and John Bradshaw's stunning assessment that the average American childhood is equivalent to the Nazi holocaust.

And further inspection reveals distorting overusages of more common words such as *anger, unmet needs, wound, grief, pain, caretaker,* and *abandonment,* encased all together into a head-nodding and rather maudlin jargon. Thus, to the onlooking media the term *therapeutic culture* does not connote a healthy culture but is instead a derisive jibe at those whose chief joy is in complaining.

Via metaphors that characterize reviewing the client's childhood as a "reaching down," a "going deeper," and an "uncovering of the 'real' truth," the basics give itself further appearances of being "truly foundational work." Yet, these metaphors overburden the (psychoanalytic) past, and skew our gaze on the present and into the future in often barely detected ways.

For example, therapists of various schools of thought are trained to suggest to their clients, "You seem to have another *deeply buried emotion "X" beneath* your expression of "Y" (where X is typically "anger," "sadness," or a "sexual" sentiment and Y a smile or off-hand remark). Following the basics, therapist and client then proceed not only as if on firm ground, but as if moving onto more firm ground ("deeper," i.e., bedrocklike) than was being initially presented by the fleeting immediacy of the client's smile or quiet warmth of the casual remark where, now, the "real work" will take place.

The possiblity of distortion or iatrogenic side effects of such metaphors and the suspicious searches they engender becomes hardly worth considering. Beginning with Freud, the model of the therapist as courageously digging into the past and avoiding the "superficialities" of the present and, often, anything that does not fit his psychoanalytic theory, still prevails. As Freud instructs:

> [A]s a rule, the [forehead] pressure procedure fails on the first or second occasion. The patient then declares: "I expected something would occur to me, but all I thought was how tensely I was expecting it. Nothing came." . . . We can say in reply: "It's precisely because you were curious; it will work next time." And in fact it does work [*sic*]. . . . The work keeps on coming to a stop and they keep maintaining that this time nothing has occurred to them. We must not believe what they say, we must always assume, and tell them too, that they have kept something back they thought unimportant or found it distressing. We must insist on this, we must repeat the pressure and

represent ourselves as infallible, till at last we are really told something. . . .

There are cases, too, in which the patient tries to disown [a thought] even after it returns. "Something has occurred to me now, but you obviously put it into my head." Or, "I know what you expect me to answer . . . it seems to me as if I'd put it in deliberately." In all such cases, I remain unshakeably firm. (Freud & Breuer 1955, pp. 278–80)

Pressure (now merely suggestive), suspicion (often hidden subtly in "empathic inquiry"), unshakeable conviction in one's theory as if it were a proven fact, discrediting of the patient's doubts (and any Experimenter's Effect), "till at last we are really told something." This is the spell-casting, traditional way into analytic depths.

Indeed, the *metaphoric sense* of equating "depth" with analyzing the past is typically lost to the *seeming* literality of the image it has conjured. The significance of the fleeting immediacy of the client's smile, the evanescent pleasure of the shared pleasantry, coup d'oiel, are eschewed (with a chidingly authoritative raised eyebrow for the "naive" therapist who would be "distracted" or "seduced" by such "superficialities" and miss what they "hide") as trivial coverings.

There is scant room for the mystery of life unfolding with its alluring/daunting uncertainties and ever-emerging novelties. The image of "reaching upward," for example, is rarely to be found, as if only Freud's "future of an illusion" or predictably pathologized "idealizations" lived in the metaphors of heights. Even his inmost soul, no longer the profoundly resourceful mystery of immortality it has been for centuries, is merely another differentially diagnosable stratum of psychiatric vulnerability or, at most, a taste for umbral art and melancholic poetry.

Yet, perhaps those nervously hopeful smiles and impermanent pleasantries have a far more useful and profound clinical purport. Perhaps within other, haikulike depths—those of the mercurial present—is much of the very health we seek. As those inspired by Wittgenstein's acute linguistic studies have noted, "Attention to surface detail can, if done rigorously, be radically transformative" (Scheman, liner notes in Genova's *Wittgenstein: A Way of Seeing*, 1995).

Furthermore, what about the engendering of any anxious or even gleeful suspiciousness regarding unsuspected things insidiously—that is, with "unconscious" prater-intentionality—hidden and "buried within" *by* us, by time passage itself or by *something*? In what ways might this backward/downward suspicious mood, sustained (via the regularly deployed metaphors) week after week for years on end, effect (iatrogenically?) the client's habitual regard for his contemporary world? No wonder he comes to agreeing with his therapist and sees past patterns throughout his current life! No wonder he looks more to his inner child (or, rather, is attracted to such metaphoric devices) for resources than to his contemporary adult life. His therapeutic narrative has come to constraining his descriptions of the present-future. Having given up on the possibility of untapped adult potentials, psychology pins disproportionately all its hope on the infant and child, literally and linguistic-metaphorically.

The chronic pose of self-suspicion and the temporal domains of a bloated "past," an attenuated "present," and a minimalist "future" into which the client's life is shaped is the playing field for this so alluring truth game. Here is the fashioning of the generic psychotherapeutic lifestory: the erstwhile schizophrenigenic mothers and primal scenes; the abuse histories and the singular past trauma therein which now shapes nearly every aspect of the present; the adult-children syndromes, issues, patterns, baggage. Thus, transpersonalist Ken Wilber (1996) has critiqued conventional psychotherapeutics as a "hermeneutics of suspicion."

But what if as stated in Taoist and tantric metaphysics, Buddhist *anicca* (impermanence) doctrine and in existentialism, the temporal foundation of existence is itself shakier, more fluid, and emptier of precedent "explanations" and "causal agents" than therapist and client have come to believe? And how does the phenomenology of temporal impermanence itself—nostalgia, expectancy, uncertainty, indeterminacy, evanescence, aging—permeate all psychological events and hermeneutics? As philosopher David Wood notes in *The Deconstruction of Time*:

> ["Eternal recurrence" time] can be treated as a description not of repeated *content* of experience, but of the dynamic structure of experience—the rhythm, the pulse of excitement and fatigue, of arousal and consummation, of exhilaration and passivity, of the rising and setting of the passions. . . . It is this *movement*, the movement of becoming, that is repeated eternally. Or, with Deleuze, one can say that it is *the returning that returns*. (Wood 1991, pp. 29–30)

Yet, if the temporal ground of relationship, emotionality, and the "real psychological meaning" of time and its "developmental" events are shakey *ontologically*, the conventional therapist might never know. For his method of inquiry sways and merges exactly with the nostalgic pathos his very queries engender in his client: "What, I *wonder*, is *beneath* that 'smile?'" inquires the therapist; "It must be *something*!" synchopatedly shudders every client so questioned.

That impermanence—with its fleeting and ever-aging body language of charming innocences and mortal vulnerabilities—underlies each moment is missed. And from this more mercurial ground, the bedrock of analytic "certainties" begins to shimmer disconcertingly. As Lyotard admonished regarding trying to remember the indelible holocaust, "memory" at best must not be asked to bear too much in establishing an emotional truth, as if a final recovery will then ensue:

> [T]o fight against forgetting means to fight to remember that one forgets as soon as one believes, draws conclusions, and holds for certain. It means to fight against forgetting the precariousness of what has been established, of the reestablished past: it is a fight for the sickness whose recovery is simulated. (Lyotard 1990, p. 10)

Where the present is precarious and mercurial, so does the past become a mutable ground for soteriological redemptions, and not merely etiological analyses. To learn the lessons of history so as not to repeat its worst nightmares is far more a matter of awakening to shared hopes buried beneath any tragedy and learning how to cultivate them. While reviewing the past may awaken insight and release pent-up emotions, the former awakens the soteriological powers of the soul, a difference that can open up another sort of past, present, and future time altogether.

Thus, from this other temporal ground, one that is self-admittedly shakey, uncertain, and endlessly fleeting, existential psychiatrist Medard Boss discerned the pervasive iatrogenics of what he only somewhat facetiously called "psychoanalytis," a chronic and global mood of self-analyzing suspicion which can impair personal action.

> Instead of staying close to the immediately observable appearances of the world, [those with psychoanalytis] disregard them and speculate about what is "behind" them. . . . Instead of dwelling in openness toward the things and people they encounter, they "interpret" these same phenomena . . . [and are unable] to penetrate beyond the concepts and interpretations of psychoanalysis . . . [while] genuine freedom and openness is always experienced as a threat. (Boss 1963, p. 236)

The client barely learns to walk and create on the grounds of existential uncertainty, temporal impermanence, and soteriological possibility. How can he, when so many contemporary happenings receive the therapist's backward spin and "the past" he discovers has little bearing on the powers of his soul and their worldly maturation? Must therapy always aim low?

FROM AN OVER-DETERMINING "PAST" TO THE FLEETING IMMEDIACIES OF A "DEEP PRESENT"

Yes, there most certainly are side effects to this psychoarcheologist's metaphor. Without any check or balance or self-critique, "going deeper" into "the real work" comes to mean always a going into the etiological past—thus it is always a malevolent, subterranean past. Like the superficial smile of the present, reported positive, inspirational events from the past are often pathologized as a denial of something else, a covering over or evading of the "real" matter. Or, at most, anything good is to be known only tragically as what was lost or taken away so that even this goodness is made into a mournful pain. That the sheer novelty and wonder of the present should have any inherent (nontransferential) "depth" often becomes unthinkable. In the psychoanalyzing narrative, anything redeemable from the past and life in the haiku-present typically slip into oblivion.

The health that lives as the aesthetic-affective movements of presencing itself is missed. For its hermeneutic of mercurial immediacies, shy blushings, trepid hopeful smiles, and sheer impermanence does not exist for the conventional basics. But what if Freud had not been an amateur archeologist but had instead been a rockclimber, a white-water canoeist, or an improvizational jazz musician whose attention is constantly drawn forward into the uncanny depths of the never happened before NOW? What basic metaphors and practices of therapy might have been crafted then?

Another economy of time would now prevail in psychotherapy where "the past" is overlit by and consumed in the ever-fleeting opportunities and ideal possibilities of the emergent present-future. In such present-focused activities, one looks for possibilities in every newly emergent crevice or hears opportunities in every warbling tone and quivering smile. Imagine a therapeutic commitment unswervingly threading its way from one glimmer of hope to the next, amid even the most threatening turbulence.

Here the clinical hermeneutic is one of unfolding mystery, transmutable crises, and uncertain possibilities. The conventional aesthetic of "wounds," "boundaries," and "patterns" is replaced by one of "difficulties," "respect" and "novelty." Focus is on the subtlest increments of progress and what the client could learn to say or do or think in order to sustain that subtlest increment of progress and, with the therapist's help, to build from it—again and again and again. Perhaps it is only in the poignantly elusive eye-to-eye present that past tragedies can be redeemed, that vengeance bows ashamed and quells its echoings. So uplifted and free, we would have to begin to wonder: How far can love, hope, and forgiveness go?[1]

Lines of therapist dialog that begin, "I really admire you," or "Thank you for trusting me," and move through the layers of disbelief, fears of obligation, resisted blushes of shyness, pride, nourishing-then-clinging-then-releasing appreciativeness, and further into a matured awakening into evanescent, shared presence, renewed optimism and the regeneration of the life-web of aspirations, involvements, and relationships. Beyond the conventional horizon, beyond the habitual retrospective gaze, another therapeutic ground can emerge: the moving ground of YHWH, continuously emergent Is—a naming that, strangely, embarrasses us as if to call time "God" were grandiose or mere new-age fluff! As Dionysius the Areopagite wrote in the late fifth century: "For He Himself is the Eternity of the ages and subsists before the ages" (Rolt 1966, p. 135).[2]

In a soteriological therapy, the skills of observing for and engaging with even flickering or ambiguous innuendos of hopefulness overarch all empathic listening and replace much mirroring, uncovering, and etiological interpreting. These innuendos are often found in the intricate folds of irony (not mere repetition) or hairsplit compromises between one degree of progress and the next.

> TOM. It's been going on poorly for ten years. I feel all this hostility from you and yes, although I'd like it to get better, I don't need it to anymore. It's okay if it doesn't, it's really okay! Maybe it should end, that's another possibility, while we're still in our thirties. I don't know.
>
> THERAPIST. I'd like to ask you to do something, but it's okay if you don't, if one of you doesn't want to, but would you each be willing to reach across and touch finger tips to each other.
>
> TOM. No, I don't want to. No. (Pulls away)
>
> JIM. (simultaneously): Yes, okay.
>
> THERAPIST. Then Jim, can you reach out and just allow Tom to look at your out-stretched hand and just keep it there? And Tom, you can just see his hand there.
>
> JIM. Okay. (Reaches out, two [long] seconds go by)
>
> TOM. (Suddenly reaches and clasps Jim's outstretched hand)
>
> THERAPIST. See, this is acting now, in real time, outside of all the generalizations of those ten years and what they tell you how you should act. Consider the last fifty minutes of this session as building to this moment. This is the gold, yet it will slip away. Jim, thanks for reaching out alone and Tom thanks for bearing watching without reaching out as you had said you would do, until something else happened and you reached out.

Within these more convoluted "yes, no, yes, no, yes" narrative forms hopefulness dimly glimmers its futuristic ideal possibilities, now, outside the oft-nightmarish history from which clients are trying to awaken. Treatment consists in naming these observations and cultivating their further emergence to the point of breakthrough.

Sessions continue escatologically, that is, drawn forward by an alluring/daunting sense of the uncertain yet hopeful present-future, rather than backward, as an archeological dig. But equally daunting and enough to send us scurrying into past-tense narratives for some shelter is how moving forward (soteriological progress) makes evermore vivid the relentlessness of our mortal impermanence. (Those ten horrid years! Dare I reinvest yet again? And then what?) Apology and forgiveness can open doors long shut, but then what? Just the rest of one's life. Divorce papers get filed and then unfiled. Incendiary child custody transfers no longer occur at police stations but unsupervised at park playgrounds. (How far can this go: [Remarriage? Never! But why not? I'll forgive and cooperate, but not *that* much!]) And then what again and again? Who wants to sense the reversability of problems, to go forward week after week after week when a vengeful or hopeless "stuckness" can preoccupy and bitterly, enjoyably justify how impossible one's wife, husband, parents, past was/is? They're why my life is so hard now. Therapy told me so.

Dare I raise my hopes yet again and again? Wasn't it easier before, when I was merely the struggling protagonist in my family history? Not merely another analysis or tearfully "reexperienced" childhood catharsis can show us the way to move forward. Why should it be able to do so?—there is no necessary connection between the two realms of experience. Even those who discover the root of their water phobia must still learn how to swim.

Like propeller aircraft facing a possible jet age, "the basics" and their psychoanalytic justifications are to be seen as mere first inventions of a rather young healing technology. Let us believe that they can be improved upon in ways unthinkable to their creators and even to many contemporary innovators. Even the time-honored "transference" is to be seen as a limited working concept and not as a discovered, all-explaining fact. Certainly, "family history" must face the same critique that "world history" faces in the postmodern age. For any rendered story is dependent on the type of soliciting questions that are (or can't be) asked and the type of trained, etiological ear that does the listening, interpreting, and probing.

In this questioning of clinical practices and theory, time itself becomes more alive than the basics of conventional psychotherapy grasp. The iatrogenia of its healing metaphors, grounded in its deadening *kind of* temporal hermeneutic, can also be raised. In a variety of ways, Crews (1993, 1994, 1995), Grunbaum (1984), Hillman and Ventura (1993), Kaminer (1992), MacMillan (1991), Rubin (1996), Spence (1982, 1986), Webster (1995), and others have already done so.

ANOTHER, MORE TREMBLING GROUND

Gratitude, (praise), forgiveness, apology, faith, hope, awe, humility (perservering nonomnipotence), reverence, ecstasy, hellish dread, compassionate love, and longing comprise the terminology of core sentiments common to numerous spiritual traditions. Consider these words as pointing toward flickering feeling-traces which might reliably guide our possible development as embodied souls toward some ultimate maturation. Consider the terms as pointing to sentiment-radiances that issue throughout the body as efflux from the soul: "And to imagine a language means to imagine a form of life" (Wittgenstein 1968, p. 8).

In *yogic* psychology, these spiritual sentiments are found in the *yamas* (regulations) of *ahimsa* (nonharming love), *satya* (honesty; idealistic truth), *asteya* (respectful nontaking), and the *niyamas* (cultivations) of *kshama* (forgiveness), *daya* (compassion), *santosha* (contended optimism), *astikya* (faithful optimism), *hri* (apologetic contrition) and in the Buddhist psychology of meditatively discerned anicca (poignant impermanence) and yogic emotionalities of bhakti (devotional longing.) These sentiments are also found in the Judeo-Christian tradition as *soteriology*: forgiveness, faith, and gratitude as a spiritual or redemptive path. Here, "redemption" is the moment-to-moment, ever-truing of development—as guided by these radiances, sentiments, or words—toward ultimate maturational possibilities: toward eternal impermanence lived as such.

Here powers of forbearance and compassion can heal the psychological effects of abuse or strife through forgiveness of self or the other with only fleeting vengeful angers, grievings, or victim identifications. *By forgiving, we become forgiving.* Our glands secrete soteriological chemistries into the poignant fires of compassion, forebearance, and forgiveness, and this emotional alchemy matures us. Little by little, embodied character—not mere ego—development is fostered. Thus, according to kundalini yoga, the embodied soul is the foundation of this path—this path of felt time passage, called "a lifetime."

The greatest opportunity of a relationship is to share love and gratitude. To the degree that other sharings are not for the sake of this greatest opportunity something feels missing. This missing, however, can guide us to such opportunities, for missing, longing, or even despair is love or hope felt at greater and greater distances. If this distance is traversed, the greater sharings can happen and one awakens more to the sense that time is passing, that within the long penumbra of the infinite, his finite life is happening now. This difficult awakening to moods of awe, within which flicker awkward sentiments of shyness, arising hopes (within dashed hopes), and (the old) longings is the essence of clinical progress. The difficulty rests in the inherent impermanence (not mere resistance), the constant draw of time unfolding, and the unfamiliarity of new degrees of hopeful awe.

This awakening can be alluring/daunting both in its vividness and in its uncertainty (compared to the [pseudo]certainty and [pseudo]familiarity with [pseudo]patterns fashioned in past-referencing narratives)—the undetermined, awesome uncertainty and impermanence of the present moment and of all future moments. To foster new moments of progress, the therapist becomes a kind of poet, coach, or empathic guide in his client's awakenings from reluctance, doubt, and cynicism.

> WIFE. He says he loves me now and I feel encouraged, but then, but how long will it last?"
>
> THERAPIST. The love and hope are awakening you to one another. and it is *sheer impermanence* that you are experiencing, and the real uncertainty and impermanence of each new moment that makes you ask your question, not the weakness of this just-achieved hopefulness. Leave it at that and share impermanence and uncertainty *with* each other, instead of converting your joyful wonder and awe *into* a mood of interrogative suspicion, and him (or fears from the past) into a (false) "explanation" for the just-awakened-to unsettling sense of impermanence. Share it by looking at each other now. The impermanence and uncertainty are here, now, equally, for us.
>
> Converting joyful *wonder* into moods of interrogative suspicion and doubt via mere misnaming of the wonder throws you back into your own bad dreaming about things that have nothing to do with Now and its unhappened path into the future. In freeing yourselves, you can go into past memories, but not lost to the present sharing.
>
> Instead, stay awake and perform the difficult task of persistent sharing of this innocently human condition of mortal impermanence, uncertainty, awe, and shyness—perhaps by just looking at each other in silence, feeling together the unstoppable flow of time and how this sharing erodes further and further any chronic sense of isolation or being stuck in the past. And thanks for trusting me with this guidance, for using these words as stepping stones into the open time of the present.
>
> If you want this openness to last, speak it into words, again and again in dozens of ways, and wisdom, not cynicism and doubt, will grow. If you err, apologize, and forgive and go on. Now will you vow to be helpful to one another whenever one of you wavers, that you can count on one another to be a helper and not a mere blamer or ready victim? And will you vow that you can be counted on to receive and make use of your partner's help?
>
> WIFE. Yes, but I'm afraid this won't work.
>
> HUSBAND. Yeah, I'm afraid it will just revert.
>
> THERAPIST. Okay, look at each other. Wonder if it is not the same fear that you feel that the other is also feeling. See that you are in it together. You're not alone. It's the same fear. In sharing it and the hope and the wonder, see that this sharing preserves you from seeming to be alone in the flow of your emotions. And next comes the sense of sharing in the flow of the time of your very lives. And doesn't that lighten your burden a little more?

WIFE. I never thought of you as being in this fear *with* me before. I always thought of you as abandoning me and causing me to be afraid and alone in my fear. Now I am seeing you afraid too, and that we are both as uncertain as the other. It makes me feel even closer to you in this moment.

HUSBAND. Well, I feel a great deal of relief as you say that, that I am with you, just as uncertain and hopeful and fearful, and not causing it. Instead I do feel what I never thought was possible—to have someone be accompanying me, with me in such moments. I always felt I had to be responsible, even if that meant coming up with a convincing explanation of how you were causing us problems. Instead, I feel sad that I used to do that, because that's how I would end up missing this sense of sharing the difficulty with you.

There is a great deal of hopefulness and hopelessness about the prospect of spending very many moments of life feeling love or gratitude. The hope seems to stir a sense of hopelessness, of the "yes, maybe" of moments that seem too good to be true, and so many other sentiments somehow emerge, that take up our lives, to say, think, enact. We end up rarely getting around to praising, thanking, apologizing, forgiving, or sharing the poignant impermanence.

As doubt and cynicism set in, a cognitive *conviction* shifts the ambiguous hopefulness of the "too good to be true" toward a pessimistic scoff: "anything *good* is *too good to be true*, and is therefore [*sic*] *false*." The act of coming to a therapist is often a latter or last resort, a hopeful kind of hopeless hopefulness that things old (and less good) will end and things "new" (and too good to be, but, *possibly*, true) will begin to happen. "Ask yourself 'For how long am I struck by a thing?—For how long do I find it *new*?'" (Wittgenstein 1968, p. 210).

Fundamental to the therapeutic project is the *sense* of any moment being a new moment, a change. Ironically, *every* moment *is* new. The tolerable *sensing* of this inherent quality of time is often called "hopefulness" and this name gives us confidence into the next new moments; almost intolerably it becomes "awe," "grace," or "infinity," and these names can inspire or daunt us; intolerably, during sudden breakthroughs into a greater sense of impermance via "crises"—for a crisis is merely anything that awakens us to the crux of the matter: the irreplaceability and true evanescence of each moment. At these times, it gets named "anxiety," "horror," "insecurity," "abandonment fears," "panic," or "endless dread," and these names swamp any subtler, tolerable tonalities of the new.

Once misnamed and put into a coherent, justifying narrative ("Don't get your hopes up [again]! Remember what happened the last times."), who is there to correct our error? Once misnamed, we are off to the explanative races, the wrong races. Who is to stop the comic tragedy of linguistic and emotional errors that, like in *The Sorcerer's Apprentice*, mushroom boundlessly.

> You are cruel
> to make me feel bad to think
> I am cruel to make you feel cruel
> by me feeling bad that you can be so cruel as to think
> I don't love you, when you know I do.
> If you don't know I do there must be something the
> matter with you. (R. D. Laing 1970, *Knots*, p. 12)

From misnamings to convolutedly "logical" generalizations based upon the misnaming, misgeneralizations, and then harshly "true" diagnoses of who each other "really" is, and then dooming predictions (admixt with vengefulness) of how each other will act, based on these generalizations, and the escalation: *A*:"Yeah, you say you care, but you don't!" *B*: "It's useless to tell you anything nice, you just trash it!" *A*: "Well, I wouldn't trash it if you really meant it. Which you don't." *A* and *B* fall into the acrid sadomasochistic pleasures of exchanged humiliations. Thus both alluring hope (health) and daunting fear (psychopathology?) flicker within the awe of time, at the whim of one word choice after another, and what that word calls our attention to in the next and the next moments.

SUBTLETY CAN BE PREEMINENT ...

If "anxiety" is dominant and "awe" is subtle, we may need to name that which is subtle in favor of what is dramatic, if we are to get anywhere outside of anxiety. Therapists, however, are often trained *not* to do this favoring or to become aware of the subtler emotions—especially subtler "good" emotions—but instead to have clients stay with *the* anxiety (or the same few other troubling sentiments: anger, grief, or fear) and find out what it means (from the past), to create narratives about it (etiologies), and then to measure future anxiety against these narratives (the "patterns" and "issues").

Focusing (frequently or occasionally) on subtle awe, shy hopefulness, and uncertainty, however, can yeild present-future narratives of novelty and alluring hope. How much subtle awe does a therapist need? How potent is subtle awe in ameliorating hopelessness? How potent can impermanence be? Dreadfully potent, inspiringly potent but impermanently so. Eternally.

UNCERTAINTY AND ONTOLOGICAL HOPEFULNESS...

Our "being" and time passage are one. We can sense ouselves *as* this flickering-with-possibility time sense, awaiting and *being* "*what*" is next. *We* "become" hopeful; or *we* "become" anxious (concerning, ironically, being *adequate* to tolerating/abiding in our *own* larger-than-before nature: "*Can* I/we *really* do it?"). In each case, we are merely feeling time passage more fully. Marriage proposals, job promotions or terminations, child-custody mediation sessions, the forty-ninth minute of a fifty-minute hour, budgets and income, lovers' separations, funerals, births, verdict waits, executions—all these shake/invigorate our current sense of adequacy and heighten the time-passage sense with flickers of wonder, allure, awe, terror, or dread.

> It looked as if he had only five minutes to live. He told me those five minutes seemed an eternity stretching before him, a great abundance of time; he felt that in those five minutes he could live so many lifetimes that there was no need, yet, to think of the final moment.... Then when he had said good-bye to his comrades, came those two minutes he had set aside to think about *himself*; he knew beforehand what he was going to think about: he wanted to conceive, as fast and as vividly as he could, how it was that he was here and alive now and in three minutes he would be *something*—something or someone—but what? And where? And he thought he could resolve all this in two minutes! Not far away there was a church, and its gilt roof gleamed in the bright sun. He remembered that he gazed with terrible intensity at that roof and the rays of sun that sparkled from it; he could not take his eyes from those rays of light; it seemed to him that this light was his new nature and that in three minutes he would somehow melt into it. His uncertainty and revulsion against this new thing which was bound to happen at any moment were terrible; but he said that nothing was more awful than the incessant thought, "What if I was not to die! What if life was given back to me! What an eternity! I would turn each moment into a century. I would miss nothing!" He said that this thought finally filled him with such rage that he wanted to be shot as soon as possible. (Dostoyevsky 1969, pp. 80–81; based on the author's experience of his own near execution)

Utter hopelessness is unreal, for there is always some degree of hope, even in horrendously worsening situations. Why? Because there is always the next moment and always there is an (at times, "unbearable," or *so* we *name* "*it*") uncertainty about it until it happens and, even then, an indeterminacy as it happens and then about what happens next, relentlessly next. This *uncertainty* or "not knowing yet," called as well, "the future," is the "basis" or temporally nuanced synonym for hope. *Particularly* regarding the "what happens" we call "death" and its mysterious next moment, we are most uncertain.

THE FORWARD EXPANSE OF ENDLESS
IMPERMANENCE AND SOTERIOLOGICAL TIME

Imagine growing older and older, but not dying and still again, after ninety, then one hundred, twenty, thirty, fifty, two hundred years. Will there come a time when one would stop waiting for "it" (some ending) to happen? Stop waiting for the other shoe to hit the floor? If the "it," or the "this" of: "When is *this* going to end, so that I can then start to live fully" and its spawned narratives of etiological retrospection and suspicion wither, is it not an endless impermanence that thrives unencumbered as Real Time?

In kundalini yoga, we encounter advanced stages of spiritual (as *spiritus*, or breath as living spirit) maturation where a breathless type of respiration emerges in the spellbound awe of the infinity of Universe-Time-consciousness. Thus, too, imagine living through minute after minute after minute of breathlessness, without panic, without anxious gasping, in a matured beatitude. Imagine the freedom therein, a taste of unending, literally *in*spirational, regenerativity (see p. 169).

What is the effect (danger?) of not naming this ongoing background of real time "Endless Impermanence" and it whirring on anyway? What other things or people do we blame for our vague feelings of uncertainty, indeterminacy, and slipping away? And even if we do name it, what dangers can still remain? What are we afraid of here? How safe do we expect (someone to make) it to be?

The bodily "I" that dies, does she not live in a finite episode of an eternal impermanence that extends before her birth and after her death? Here is the challenge: to feel one's life as a finite "segment" of the *eternal*. As the original "psychologist of spirituality," Ludwig Feuerbach noted in his formula that all predicates concerning God are predicates of the person. Human consciousness is itself infinite:

> Consciousness, in the strict or proper sense, is identical with consciousness of the infinite; a limited consciousness is no consciousness; consciousness is essentially infinite in its nature. The consciousness of the infinite is nothing else than the consciousness of the infinity of the consciousness; or, in the consciousness of the infinite, the conscious subject has for his object the infinity of his own nature. (Feuerbach 1957 [1841], pp. 2–3)

Mature participation in eternal impermanence is not best characterized as time*less*ness, but as infinite time; as an immature escapism, the sense of a vacuous timelessness without duration might be shallowly conceived. Yet, the daunting depth of the situation is better phrased as "the fullness of time." There is no exit, no escape from time. Wanting one is hell, liking this is heaven. As Friedrich Schleiermacher noted two hundred years ago in what theologian Rudolph Otto called "one of the most famous books that history has ever recorded" (Schleiermacher 1958 [1799], p. x):

> [T]he true nature of religion . . . is not the immortality that is outside of time, behind it, or rather after it, and which still is in time. It is the immortality which we can now have in this temporal life; it is the problem in the solution of which we are for ever to be engaged. In the midst of finitude to be one with the Infinite and in every moment to be eternal is the immortality of religion. (ibid., p. 101)

Thus Eternal Impermanence gives rise to both heaven-bliss and hell-dread as emergent from the same phenomenon of UNCERTAIN NEXT MOMENTS TAKEN ENDLESSLY. Thus, spiritual "emergence" has often been no continuous picnic, whether for the crying infant or the midlife adult, even with the best of childhood parentings.

Time is passing, relentlessly. What do we most want to say to husband, wife, child, parent, neighbor? **Go ahead, break the flow of the paragraph**, let's tell someone we love them, we want their apology or we're sorry, or how much we admire them. What is stopping us that the soteriological sentiments could not passionately dissolve? For all relationship is a loosely held impermanence. In the poignancy of impermanence is the freedom to create anew. What expressed sentiment would we want to be with at "the end" and for (what may feel like an) eternity thereafter?

To sense this temporal reality, an enlightenment in itself that is always available, seems at once uplifting and liberating, "What an eternity! I would miss nothing!"—and then, shuddering under the weight of our own gratitude and profundity, the moment swerves pathogenic— ". . . this thought [this inspiring, "too late" enlightenment] finally filled him with such rage that he wanted to be shot as soon as possible."

Thus, it is not our problems that are the most difficult, it is how to handle the daunting press of our own enlightenments. With the right words to serve as stepping stones, we go onto these new grounds of endless impermanence."What an eternity! I vow to never miss another moment! And those who would shoot me, forgive them, for they are caught in their strange narratives and know not what they are doing. If I must die now so tragically, let me not miss my own death by being caught to the end in such narratives."

The quickened impermanence sense can liberate us not only from certain limiting narratives (into newly chosen *actions*), but from the subtle "grammatic constraints" of verb tenses of past, present, future, conditional, subjunctive, and so on. The narrator's pose as determined by the punctuation of the commanding "!" or the so-certain (.) and the ambiguous (?), also unwinds. But into what? No (?) is left, no (!) or even ([ ])

Thus, "resistance" in therapy or elsewhere, is to the daunting glimmers of this vast eternal impermanence, with its surrounding soteriological aesthetic of feeling-imports and their potentially redemptive-transformative effects on (ordinary?) history.

In accepting, pardoning, and feeling gratitude for our parental conceptive origin, regardless of personal history, to "honor mother and father," is one way of opening the door to soteriological time. To break the "oedipal complex" means to grasp our own transpersonal origins, *procreative* (*pro*, on behalf of the Divine) origins that exist in a time sense that transcends ordinary historical time. Love of God is another door. What difference does it make?

We resist our own enlightenment and maturation into the actualized soul powers by clinging to historical time, and biographical-historical time is certainly a most convincing narrative history to become enamored with. Yet, these histories are rarely the whole truth. They often occlude the truth of the soul's history-shattering love. ". . . they know not what they do" is an anguished utterance of compassion from the level of soul describing life on the dark side of this occlusion.

THE NARRATIVE, ITS TIME, AND ITS EGO NARRATOR BEGIN WHERE *WONDER* OF THE ETERNAL IS MISASSOCIATED WITH ORDINARY DOUBT

"But how long will it last?" We have come to thinking of the narrator of any such interrogative sentence as preexisting and then merely raising an honest question. But consider the reverse lineage: It is the grammatics of the interrogative that give rise to a precarious narrator who now must await his answer, his fate. It is the interrogative sentence that "sentences" us, but it will be certain innuendos therein that can free us.

A "kind of" future is construed that is mere doubt. The soul gets backgrounded by the ego intelligence of doubts and answers. There might be faith, but subtle Wonder evaporates. Indeed, wonder will seem naive to this growing sophisticated intelligence.

Misconstrued impermanence begs the question intoned too seriously. For it will be the enlightening *wonderment* and awe in the face of sheer uncertainty and the mysterious play of time—which allures us—that will transmute this so serious doubt and suspicion. Thus, when progress is granted, psychotherapists must be vigilant in protecting awe, wonder, and sensed impermanence from the subtle deteriorations, by innuendo, into suspicion and doubt, and the evermore solid-seeming narratives they construct.

> CLIENT. Yeah, but this has happened before, I've said I would call my parents and it got all messed up.
>
> THERAPIST. The similarity you are noting is not the same as this being "the same as it was before." And every time you become optimistic, you will feel something similar to this feeling, so please do not get discouraged at the similarity. This is unique. Now on May 10, 1996, at 2:12 P.M. And let us consider that there are myriad ways of speaking to your parents that you haven't yet tried and that your parents haven't tried. And, of course, I will, hopefully, be with you all in that meeting, guiding you all out, and into that which is most hoped for by all.

(There is something elusive and slippery about eternal impermanence making me feel I must repeat the same observations over and over again and again, that forgetting even for a moment this ongoing current of time passage seems to re- and re-require.)

Another name for happiness could be "impermanence." The Greek, *ekstasis*, "out-of-stasis" or impermanence, suggests that the accurate experience of the flow of experience itself is felt as a kind of poignant or sublime ecstasy. This is another reason why perceived subtle, fleeting phenomena are so crucial to the therapeutic endeavor: they show the thawing into life of the perceptive powers, powers that reveal a world of uncertain possibility and poignancy. The warmth of the soteriological sentiments contributes to this thawing, this at-one-ment with time passage.

How ironic that, interpreted one way, time passage is named "depressing," interpreted another it is named "ecstasy." (A sense of irony is often a doorway to a psychological maturation, being more complexly nuanced than "paradox" or "causal explantion.")

The fundamental problem has always been there—"Will it last?"—just as impermanence has always been there. At the moment of granted progress, the question surfaces in this ambiguously optimistic/pessimistic query. The innuendos of this interrogative range from ecstatic enthusiasm to cynical despair. Instead of asking this question, which is at the beginning of so many life-robbing narratives, just look and *see* how it is next and next. Be ready to see the most subtle blush of hope, even amid far more dramatic frowns and scoffs. Then responsibly think, say, or do something that will keep "it" lasting yet another moment. "I don't feel like it. I'm the one who *always* does it. It isn't real for me to do that. I am still enraged." And so it goes.

A therapist is someone who can help us see the phenomena of hope in real time, convincingly, encouragingly, and assist in its continuance. All else rises no higher than diagnostics. And diagnostics often poses as therapy: *Ther*: "You're in your pattern?" *Pt*: "Yes, damn it, I see that I am."

TEMPORALITY AND DEVELOPMENTAL TIME

Imagine a punctuation mark like t created by temporal grammarians to remind us of the ever-passing "while" that it is taking to read (t) and (t) ponder (t) any (t) sentence (t,t,t,t,t,t,t,t.).

All t therapeutic t "development" took, takes, and will take place at this "edge" where progress t or hope was/is/will be granted, and wonderment t emerged/emerges, quivering t in the face of endless impermanence. t,t,t,t,t,t,t . . . t—even "back then," it was in *this* kind of passing time.

SPIRITUAL DEVELOPMENT,
THE GOOD DREAM, AND PROGRESS

"Progress" in therapy, *un*familiar degrees of progress, contain just this very uncertainty of t and its most daunting problematic that calls for wonder and awe, not querulous interrogation or exploration and uncovering. And truly, any *real* progress always yields us an unfamiliarity, even if it (some image of it) has been long desired. These subtle "problematics of attained progress," not conventional psychopathology and its developmental past, is to be mapped out and worked with as the recurring focus of psychotherapy. For *development* is to be thought of as a verb that lives fleetingly in the present as an activity, and not a fait accompli, not merely a formed product of the past.

The constant ego sense (the dreamer) dissolves when narrative dreaming withers and eternal impermanence blooms. Thus the importance of having great and beautiful dreams: "We say we pronounced the word with *this* meaning. . . . Call it [the act of meaning something] a dream. It does not change anything" (Wittgenstein 1968, p. 216).

The client interrogatives, "Is this *for real?*"—that is, "Can this last?"—greet certain moments of progress. *Realness* (or our willingness to use the word) and *duration* get correlated, even equated: That which by lasting proves it is real. This linguistic equation—of matters so filled with uncertainty, the regressive lure to familiar cynical disbelief and scoffing, and the daunting awakening to eternal impermanence—deserves careful clinical involvement. Since all events pass, this definition of "reality" is precarious, while progress itself will only be as precarious as the degree of skillfulness needed to further further it in time ttt.

Whatever the previous chronic problem—drug abuse, criminal recidivism, hopeless depression, family strife—when some moments of some degree of progress is granted there will be a shift onto this primordial problematic: can I have faith that these two minutes of progress are more significant (and more *real*, since they are the moments happening now?) than the previous decades? Furthermore, perhaps their *greater* "spiritual reality" is *verified* by how much better life is just now beginning to feel. Here *the ideal* is to be granted as being more real than the tragically twisted Laingian-knot enacted bad-dream actualities of the past. What to do next and next and next? This looms in front, as always, but progress awakens us to the matter.

> Where the Mystery is the deepest is the gate to all that is subtle [t,t,t,t,t] and wonderful. (Lao Tzu, *Tao Te Ching*, 1962, p. 47)
>
>> Before one goes through the gate
>> one may not be aware there is a gate
>> One may think there is a gate to go through
>> and look a long time for it
>> without finding it
>> One may find it and
>> it may not open
>> If it opens one may be through it
>> As one goes through it
>> one sees that the gate one went through
>> was the self that went through it
>> no one went through a gate
>> there was no gate to go through

> no one ever found a gate
> no one ever realized there was never a gate
> (R. D. Laing 1970, p. 85)

There is no (singular) "accumulated past development," there are only various ways now of looking at past events. Making connections of past to present creates *types of* pasts and presents. There are various ways of making connections. Each is *a way* of looking at events, with each shaping the archiving of the events, shaping the events. Seeing one's developmental history comes from *looking for* one and crafting a coherent-enough narrative of this history. These histories trace the *criteria for coherency* being obeyed by the clinician, per psychoanalysis, self-psychology, self-help psychology, soteriological psychology, or whatever.

Sustained via ruminations, unreal hopelessness attains the status of a kind of semiwakeful bad dream, which blots out (misnames) or misconstrues (often as fear) the flickerings of impermanent newness. Its ever-new flickers of awe-wonder-hope-possibility are overshadowed by the past ruminations, via focusing on the familiar, and thus missing the blushing dance. The flickers of infinity-as-dread are misunderstood as related to the *fantasied* catastrophic-future *scenarios*, which makes these fantasies seem overwhelming and supports evermore catastrophic fantasizings (narratives).

Fearful fantasy to fearfulness to troubling events to unforgiving/unapologetic memories of troubling events to expectation of more such events to cynical certainty and diminished soteriological courage to angry-fearful fantasies to memories to more events: start anywhere and be in the picture-worded labyrinths of an illusory hell become ongoing and "real."

We can scare ourselves (and each other) with the pseudocertainty of imagined disasters, rather than live with the sheer uncertainty of "not happened yet." Perhaps something of the mortal sense of one's own finitude flickers there too and contributes to our unsettling awe, which becomes evermore unwieldy if (mis)interpreted "backwards" as some specific unresolved fear or childhood wound that has nothing to do with the living moment. Or does it? Do conventional therapists even have both alternatives before them?

At the end of the hour the client would always make some kind of discovery, or present some new problem. At first I named this a "manipulativeness." But then I looked at him as if impermanence was suddenly awakening in him to some heightened degree. We talked about sharing those heightened moments *together*, and *equally*, which was news to him: he imagined that I had no such similar feelings. Our ability to share impermanence strengthened and, for the client, the end of the hour lost its sense of isolated desperation. It was just the unstoppable flow of time against which he had been guarding himself, and our immanent missing of each other which he feared being unequal to, or alone in.

Hormonal secretions correlated with these *temporal* emotions, and various physio-cycles as "the bodily juices of time passage," and as the basis of yogic hormonal alchemy: the body(-substances) as a material "path" to eternal time—the "nectars of forgiveness"; medication as allopathic neoalchemy. Emotions as the ripples and cross-ripples of temporality. Neurotransmitters, hormones, and their ionic/molecular precursors "alchemically" mutable elixir mood states.

Perhaps meditation can cultivate in therapists the skill to see/hear subtle phenomena of impermanence with their clients. But they must also have (nonretrospective) present-future clinical terms to name what, in this heightened perceptivity, they see. "What if what you call 'fear' is merely the real uncertainty about the next moment? We can't even know whether or not that next moment is frightening. Perhaps it is sheer uncertainty and not fear that your confidence and progress has brought you to in this moment. Feel the spacious uncertainty, share it with me, and, in it, free of self-induced, misinterpreted 'fear,' feel time carrying us somewhere."

As the martial arts proclaim, such an open perceptivity is even the most optimal of all to deal with any emergent dangers. Past-event conditioned fearfulness can be surmounted by a combination of compassionate patience and gently repeated guidances to "Keep looking. Use your perceptions by taking in the surroundings now. Am I telling you the truth? There is sufficient safety for you here and now. Keep looking. Do my words coincide with your perception? Is there something you want to know about that will help you to see any of this possible safety, now?"

If a "safe" situation is made into a sample or example of a dangerous situation, based on past-conditioned, emergent fear that is being agreed with (by the therapist) and followed as the "client's process," then more and more of the "safe world" can be lost to the client.

If there is no actual danger, then empathizing with a client's wording, "I don't feel safe," in certain situations can approach a folie a deux. Yet, this is exactly what conventional therapists are trained to do, drawing chalk circles (boundaries) around clients to help them feel safe, guiding

34 WORDS FROM THE SOUL

them to cease communications with parents and others to "create safety." Instead, with firm focus on the ideal outcome of moments of shared apology, forgiveness, gratitude, admiration, love, and future hopefulness, be allured by great possibilities in uncertain time t t t t t.

PATHOS, PSYCHOPATHOLOGY, AND SPIRITUAL MATURATION

"But having fun [together] is a waste of time, because it doesn't help to figure out why they're *not* having fun" (Laing 1970, p. 2).

Consider this narrative: "This 'temporal mystery' t,t,t,t, is what quickens in the urgent emotionality of the infant just separated from her mother. Her outreaching cries stretch her forward into uncertain time, gestating the sentiments of longing, hope, and sheer *pranic* (life-force) intensity and undergo a reductionism when labeled as 'pathogenic separation anxieties.'"

The exchange of "temporal mystery" for "separation anxiety" alters fundamentally the psychoanalytic healing/developmental narrative. The tears of the infant on being merely separated from her mother are more complex than "fear of abandonment" grasps: they include the beginning of a spiritual struggle toward an infinitely sublime zenith Rilke hauntingly described:

> Who, if I cried, would hear me among the angelic
> orders? And even if one of them suddenly
> pressed me against his heart, I should fade in the
>   strength of his
> stronger existence. For Beauty's nothing
> but beginning of Terror we're still just able to
> bear. (Rilke 1939, p. 21)

What is the infant who does not stop crying experiencing? If "it" is a spiritual terror regarding the chasm of infinite time, then the parental hug is one admixed with comfort, awe, and protective pride. If "it" is deemed/named "separation anxiety," then the hug is a comforting apology, a salve on a wound, the termination of a trauma. The difference between these two hugs, is it not all the difference in the world?

Winnicott believes that in the gap of a crying baby's "need" and the mother's "failure to adapt to her baby's needs" (Winnicott 1989, p. 156), the baby develops his ability to think, which "becomes a substitute for maternal care and adaption." The mother can thereby "exploit the baby's power to think" by continuing to fail to come to her crying baby. Thus thinking becomes a "defence against archaic anxiety and against chaos and against disintegrative tendencies or memories of disintegrative breakdown related to deprivation" (ibid., p. 157).

The pathos of Winnicott's depiction feels impenetrable and utterly persuasive. Yet, if we believe in a spiritual profusion, thinkable but also beyond thinking, this scene becomes more complex and we must find a way into this complexity. Otherwise and in spite of the Winnicottian "good enough mother" (itself a sensing of the merciful), the spiritual-temporal potency of this gap where urgency reaches into the uncertain, into the endlessness of time, is missed.

Should we care if *something* is being missed in the overpathogenicizing of such cries? Faith, its possible growth, and the possibility that there *is* [S]omething being missed asks us to care.

There can most certainly be the temporally mounting terrors of abandonment, or worse, *much* worse. For much worse happens. Yet there is also the barely thinkable spiritual dimension into which only an ever-increasing sense of urgency is *able* to reach. If there is "archaic anxiety," "chaos" and "disintegrative breakdown," there is also the terrible and beautiful uncertainty and temporal endlessness which humbles infant or adult thinking, yet permeates us with wisdom of the infinite and can mature us into its vast security. Hug a crying baby, but with comfort *and* respectful admiration, and feel the difference.

Inklings of a wisdom *beyond* word-thoughts: an *auspicious* kind of chaos-breakdown-disintegration of inherently limited linguistic contrivances; an auspicious breakdown which reveals, not an unequivocal archaic terror, but the archaic-primordial All. The child must still be hugged by a "good enough mother," yet it is a different child—a frightened, vulnerable, yet also noble and spiritually initiated child—who is hugged, and thus a far more honoring, not just soothing hug that he receives. And it is a mother who receives an infant's blessing, not just his gaping need. And the child who is not then hugged? His possible cry calls us even now. Yet the hug that comes to him, as soon as possible, let it be such a soothing and reverential embrace.

And the adult whose "intelligence" seemed to Winnicott to be susceptible to such "breakdowns" (/"breakthroughs?") must also be understood within this greater spiritual complexity.

This complexity renders the ground of psychotherapy spiritual. This subtly more complex infantile cry, not merely an empty terror but a cry also resonant with Rilkean or Christlike (or anahata-nadic, see pp. 169–71) passion, is the unverifiable, nonomnipotent, yet inexhaustively radiant apex glow of Hope, around which all else prayed for or beseeched, circles. Anyone who *has ever been helped,* has been helped by inklings from this glow. (And, this is why we answer anyone we *ever* answer who cries.)

Anxiety, panic, object constancy, fear of abandonment, and separation anxiety are all related to difficulties with experiencing the vastness of time passage. All resulting hormonal imbalances reflect physically what is being felt psychologically, for neuroendocrine secretions are time-flesh correlators: Body-maintenance urgencies (hypothalamic appetitive-drive regulators); wake-sleep and seasonal cycles (serotonin, melatonin release and uptake); maturation or growth correlators (pineal, pituitary, thyroid monitors), lineage urgency (menstrual/spermatogenic, and sex-arousal hormones): And temporal-poignancy secretions (lachrymose tears expressants)[3] As in kundalini yoga, neuroendocrine secretions are to be understood spiritually or transpersonally (correlated with soteriological time).

WISDOM BORN BY TIME PASSAGE

What Alan Watts called "the wisdom of insecurity" is the maturing grasp of how temporal passage carries us always to the brink of not-happened-yet. We get "baptized at the fount of eternity," as Nietzsche said. As all the hormones perform their mystery we, bodily, gather age and mature—gradually and, at times of crisis, in overwhelming spurts. Thus, so many enlightenments or spiritual maturations have occurred during moments of great trial. We see "uncertainty" as how it is in real time, and humbly and inspired, we feel more equal to "it" because we *are* "it" too. A kind of invigorated peace and the inner (endocrinal) secretions of this maturational state fructify.

A lack of spiritualized languaging of these phenomena leave us with the lop-sided "negativity" of all psychopathologies and etiologies. The inclusion of the spiritual import of all psychopathology prepares the way for the redemptive review of personal history, not merely an etiological review.

> In the culture of victimhood that exists today, people feel a *mandate* to be overwhelmed by their feelings.
> We need a much broader conception of the human spirit and its capacities. We—and by "we" I include mental health professionals—

think of our psyches as fragile when, in fact, we're very hardy people. . . . So what I'm saying is that the human spirit is extraordinarily durable. (Lillian Rubin, Senior Research Fellow, Institute for the Study of Social Change, University of California, Berkeley. In Beneke 1997, p. 14)

MORE THAN EMPATHY IS NEEDED: BREAKING THE PSYCHOANALYTIC SPELL

Compassion, the only soteriological sentiment encouraged in therapists (and critiqued curtly as a departure from true analytic technique) as empathy has overgrown to the point of ridicule as the term therapeutic culture now pejoratively connotes. As other soteriological sentiments are given a place in psychotherapy, the role of clinical empathy can normalize.

> When [the patient] cried out that [the therapist] was "blocking" her . . . he told her that he was *deeply sorry* [my emphasis] she was experiencing something so terrible because of what he had done. . . . The whole delusion [that the therapist was sending rays from his eyes to "block" the patient] in fact began to recede at this point. (Stolorow et al., 1987, p. 167)

Psychoanalyst Robert Stolorow assigns the effectiveness of this intervention to the "validating acknowledgment" of the patient's experience, rather than to the soteriological power of apology. Because his theory pedestals empathic "validation interventions" and does not allow for "therapeutic apologies," the therapist's actual apology is recast as a "validation." This is the power of the psychoanalytic spell. Since "apology" names what was done, why not continue breaking the spell and study how therapeutic apologies, forgiveness, and so on, can work as valued interventions? "The spell" makes me feel I have done something wrong in calling Stolorow's apology an apology. I must go along with the spell, for "an apology" would be too intimate and countertransferential.

When next stymied by this psychotic patient, the therapist speculates in utterly programmed, psychoanalytic fashion that her insistence that he "know her *whole* life" is a trick-clue that he become aware of some specific incident, a "secret" from her childhood. First he offers the suspicion-born intervention of suggesting a possible incesting. This is loudly rejected by the patient. Then, sleuthlike, he rehears "whole" to mean "wholeness" and not her "entire" childhood history. Seeing her now as a *whole person*, not yet *admiring* her outright, proved beneficial. After plodding through the stock analytic suspicions, soteriological admiration emerges. Yet the admiration is only allowed into the therapeutic dialog through the approved route of decoding a double entendre by the characteristic psychoanalytic cleverness—not through warm, deserved admiration plain and simple. For such are the time-worn ways of the spell.

The therapist whose empathic perspective has been enriched with the array of soteriological sentiments can see numerous fleeting emotionalities in the cathartic tears of her client while recounting some personal trauma from his past. Before the tears emerge, glimmers of forebearance are visible as a humbled looking up, as if from under a burden. The therapist will feel admiration and respect for the client at that moment, *not* a diagnostic cleverness-certainty-feeling in [mis]naming forebearance as "holding onto the feeling" or "repression" nor a clinical empathy that, devoid of admiration, can swerve toward sorrow-pity.

In recounting trauma, the client's tears include those of longing for help (not mere "pain") and can inspire the therapist with their seemingly fragile but certainly courageous plaint. Tears of privatized loneliness emerge as the burst of relief in finally, at long last, crying and the therapist feels a poignant intimacy in being now with this person who is now reversing this privacy with her. Thus, tears of closeness too emerge.

She is aware that the dramatic poignancy of such tearful moments requires the full soteriological response (admiration, feeling trusted and moved, seeing the longing, hope, sorrow, forebearance [not "blocks" or "stuffing down"].[3] A steady diet of empathy alone can lead to a debilitating client victimism and, via the humbling pleasure of tears, into a masochism of ever longing to cry again on the client's part matched by the hoped-for decisive sense of "competence" or special intimacy that a therapist can feel, particularly when client tears flow.

When do client recountings of past abuses and their sorrows, forebearances, longings, and lonelinesses go on to consider the frailties of the abuser, in order to further the tears, now of universal pathos and ironic shared limitations? And then the horrible, anguished and, finally, relieving tears of forgiveness? The client does not lose himself in concern for the other at such times, but expands himself. The therapist is not necessarily siding with the abuser either. Beyond the binary lens of "sides" is a simple, tragic wholeness. When can the tears flow regarding the buried ideal interactions that everyone involved would have preferred to have created and, had they known how, would have created: the burst of fully redemptive tears?

Invite those concerned (parents, exspouses, abusers) to join in the therapy to be guided in creating future-changing, impermanent moments of redeemed relationship. "This can't happen; accept it." Who knows that much?

There is a clinical-soteriological stand whereby concerns for "triangulation" (one family member pitting the therapist against another family member) evaporate. Taking the persistent stand on high ground for family wholeness can draw the family out of such lesser activities toward that very wholeness. For when therapy aims for what therapy is all about anyway, various theoretical concerns that aim at lesser objectives fall off to the sides.

FAITH, HOPE, AND THE FUTURE

Consider faith as a predisposition of ultimate optimism rendering all difficulties as temporary and/or somehow valuable. Faith, sustained meditative concentration, ek-stasis, and impermanence are all synonymous with wakeful or thoughtful *dasein* (being-here-in-time). They each give us a sense of the undetermined possibility continuously arising in this moment and/or the next. The angels of the infinite, the subtleties of hope that, glimmering, live in brief moments of indeterminate time. The possibility that salvation and matured well-being *are* our destiny (*destiny*: where all things tend toward: the ultimate psychological tendency). Consider the effect of merely believing this, no matter what. How do we know what happens next? (During the interminable moments of dying, how will it all seem?)

The "future of an *illusion.*" Who knows *that* much?

This "mystery of continuation" or "eternal recurrence" is sheer hope given as infinite time. It is akin to the mystery of procreation, of young life coming out of older life into successive generations, potentially (perhaps) forever more. (It is also seen in the evolutionary process known in yoga as kundalini *urdhva-retas* developmentalism.) It is seen in Christ's invitation to "believe in Me and have eternal life," where Christ is Eternal Time entered into historical time: that which lives yet again.

We must grasp all procreation/reproduction (life forms) as sheer hope reaching into hope (hope-as-future-time) as an ominous time-flow mystery. (The first Greek word *mu*, the bellowing sound of an animal becomes *mysterion* and then, mystery—*mu* and *aum*.) We don't know what happens next: *That* is the mystery we live *as.*

SUE. I've wanted us to create a family and I keep waiting for Tom to "feel ready," as he puts it. I think I've been pretty patient for a year now, but I'm starting to think that if it isn't going to happen then I will have to make other plans, as much as I love Tom and would want it to be with him, I feel I will have to take care of myself and, well, separate pretty soon, if I am going to do this. That's why we're here in counseling, to get some help.

TOM. I can't just make myself be ready, I am taking all this very seriously, and I have to be honest, say my truth and although I love Sue and it would be nice to have children with her, I also know what I feel too. It just seems that we're in two different places. Sometimes I'm not even sure I want to have kids.

THERAPIST. You are both talking about having children as a kind of "want" that you either want or don't want. I'm not so sure you have given yourselves a chance to grasp what it is that you are deciding *about*, that *it* has gotten lost in all of your asking and questioning. I think it might be a good thing to at least get a sense of *what* this having kids might actually *be* like, at this time, yet free of either the necessity to do it or not to do it.

I'd like you to look at each other for a time, if you will, and let me speak and you can just see each other and yourself from these words. You are each looking at someone who, whether you do so or not, has stated that he/she would choose you to have children with. Without being afraid of the consequences of such a feeling, just let this in: of all the men, of all the women, this person would now choose you, and Tom, see how much Sue believes that you could be a great Dad—isn't that right, Sue?

SUE. It most certainly is, a great Dad!

THERAPIST. So, yes, Tom, if you can let that in without worrying or feeling obligated in any way, feel the difference it makes.

TOM. And I have no doubt that Sue would be a great Mom.

THERAPIST. Sue, see Tom's admiration, his belief in you, and now Tom, you can see the glow of enhanced confidence your mere belief in Sue has prompted in her. And Sue, see that just now Tom has seen you *merely receive* his admiration of your potential motherhood, and see the effect you are having on him by merely receiving his admiration. In fact, you might notice a kind of glow about each of you now. And just feel that it is very true that between the two of you is the profound mystery of possible fertility, and family creation.

Without worry, give yourselves and each other that gift of what fertility and believing *in* each other at this level of potential parenthood is like. See how being *believed in* regarding this matter affects you, independent of enacting anything. See how it affects your sense of womanhood, of manhood, and of the spiraling respect for each other. It may sound dramatic, but it's true that you hold the potential to life itself and the creation of new life, as a potential. Please, take some time and put into words what giving yourself and each other this gift of the perception of potential parenthood is like. Free from obligation, see what *it* is that you have been talking *about*.

> TOM. Well, that was really different, I hadn't even registered what we were dealing with, I was so ready not to do it. I felt more confident. I see how being afraid of parenthood foreclosed me from the very experiences which could make me feel less afraid and even inspired enough to feel ready for it.
>
> SUE. Even if we don't go ahead with this, I am glad that we got to share this moment. I had gotten pretty carried away into making it happen or else, and I didn't get to share what a gift it is to even feel this way with you.

What does one "feel" as sheer time passing? As the hope of life living itself out, uncertainly, but relentlessly? Is it to be named suspense? Inner emptiness? Or joy? Or dread? Or impermanence? Perhaps it will emerge strongly at a certain age with another person to be named "procreational urge," "oedipal tension," or "*this* has gone on too long!" What words do we choose? What sensation do we tune into is also a matter of which of the many possible words and narratives we can choose from.

The sensation ages, *it* changes; what name to give it now, and now and now? When might we call it Mystery? We have a vocabulary and various narrative technologies of demystification; what is the vocabulary of mystery and what methods *reveal/depict* it *as* mystery?

> And to imagine a language means to imagine a form of life. (Wittgenstein 1968, p. 8)

CULTIVATING PROGRESS

So seen and worded, so are glandular secretions encouraged and the body grows in the soteriological direction, or somewhat away from "it": the body's own greatest hopes and happinesses.

All therapeutic interventions should foster progress toward the greatest of opportunities and their attendant existential awakening, as well as support the individual in his/her creative ways of being in the world. Thus, therapists must be attentive to subtle and mercurial increments of progress such as "hope buried in cynicism," quiverings of the voice and fleeting glimmers of daringly-resentful-playful-hopefulness in the eyes.

When unfamiliar degrees of happiness or even momentary switches from pessimism to optimism occur, the truism that we do not know what we don't know (in this case, about how to proceed at such times) wields its innocent ignorance with a peculiar backsliding effect: We are happy or optimistic, yes. But it is an *unfamiliar* degree of (dare we trust it) impermanent happiness all the same.

There may be (or are) ways of building upon this optimism and happiness and the world of possibilities that now emerges. There are ways to do this building, but we just don't know what we don't know, so these ways remain hypothetical, they remain inaccessible. The therapist can be most helpful if he knows many ways in which to sustain and thus *build upon* subtle or dramatic degrees of progress, of happiness. "Build upon" can mean: keep the hopeful conversation going another and another round, without distractions. Like building a fire with one twig at a time. "What did you think when you felt hopeful? . . . And what did that make you feel? . . . And what if it could happen? . . . And what would be a next easy-enough step to take? . . . And how does it feel to wonder about this? . . . And you inspire me with your willingness."

Unlike the techniques of "reframing" from narrative therapies, Soteriology asserts that hopefulness is *actually there*, even if we do not see it, and is revealed through faith and devoted (sustained) looking. Reframing emphasizes the reassembling of the words as deftly respinning the situation positively. It makes little claim to revealing any hidden goodness and is thus an honestly naked clinical technique. Soteriology brings a sense of mystery to its action and gives the illusion (or is *it* the "truth") that the hope was really there *anyway*. It is this uncertainty about the hope perhaps being there, even if we don't see it, that makes the soteriological emphasis uncanny.

Named as "uncertainty," "*it*" (something hopeful?) lives in the cracked door that Wittgenstein left a little bit open in his last sentence of the *Tractatus* ("Whereof one cannot speak thereof one must remain silent")—open to the very silence about which we can only say that there is such a thing, a "silent thing," and that we linguistically (which is the only way, if we are intellectually honest in our use of "to speak" [which is a verb, a word, after all]) can't talk (much) about *it* otherwise.

(Perhaps someday many people will act as if the [now rare] truths which emerge in meditative silence and in *khecari mudra* [a yogic maturation of the hypoglossal nerve toward postlinguistic capacities] have always *been there*, thus are here now in your and everyone's spine-heart-throat-mouth-brain, reaching in some cellular way, as you now read this, into that knowing silence. The *it* as a spinal-heart-throat-mouth-brain, hinted tingle.)

So, the therapist is to be experienced in *seeing* hopefulness (where others might not) and in being able *to* mentor clients in each next step forward toward happiness and creative optimism. Most of these steps turn out to be the simple acts of thanking and receiving thanks. They are so simple that they keep being overlooked, or are done shallowly. So the therapist merely keeps the ball of gratitude rolling and keeps seeing progress in its many disguises. Many times progress or hope has been disguised by misusing pop psychopathological concepts.

For example, even "denial" is a kind of hope-against-hope, as if to say, "I wish everything were okay, so I say it is." A denial of something from the past can just as well *be seen as* an affirmation of some hoped-for possibility in the future. Then comes the matter of learning (from the therapist) what one did not know that he did not know (or knew but did not know how to see a next incremental step that he could take, from which other incremental steps would then be possible). So the therapist describes "incremental steps" that the client might not be perceiving and wording as such—increments such as "the glow of quavering hope," or "the (deeper) significance of a 'your welcome'" (to be welcomed, to have free access to the goodness of another) otherwise hidden under taken-for-granted, merely perfunctory, polite (weak) statements. Yet, thanks and welcoming are long-standing, core spiritual sentiments.

GETTING FURTHER INTO THE DETAILS OF CULTIVATING PROGRESS . . .

I want to emphasize that, in the "talking cure," the word *to* in *how to* has great significance. It points in a direction, a for-the-sake-of, that gives the skills of the *how* a purpose, a raison d'etre, and that the skills are definitely going to be applied *to* something that will make the how worthwhile. The *to* focuses the *how* into an even more specific means of doing, leading to and fulfilled by the for-the-sake-of, which is its end. The *to*, of course also points to hopefulness in the form of some kind of *doing* or action that *works* when done.

(We must regularly remember what therapy and its guidances are *for*: that the remaining moments of this life be as poignant, creative, and joyous as possible. Or else the subtended and even iatrogenic conventional goals of "getting in touch with grief," "creating boundaries," and the like, get left standing as if *these are* some type of great or final achievement.)

AND FURTHER INTO THE DETAILS . . .

I point out this humble *to*, to make vivid the level of perspicuity that has enough ferreting-out grasping in it to find such overlooked significances.

When the therapist is *hearing* such soteriological nuances in the obviousness of the overlooked (prepositions like: *in*, so closely related to *intimacy*; the giving denoted by *for*; the unifying *with*), he can hear buried redemptive meaning in his client's presentations and can then bring them (back) to life with his words. For through such perspicuous hearing, intelligence is awakened to subtleties that live during brief durations of time. And in the more hopeless person, it is likely that hope will only be found or be tolerable at such subtle (spiritual?) levels.

AND EVEN FURTHER...

Furthermore, this (how) *to* will take up the very time and energy of the client's *life* in performing the "how to," the clinical guidance. Now it is the *of* that becomes important. This time and energy is *of* something called "the client's life." And in this *of*, in this *of what* we *now* consider, we begin to hear the soul, the soul for the sake of which all this effort is expended, and from which all expendable energy emerges: the uroboric play. TO, FROM, TO, FROM, TO.

NAMING SOTERIOLOGICAL FEELINGS

Therapists can overenjoy pointing out what is being done wrong, if their nosology does not include the healthy ambiguities, or positive rephrasings, of any pathology. They function with a limited vocabulary of hopefulness and cannot see much hopefulness and are stranded with the joy of eureka! in pointing out negative patterns and their etiological histories ("You're caretaking again!") Not knowing or being trained in any other, different (better) skills, this is called no longer mere "diagnosis," but "therapeutic" intervention. Skills like carefully accurate compliment giving or admiration ("clinical admiration") and their assiduous follow-up interventions are absent: the goal of giving and receiving (and getting better at it to the point of the high gratitude and blessing-giving of loving life).

Hyphenated, multitermed emotion descriptions may be more accurate to the lived phenomena of emotionality than singular-word descriptions. Rage shifts to fear, to hate, to shame, to fear—perhaps in the space of a few seconds. The therapist can box in his client's living, fluid emotionality by requiring the client to "identify *the* feeling," or to "stay with *the* identified feeling." If "*the* feeling" changes, will the therapist tell the client to "go back to *the* feeling," "stop avoiding *the* feeling," "stop denying *the* pain"?

We must be aware that encouraging a client to "have your own feelings" is tied to the permission of getting to choose whatever *word* he wants to use to describe his feeling (It's *this kind of* a feeling), or to represent it (I feel scared). And, if single words are further integrated into word neighborhoods, we must see how a word choice hangs together with its neighbors: We can (mis)call uncertainty as "unsafety," although it may impugn the character of others around us as *being* dangerous—but *are* they? We may call longing "unmet needs," although it denotes that others deprive us, perhaps irresponsibly, but *do* they? We may call loss or missing "pain," although it may sound like the missed one has *actively* injured us, but *did* they?

An advanced intern is seeing a family consisting of a mother, father, and a seven-year-old daughter. The father is crying as he talks of another child who died in infancy. The daughter acts concerned for her father and the therapist says to her, "It's okay, just let him be in his pain." The daughter gets even more upset, and confused, "What? Why? That doesn't sound good!" she says. The therapist, says, "It's okay, he needs to be in his pain."

The intern has been so completely trained in the strange clinical language that she does not realize the child is relating the word *pain* to the agony of an injury like falling off a bicycle and bloodying one's knees. "Let him be in his pain" sounds horrible and cruel. My suggestion is to use the phrase: "Your father is feeling the loss of that baby brother of yours, he is missing that baby, he is feeling his love for him and missing him greatly." This comment will help father, daughter, and mother to enter the complex emotionality of grieving. I am guessing that therapists, thousands of them, use the words *pain* or *hurt* when they might better use a set of several descriptors to grasp some complex emotionality. I infer that they unwittingly introduce iatrogenia into the therapy due to their limited and overused, unexamined vocabularies.

Wittgenstein says a language is a form of life. Consider the magnitude of the effects of the therapist's word choices: One kind of family life gets built while the possibility of *other* forms of family life are barely missed.

Is the client's emotionality dependent on the range of his or her therapist's emotion vocabulary? or his therapist's theory and his priority of emotions? (All is sexual, repressed anger or unexpressed grief, unempathized woundedness, etc.)

Stay with that feeling of love, forgiveness, gratitude. Do therapists only box their clients into "pain"? "Stay with the pain. Sink into it." (Stay with the love, uncertainty, awe, flow of emotionalism, sink into it.) Here, patience can be taught, patience with the inherent *flow* of emotionality, not an artificial freezing of this flow for the sake of building up "the" (*sic*) feeling for full catharsis. And even those tears that come will be more complexly nuanced and fluctuating than a single term grasps. The first bright "tears of hopefulness," lasting only a half second or so after some breakthrough must not be missed (and thereby lost to further cultivation) amid the more copious, soggy tears that emerge as the breakthrough is displaced (at the moment of intolerable hopefulness) by some past memory of upset.

Be careful not to make "grief" or "rage" or "getting in touch with your pain" an end in itself. Pain in the service of further pain is often the beginning of masochism. And masochism should not be considered some strange eroticism, but the most ordinary plaintive innuendo, which has come to enjoy complaining. Often this masochism is disguised in phrases like, "This is *my* truth, I *must* speak it." "This is *my* feeling, I am *entitled* to it."

This red-white-and-blue disguise of inalienable rights not to be tread upon should not distract us. Seceding from a relationship as one's strident right to truth often proves the "truth" to be more of a sign of the partners' limited capacities to share and to express the soteriological sentiments than a noble pursuit of happiness or personal truth.

The greatest opportunity of moments of grief is not to feel the depths of anguish or pain but the incomparable preciousness of our finite and particular time together. Grief is, after all, an amalgam of love, missing, and believed loss. Perhaps death can be seen as part of life, a contribution to those still alive here, more than its sense of terrible *loss*. For the loss too is *of life* that thereby conveys life's preciousness. Be wary of sentences that end with mournful nouns like *loss* or *disappointment*. Listen to how the noun changes when we hear what it (the loss, the disappointment) is *about*, *of*, or *for*, when we continue the sentence with a few more words. With a little more listening, and wording, something (falsely depicted as) *totally* lost begins to be redeemed. "Because you *hoped*, you risked this disappointment."

DEVELOPMENT NOW

The final edge where progress/development takes place is the edge of impermanent subtlety in the now-to-next moment. Here is where developmental history has always taken place with each new moment, again and again, altering all the way back through the history-so-far with its contribution, contribution, contribution.

Here each of us wobbles, stands, and moves on our newest legs of newly developed confidence. It is the same situation over and over again that the therapist engages with: To help the client walk forward on these new legs, to forgive what minutes ago felt unforgiveable, to apologize for what moments ago seemed so righteously justified, to avow an intention when minutes ago such intention felt impossible. Then to enact the first step of the vow, and then the second and third, while all the while aware that impermanence withers the effects of each gesture and we are required to create anew, jerryrigging our way from niche to cranny, from this irritating backsliding to the next renewed effort, or faithful surrendering of effort.

Thus the glandular chemistries underlying "mood" and "emotionality" keep altering. Thus, a body (capable) of greater hope, gratitude, and forgiveness grows. Where there is more hope and gratitude, there is less depression; where there is more forgiveness, there is less hostility, humiliation, and vengefulness in us and in the world.

FROM MISSED SUBTLETIES TO THE COLLAPSE OF MASSIVE SOCIAL PROGRAMS

Failures in efforts to help are so often successes up to the point where the subtlety of the *next* necessary step is missed where, after some more dramatic, flailing effort, it is now the more subtle phenomena that we must pay attention to: the quavering of the lip, the near-inaudible tremble of the voice, the faint tinge of a self-doubting blush and apology.

"The expected value for any measured effect of a social program is zero" (Peter Rossi, "Assessing Family Preservation Programs," quoted in Moynihan, 12/11/95, Congressional Record). At some point massive social programs to help people/families become "functional" or "working" must enter these terrains of subtlety to help. Measured failure of social programs, over and over again, merely demarcates where the phenomena of human progress that needed attention were more subtle than what the helpers/program evaluators had been trained to detect, engage with, measure, and build on.

The programs were perfectly good, they just didn't go deeply enough into the soul. But since psychoanalysis is the prevailing paradigm for all soft services (empathy, active listening, boundary setting, etc.), we encounter in many of these programs all the iatrogenic problems I have been describing. Thus, we have the backlash against the "whining poor" and the cutbacks, as if they should just "do it on their own!" I wish that the soteriological model of seeing and mentoring could have been the counseling method active in those decades of massive programs.

For the current doubts in the validity of the liberal agenda are more of a sign of the inherent weakness of conventional psychotherapy that has served as a primary foot soldier in the liberal efforts seeking a "great society" and "wars against poverty" via youth programs, public school child study teams, criminal "diversion" and rehabilitation programs, alternative mediations, and many other social services. But the cure wielded by these well-meaning foot soldiers in these many programs was too often riddled with the iatrogenia I now discuss. Yet, as early as Lasch's *The Culture of Narcissism* (1978), these weaknesses in method, not in the essential liberal attitude, were being noticed. The Menendez abusive childhood psychological "defense" must have put matters over the edge for many people.

What would make the difference between "failure" and continued progress is overlooked because it is so subtle. "Where the mystery is the deepest is the gate to all that is subtle and wonderful": This is not mere poetry. The whole of a national response to human deprivation might rest on the belief that this is truer than the (evershifting) value of the dollar. What are dollars *for*, anyway?

As a juvenile probation officer in Atlantic City, I was called to the pier of a deep sea fishing excursion boat located near the edge of a dangerous neighborhood. The boat captain told me that for decades local kids earned money cleaning the fish caught by the tourists, until one windy day. The knife-waiving kids' calls, "Clean your fish, clean your fish!" pealed out into the wind toward the incoming tourist boat and were misheard by a tourist as "Cut your throats, cut your throats!" The tourist demanded a police car be sent to the scene, and by the next day the only signs of twenty years of previous kids' fish-cleaning business were the circular holes in the boardwalk plankings where the fish-washing sink pipes had been.

An immigrant with no English is coached by his friend on how to order lunch at a restaurant. (In the foreign tongue) "Tell the waitress (English phrase, unexplained to our immigrant): 'Apple pie and coffee.'" For three weeks the immigrant did this. But he grew tired of pie and coffee.

He told his friend this. "Tomorrow, tell the waitress, 'Ham and cheese sandwich.' This will get you another lunch." The next day when he ordered, the waitress asked, "Wheat or rye?" He boggled. He could only say, "Apple pie and coffee!" (As told by Danny Thomas.)

Conventional psychotherapies do not attend to this realm of trembling as a fresh movement forward. Under the sway of psychoanalysis, they use past-oriented (mis)interpretations to (mis)name and pathologize such tremblings. This is of course true for the most priviledged as for the most underpriviledged for, at this edge, there is no historical-socioeconomic explanation. Here we are *all* equally in the unknown, shaking with uncertain hope, with our new intentions. What happens if we believe in this statement of human equality?

FAITH, OPTIMISM, AND SOUL

Consider "implementing optimism" to be the goal of all therapy. The therapist implements optimism with the client, the client implements optimism with the others in his life. Consider *love* to be the superlative adjective characterizing very high optimism, "we can do (almost) anything."

What the therapist estimates as possible often becomes the limit of the client's possibilities as well. If I think a marital problem can be easily resolved, this confidence leads me to persist in one direction. If I think it cannot be resolved, I am led in another direction. How much confidence am I to have? As little as the client-couple? Empathy for the statement, "This is really hard" can go too far.

> HUSBAND. I am really so tired of this.
>
> WIFE. Yes, I am really tired.
>
> THERAPIST. No, you must go on, as tired as you feel. Look into yourself and find the energy. That shred of energy that got you here today, look at each other, see that fatigued but relentless commmitment that persists, let in the recognition that is coming your way for all the hope that your tiredness is *about*, let in just enough to go on. Be proud of each other and get nourished.

A "healthy sense of self" is a structural word-disguise for the living, breathing *mood* of in-play confidence or optimism-cast-into-the-world. The latter description seems to have more vibrancy. The container word, *self*, like the object *a bottle*, begs the question: "A self of what? A bottle of what?" The operative word here is not *self*, but is *healthiness-sense*. The crucial question is "What is felt-health?"—not "What is felt-self?"

When we tell a person what he is not, we have yet to specify what he might be. "You have lost your sense of self." Or is this just *another variant* of a "sense of self"?—a sense of being lost, of being in the unknown, uncertain, or even of daunting wonder? Now we don't have to start from nothing nor to deprive our client of a sense of self, that is, of being in need of a *fundamental* "restoration," instead of being in need of improving certain capabilities in feeling uncertain, daunted, longing for greater confidence.

The clinical goal of implementing optimism is not best obtained by using the politico-military metaphor of "building (healthy) boundaries" but by the language of respect, sharing, giving, and receiving. The former metaphor breeds distrust and dehumanization. Respect is most authentic when it is a secondary response to feeling the shy awe of the other or oneself. Just have two people look at each other in silence for thirty seconds and shy awe emerges, respect emerges.

> Every It is bounded by others; It exists only through being bounded by others. But when Thou is spoken, there is no thing. Thou has no bounds. (Buber 1958, p. 4)

Conventional clinical opinions are often based on an overdefined and idealized concept of "individuation," which is a quasi-biological analog to "a fully weaned adult." In contrast, many existentialists assert that relationship, *dasein* (being-here or being-in-the-world), or I-Thou, *not* individuation, is the fundamental human condition.

> I become through my relations to the *Thou*, as I become *I*, I say *Thou*. All real living is meeting. (Buber 1958, p. 11)

> The chief concern is not with these products of analysis and reflection but with the true original unity, the lived relation. (ibid., p. 19)

There is no constant self to become or to restore (from the past). Instead, one can develop a sense of confidence (hope, optimism, faith) in relating to the world based on phenomenal experiences of improved skillful relating, communicating, risk taking, giving, and receiving. One becomes willing to use the word *confidence* to describe oneself. Via the irony of the Peter Principle, more confidence often leads to ever more challenging involvements in the world—that is, feeling more challenged and less confident.

In the rough-and-tumble world, arming ourselves with the idea of an "owned self" may feel like a worthy strategy. But, as Rilke noted, "In the end it is our unshieldedness on which we depend."

The soul (psyche) is the reservoir of endless optimism (faith, possibility, love, hope, durability, eternal impermanence). We can focus on other things and we can come back to optimism. The soul may not be omnipotent, but it is inexhaustible, and the more we draw from it, the more enobled our lives become.

A dread creeps in as we grasp the awe of the soul's *capacity to* endure all, for the implication is that if the dreadful were to happen (even death), we are *capable of* enduring it and thus we would go through such unthinkable fires, unavoidably. This is what Kierkegaard referred to as the "dread" that accompanies a sense of the infinite. It is a dread of the uniquely infinite potency of the soul, not its "woundedness." *Soul* is the name of this infinite resourcefulness. It confounds the limited ego sense of conventional psychology. We are daunted by our own, perhaps hidden, durability—the durability of time itself. And make no mistake: To endure receiving a moment of love that is so great as to awaken us into the infinity in which that moment takes place is daunting enough as to shy us away from receiving such a love.

There are many professional vocabularies in which the word *soul* does not exist, or if it does, its unique and essential eternal resourcefulness is negated. The soul becomes something, just like the ego, *woundable* and finite. The popular concept of *soul* is merely the new wine of the 'self' in an old, expensive-looking bottle. We see this to a degree in Thomas Moore's version of the soul or, worse, in Shengold's masochistic oxymoron in the extreme: "soul murder." (*Soul* names that which survives even death.)

Conventional medical-model therapy has become so uncritical in its use of the term *woundedness* that it now applies it to the Source of our being, the soul. Is this not a new version of the damnation narrative, of the original sin narrative, not as a guilty soul, but as a victimized soul? Thus, too, we have transpersonal-psychoanalytic clinical narratives coining pathologies of "original" or "primal" wounds. *Are* there *such things*? In saying there are not, I am merely championing the existence in each human being of a divine resilience, a hopefulness that Frankel and others found (were willing to put into words) even in the death camps that would not die—even *there*.

Consider too: The conventional therapist, in his creation of "*This*-Precedent-Pain-Explains-All-Difficulties" narratives, has given himself permission to characterize perpetrator actions with a never-before heinousness: of being "murderous" of the *deathless* soul. The demands of his healing narrative (its singular logos) and the demands it places upon its curative empathy solely have grown so great that it requires the client's soul to surrender its eternal resiliency. In this healing narrative, the soul is to be made "dead" (not just wounded) by the events of the past. But, in exchange, the client receives the resurrective degree of empathy from the therapist who, *by being willing to speak like this and only like this*, gives his unflinching empathy for his client. To call it "soul murder" *is* the empathy. The narrative taketh, but it giveth back again.

If *I* lose my soul, then *I* am left, and my soul is gone. Yet, *soul* names what is eternal. This *I* that is left is really the soul (*deserves* the name *soul*), the soul which, by definition, never forsakes and is always there. Whatever happens, *it* is still there, and let's always call that so unique and fundamental *it* that remains "soul." It is the clinical vocabularies, unchecked in their endless psychopathologizings, that have lost their commitment to such linguistic integrity. The sense of something being *lost* is experienced *by* the everpresent soul. *Lost* is, for all that, only a word trying to express a very bereft state. Soul names what in the final analysis, in the endless flow of contemporaneity, consciously, even catatonically, is never lost. Not even in bodily death or by capital executions.

The switch from the religiously "guilty soul" to the psychologically "wounded soul" is the shell game at play. But under these popular psychological word shells no real soul is granted: no infinite resourcefulness.

Pastoral counseling's "ministerings to the soul" refers to reminding us that we are souled beings, replete with soteriological potencies and sentiments. The phrase "doctoring the soul" can be heard in a way that implies loss of faith in the soul's infinite resourcefulness. The metaphor "food for the soul" can also be confusing, since the capacity for endless longing is part of the soul's nature. In uroboric fashion, the soul is self-nourished heartfully by feeding upon its longings-become-devotion then love.

The word *soul*, like the word *water*, should name what it is most uniquely in the theo-psychological language game. Soul is essence-as-divine-spark. If the word *divine* is to mean anything unique, in contrast to the secular or mundane, it should mean "endless refuge of hope, love, forgiveness, and grace." Cynical worldly knowing, or aging-as-bitterness, is an affront to the soul that ages us with soteriological wisdom. Is this true? I hope so, I live as if it is.

In various mystical psychologies, the naming of oneself as a worthless sinner is prized, for in those language games this extreme statement only goes to match the faith one might develop in a Diety Who loves even what we might call "the sinner." In a spiritual psychology there might be certain convolutions whereby low self-esteem (or humility) is critical in developing faith in a love greater than what we feel we deserve, which we grow into. And such extreme unlovability would seem to be the test case.

Should there be no more cynicism or hopelessness, there would be no more pejorative mundane. *Mundus*, or mundane-as-wholeness-world would be manifest. The spirituality of "the ordinary" involves the stirring of complacency or cynicism into poignancy, and poignancy into compassion, then admiration, respect, wisdom, and awe. t,t,t,t,t,t

DREADFULLY QUIVERING LOVE

Buber describes as "dreadful" the point in one's maturing capacity to love, of becoming capable of loving the consentually unlovable, the enemy, for such love seems an affront to all manners of ordinary emotionality. In whose eyes would such a developing love be seen as "denial of buried anger," or as "premature forgiveness"?

And if such love begins to emerge, how would we recognize it in its embryonic status? How might a therapist help it into sustained existence? "See how this love matures you into a risky place. Embrace the risk, and believe that a wisdom will come to you with your willingness to love this 'enemy' to keep you as able as possible to keep creating the good life. Or if you waver, seek help from those who can help to keep your relationship growing in this hopeful direction."

I can look at a "dysfunctional" family and see something I like, something admirable. Regarding this aspect, I cannot use the adjective *dysfunctional*. When I point it out, family pride quavers. The received admiration fills the room. Again and again, its permutations are described and more hopeful words, tears, shames, apologies emerge.

> THERAPIST. Do you think it is easy for your parents to be here and have a perfect stranger, me, see your family problems? No. It isn't, but you know why they are willing to go through this?
> SON. I don't know—they want us to get along better, I guess.
> THERAPIST. Yes, and look now at the tears of hope in your father's eyes. You caused that with your recognition of his hopefulness. Tell your son

what his hope means to you. (Son is thinking, "What? I don't feel any hope." But as his father's eyes brim, I point this out and in his father's eyes he sees the hope that he could only express sarcastically. *Now*, the subtlest of quiverings can be seen in his face too and I point it out, and they grow into a blush. Even in a hardened youth. *Now* I have father and son look at each other, which they can only do for one second. *Now* I say, "See, you have shared a hope for a second and you can hardly believe it. Go ahead. Believe it.")

Having recourse to temporal phenomenology as an interpretive basis lightens the therapist's use of family members (mothers and fathers, particularly) to etiologically "explain" the "why" of client difficulties. This psychoanalytic line of interpretation seems often to demonize many parents in the process of etiological analyses. For difficulty in sustaining progress in psychotherapy is not merely an archaic matter of some parents who once "wish[ed] to push the patient back in emotional development or back into the inside into the unborn state or in some way or other destroy growing points in the patient" (Winnicott 1989, p. 249)—it is fundamentally a more innocent matter of impermanence itself.

Winnicott continues assuredly, "There is every possible degree of this to be encountered in our work, in which the patient needs to reach to what in its simplest form is the mother's hate . . . or the mother's repressed and unconscious hate" (ibid., p. 250). Far more daunting, as I have seen, is for child and mother to encounter their silently trembling love, or "hopeless hope" for love, with each other. In that shakey hope-blooming moment an awakening to "what could have always been," or "what both would most want to have been" (but only rarely happened), bursts in anguish out of its cold storage.

The "hate" now seems to be a thin-skinned protectiveness from "the (agonizingly) too good to be true: the most hoped-for, long-missed" and not an actual hatred of anyone. And the shakiness is the thawing out into the daunt of real impermanence with its soteriological callings. Thus come the characteristic tears of long-missing, the apologies and forgivenesses, and the back-and-forth surge of hopefulness during such sessions where the long estranged family members tentatively discard the past (giving up their [protective] "better judgment") and then suddenly rush toward each other; At least for that while, and *whenever* they return to speak and act toward *this* uncertain new future history. Thus, two spells are broken: the spell of the past and the psychoanalytic spell that has us miss the life-altering daunt of unconscious (excruciatingly too-poignant) ideal hopes.

Questioning Words—Reviving Time 55

The therapist is like a rockclimbing guide coaxing family members onto one ledge or handhold and then another, overcoming fears and stepping further up onto this mountain of the impermanently actualized most-hoped-for, and their own development as ensouled human beings. Fascinated and consumed by psychopathology, therapists can ask far too little of their clients.

> DAUGHTER. I hate my father.
> THERAPIST. I know you won't mean it, but see what it's like to say "I love you, Daddy."
> DAUGHTER. What? You're nuts!
> THERAPIST. You can do it, try. Before he's dead and gone.
> DAUGHTER. (quivering, scoffing, smirking, thinking about it).
> THERAPIST. Father, tell your daughter you love her.
> FATHER. (shaking, sweating) I do love you.
> DAUGHTER. I can't say it, I can't.
> THERAPIST. Look at each other as you say that you can't. Look.
> DAUGHTER. (looks up and down)
> THERAPIST. Keep looking. He's just an old man, tell him.
> DAUGHTER. Yes, you're right: I do, I do. (father starts sobbing; daughter breaks down too)

Imagine a *DSM-"x"* that describes how, in a generalized way, the glimmers of health look, uniquely, in people suffering with each of the conditions outlined in the *DSM-IV*. R. D. Laing has described the "mask of insanity"—what do you really believe is behind the mask? Bad genes? Hatred of Mother? Or trapped and perhaps highly contorted unending hopefulness?

Consider giving the delusional, psychotic client the appreciation and contact that she lacks which drives her into her irreality for *some* warmth or hope, no matter how distant:

> PATIENT. I'm ready to leave this plane and go to the light. Oh, there is purple light all in this room. And my channeled guides are here now. Yes? Oh, sure. Agamemnon, Yes?
> THERAPIST. Jan, you are so very lonely, but your heart is full of love, you just want to connect with someone, you're so special.
> PATIENT. I want to, I want to. Yes I am lonely. Yes.

It is not a matter of seeing the cup as half-empty or half-full; it is of seeing the cup as even 1 percent full and 99 percent empty. For this 1 percent will become (impermanently) 2, 4, 10, 99, in the space of a few well-timed therapist interventions and teachings. And, ironically, one percent of progress in the midst of hopeless hostility and despair can be far more poignant than progress during far better times. And this soulful poignancy heroically allures us to go beyond all odds for what is best.

> THERAPIST. Given how much you resent each other and that you are both here only because of a court order, do you think it is any easier for Tom to be here in this session than it is for you? [Sue nods, "No."] And Tom, do you think it's easy for Sue to be here? (Tom: "No.")
>
> Well, then, look at each other, and you will see a kind of courage in the other that you *know* you have in yourself that underlies you being here, instead of having been too afraid or hopeless or cynical to have even come to this session. You know *you* have it because you are here. Now look—see it, grant it *in* Sue, *in* Tom. And feel that the courage and fragile hopefulness that things could get better in you is being seen by this other person, who looks at you now, in his eyes, in her eyes, for it is the same kind of courage that is in you. There, quivering, see it? Now know you are being seen—and with particular appreciation because it may be difficult to do so, given all the distracting thoughts or memories there might be. Get free of them, be in this time of this willingness. See each other striving, struggling, succeeding bit by bit in sharing this recognition with you.

Yet, impermanence withers moments of progress, requiring new looking, acting, speaking. And the remorseful sense of how nearby hope always is, the hope we merely do not speak of, and instead articulate the next logical reaction to the last reaction to some missed hope that got confusedly misnamed, and incendiarily misnamed, perhaps as "hope murdered." A reach away, not far, is another form of (soterio)logic and life, in need at times only of a midwifing from this other dimension of spiritual hope.

GOAL AS THERAPY

Congruence of the *means* (interventions, interpretations) with the *goal* (optimism, gratitude, or love, within and as felt-impermanence) is the mark of clinical efficiency. The preciousness of time evokes clinical efficiency. The sense of the eternal provokes desperate to wondrous tonalities of hopefulnesses.

The goal is to improve skills in giving and receiving love and gratitude. Do not be seduced by erudite clinical methods whose techniques stop short of learning to give and receive at least simple compliments.

Therapy can get bogged down (become less efficient) in subtended technical objectives such as trying to "diagnose the disorder," "restore a self," "create boundaries," "identify the transference," or to "achieve full cathartic discharge." For there is no inherent connection between such matters and the gaining of expressive and receptive fluencies with love and gratitude, or becoming optimistic and living in such good faith.

Ironically, getting good at talking about our difficulties can make life seem overwhelming and onesided. Especially if we also do not improve our ability to talk about our hope, joy, love, and spiritual powers of faith, forgiveness, apology, wonder, or awe.

Complaints can often be seen as longings stated in the negative, and then restated as a longing. For, within the complaint is the implied opposite: the specific hope, or the hope for hopefulness. For, negated verbs are far more difficult to respond to than positively asserted verbs and can make it difficult to take action for oneself. "I love it when you do (x)," rather than "I don't like you when you do (-x)." Or, "I'm so longing to be happy," rather than "I am so depressed."

Hopefulness grows into optimism and that into willingness. Willingness grows into desires to do, act, express. Actions bud and then involvement, commitment, and modest-to-abundant giving. Thus accrues confidence, skillfulness, knowledge, and value-in-the-world. Yet, always in the face of uncertainty.

"NEED": AN INNOCENT-LOOKING BUT MOST SEVERE WORD

Beware of the verb *to need* and the noun *a need*. Is this to be called "an unmet need" or "a longing"? Remember as you choose your words, vocabularies are forms of *life*. The authority of the expert (the one who chooses the names to be used at any move in a particular language game) has been granted to you (the therapist). What do you do with it now? What form of life are you creating in this session?

FROM "NEEDS," ALMOST INVISIBLY, TO NARRATIVES OF (UNDETECTED) DETERMINISM

Take a longing (for x in the future) and instead call it an "unmet need" (from the past) and you begin to breed a sense of deprived victimization at the hands of the (implied) one who "should have" met your need.

Innuendos of bitterness resonate in each word: "unmet" ("should have been met" is the suggested innuendo of entitlement) and "need" (desperate urgency). Call it a "longing" and the innuendo aims you into the present-future with hope and passion.

But which *is it?* If only one "satisfier" during a specific moment is deemed to satisfy a "developmental need," then we are dealing with a developmental schema with severe, exacting standards. In any situation various distinct senses of neededness and criteria of need satisfaction should be teased apart:

1. "Case of one" satisfiers: only one thing/person/action fulfills the need. (Oxygen is needed, no other gas will support life; but do we really believe that only maternal-infant "mirroring" will suffice for certain aspects of ego development? If other satisfiers are allowed/seen to foster these aspects of ego development, then maternal mirroring is *not*, in this sense, the singularly "necessary" satisfier.)
2. Temporal precision: satisfaction can occur only at an appointed moment. (The cake burns if not taken from the oven after thirty minutes.) Mirroring must be given as baby looks up curiously at 6:21 P.M. on this date/phase of his developmental passage. But can this development be catalyzed at many points in a person's life? If so, then it was not, in this sense, "needed" back then.
3. The converse condition is unfulfilling too: something useful does not occur when the prescribed satisfier is not present. But, if something useful—endurance, capacity to yearn, opportunity to forgive—is deemed to occur, then, in this sense, the "unmet need" must be qualified by what developed in its stead.
4. Recipient complicity: if the defined satisfier arrives, the recipient may also need to do something. If the recipient must do certain things on being given a satisfier in order to receive it, then *he needs* to do them. For example, the recipient saying "Thank you" might be required for reception to occur. A facility with feeling gratitude may be prerequired for need satisfaction to occur. We can imagine someone being given a satisfier and not acknowledging or even noticing it, thus having a need met *without knowing it.*

Thousands of times in couples sessions, I have seen clients complain about not getting something that was, to some obvious degree, coming his way at that very moment. "She doesn't go places with me!" (What about this very session?)

Questioning Words—Reviving Time 59

"Exacting standard statements" do not insure the essentiality of the (thing being called a) need; standards can be raised out of vengefulness alone. "That wasn't good enough." "No, it's too late to apologize or make up for it." They can be suddenly lowered as a recompense or gift for something just received. More gifts might be given than are received or even noticed as being gifts—even by the givers themselves. "There might actually be a case where we should say 'This man [only] *believes* he is pretending'" (Wittgenstein 1968, p. 229)—when he is credibly being sincerely giving. According to someone, somewhere.

The so-called basicness of something called "required" or "needed" can sound like it is *really needed* by merely couching it in exacting standard terms. The word *need* is itself pure exactitude terminology. In a world where certainty is hard to come by, the word *need* misused can give artificial solace.

Maybe we should deal with less exacting standards in defining satisfiers. Call it a longed-for or missed helpfulness, support, or admiration. If it isn't essential, then it isn't "needed." If it was essential, but has since been met, then it isn't "unmet." If it could have been met if I had allowed for this meeting, then I must figure in my responsibility, too, in this narrative of "Stuart's 'unmet need' history."

The longed for, missed matter can still be very important. We have merely deleted an iatrogenic, linguistic inaccuracy so common in conventional and popular psychology.

Many theologies speak of dieties that meet the needs/longings of the disconsolate, deprived, dispairing, or abused. The outcryings of spiritual forsakeness, how do they differ from the repeated clinical catharses?

(We cannot ignore the pervasive capitalist-consumer economy's dictum to "identify a need, go buy/market something to fill it." In such an economy, deepened appreciation for *what already is* can slow down market demand, which slows down the rate of consumption. This need-hysteria dictum has entered pop psychology.)

In the shift from the preceding Catholic confessional to the modern psychoanalytic session, the focus on abuses committed is exchanged for abuses endured: the old guilt is exchanged for the new woundedness/anger/blame. The new analytic religion competes well with the confessional, saturated with an encouraged sexuality and, here, opening up for the client an unchecked discursive flow of innocent woundedness. The client is always owed something while the penitent was always owing. Original sin becomes "original pain." The soul is more noble than all this.

In devotional spiritualities, longing itself is something to be *filled with*. As the individual accepts and then loves his longing, the strained outreaching of longing relaxes, one expands, and the longing transforms. It becomes more spacious, matured unconditional love or sheer fulfillment. In yoga this is known as *viyoga*, union through apparent separation. Thus some saints (St. John of the Cross, Shri Aurobindo) attained beatitude in prison, and most saints praise the state of longing as penultimate.

> All art aspires to the condition of music, said Walter Pater, and poetry, for one, apparently refuses to get mesmerized by human suffering, including that of its very practitioners. The natural inference is that there are matters more absorbing than the frailty of one's body or agony of one's soul. This inference, made by both the public and its watchdogs, makes poetry and, with it, all the arts dangerous. To put it differently, art's unwitting by-product is the notion that the overall human potential is far greater than can be exercised, not to mention catered to, by any given social context. In certain circles, this news is unwelcome. (Brodsky 1996, p. xiii)

THE CLIENT'S SITUATED LIFE IS THE CLIENT, NOT HIS SELF OR STORY

Via the concept of Dasein (being-in-the-world), therapy must revive optimism within the client's life web of relationships and involvements, not merely within his "self." Thus, we bring the client's significant others into sessions, instead of merely talking about them, at the earliest convenience for a series of sessions, to invigorate these others with hope and guide them into sharing it. We have created a miniculture, a "where two or more gather together . . ." language game, an interactivity of hope in the client's life world.

Early family therapists revealed the power of family therapy sessions to disbelieving analysts, at first against their wills or, rather, against the spell cast by their theories.

As soon as a family comes into the therapist's office, they deserve to be told of how impressive it is for them to come, of the kind of expression of hope, commitment, and courage that coming to the session is. Because they won't believe this, they must be told in various ways that just showing up is courageous, hopeful, and an admirable entrustment to the therapist. One member blushes with shy pride or perhaps tears up with a surge of hope as this is pointed out. For a moment, and another and another, the mood has changed, and this changed mood becomes a critical resource, for history has momentarily changed.

The therapist states his appreciation in being allowed to help with so worthy a project as bringing to life the greatest hopes of family members: that they will be reconciled, loving, and happy with one another. As the goal is described—even in the first five minutes of the first session—members begin to cry, brimming with longing and hope that this goodness could be true.

The therapist invites each to avow a commitment for the better, to stand as potential helpers to one another, and to be open to both asking for and receiving the help that one asks for. And to be perservering in growing appreciation of impermanence. A great deal of admiration emerges in such avowals and becomes the nourishment that sustains each member's efforts.

Each week, successes are praised, new refinements are devised, and optimism grows. Pessimistic generalizations from the past become more and more obsolete as predictors of the future.

Yet, few people can easily absorb compliments and admiration, and thus, the work focuses on this auspicious problem. The mood of the family is very charged and optimistic. There is laughter. Such family sessions can easily be done on a conference call with members spread out all over the country. For it is the spirit of these changes and not merely their visibility that foments the change. In fact, the barrier of the phones can be complimented as the family's willingness to "try *anything*, if it could remotely work." And the more difficult the problem (perpetrators and abused, litigious divorcees, long-estranged parent-child relationships), the greater its potential leverage:

> THERAPIST. You know how difficult this is, and yet you are here today, he's here too, she's here, in spite of how horrible this all is: that says something about courage and hope for your children, doesn't it? Look at each other, and see in the other the same struggle with hope you went through to get here, for the sake of a possible improvement in your coparenting. The pride in yourself that you feel in coming today, come out of your own self-consciousness, and see it in this other sitting across from you. There is no reason you can't create the best coparenting situation in this county. We can do that.

And feel the court that ordered you to come, not as some kind of harsh authority, but as hoping just as we can hope that *something* helpful might happen, based on something happening that is greater than all your bitterness and cynicism.

Look, see each other wondering about what I'm saying. That is the hope, and see that you are both wondering this, and look and see that you are sharing this wavering possibility, and say to each other what of this wavering, no matter how flimsy and vaporous, say to each other what it was like the moments you wondered, what if? Even for a split second. Then give something to the other on his or her terms exclusively, give something that he or she wants that you know he or she wants, give it as a gift. And don't be stingy. Your children will see that their parents can still give and they will be proud and inspired by what you accomplish.

Admiring can easily take up nearly the whole session. This is the climate in which to solve substantive family problems, and not before. There is more creativity and willingness at this time and not before. Starting where the family is at (their current resentments) is provocative and fits the cathartic model, but lacks wisdom about what people most hope for. Within a revived setting of what is most hoped for, resentments can be brought up: now there is a felt reason why *to* reconcile differences.

Since conventional therapists refer the "other" [or the couple] to another therapist, guided by the theoretical concept of "containerism" and fears of "triangulation," most will never meet these others, and the existential scope of the client's story remains unenlarged.

And when there are abuses, skillful repeated use of apology and forgiveness, unearthing buried hopes and gratitudes, here-now shared shyness and glimmers of love can cultivate a new ground for developing healthy relationships. We remember what all therapeutic efforts are *for* and aim to bring that about. Not all at once, or even just eventually, but impermanently, over and over, amid (not just after) the "processing" of any grievous feelings.

An apology can't be received from someone who isn't in the session room, thus clients can endlessly experience outrage about not being given an apology by that person and perhaps never achieve reconciliation. The impact of the abuse is minimized when the apology can be made because all parties are in the session room together, thus the aggrieved one's forgiveness comes easier.

Even then, abused and abuser have a difficult time looking eye to eye at each other for very long, and the former turns away as the abuser is being most contrite, and the abuser turns away (in shameful disbelief in being forgiven) as the abused is feeling at all forgiving. And what they turn away from, falls out of their visual-perceptual field (as if it didn't really happen), unless the therapist can return them to those glimmers of eye-to-eye contact that flicker with the soteriological struggle.

The future hopefulness of the reconciled relationship begins to peek out; the past begins to recede. Some will say, "minimizing abuse is like denial, a repression of the survivor's pain and woundedness. It *all* has to come out, and even then forgiveness is optional." But what kind of goal is it that does not include reconciliation? And the *all* that comes out, won't the injured party benefit more from sharing this with his abuser? And won't the abuser have a greater chance at apologizing and reconciling, by taking in the abused's sorrow? This "all" also includes "too good to be true" hopes for love and a happy future, even if at first crusted over with bitterness, shame, and vengefulness. And the courage and pride in trying is enough to compensate for a possibly disappointing outcome.

I once led a group at the Institute of Holocaust Reconcilation and Remembrance of Jewish death camp survivors, the adult children of Nazi officers, a Palestinian victim of Israeli bombings, and other victims of military-political violence. When the ragings emerged about the six million, about the unfair endless guilt-mongerings against Germans, about contemporary Israeli violence against Palestinians and Palestinian violence against Israelis, I enforced only one rule: If you wish to speak about these things, do so freely, but look into the eyes of those around you to see your listeners listening to you. See in their wincing responses that you are being heard. Let that in and do not speak to merely let your anguish out. Let in the present moment in which these living listeners are hearing you too.

When the listener's eyes would well up with tears, and this was seen by the agonized speaker and the wreckage of human tragedy hung in the air, the claws of retaliation and the subtle promise of sorrow would arise. All hinged upon the shared shame and horror, and the now-and-future moments into which another kind of future could be hoped for. All hinged upon this being a shared sorrow, shared in different ways, but granted by all as becoming shared and emptying out into an undetermined future. Our nonomnipotence was then the most difficult to bear, and the fact that time was still happening, in which perhaps anything could happen (again). And even if nothing of the sort happens "again," we would still be faced with the fundamental challenge: sharing new admirations, gratitudes, and the arising of optimism and its risks, senses of finitude and mortality, and finding in that strangely shy innocence (and in only that) sufficient redemption of the past.

We rarely tap the effective potencies of the soteriological and instead hover in the retributive or "explanatory." As Nietzsche decried that an atrophied spirituality "killed God," so has our atrophied faith in the soteriological powers of apology and forgiveness killed (withered) these spiritual powers. The powers are still alive and potent, but we live as if they are childishly weak and pollyannic. We, as Nietzsche would say, must "overcome ourselves."

Forgiveness drops out of the clinical narrative: "You don't have to forgive," the conventional therapists announce, "Get into your anger." In conventional therapy, there is far more concern for premature forgiveness than there is for perseverated anger. Are we afraid of our nonomnipotence in the face of a future of uncertainty and thus we arm ourselves with this flow of anger about the past to feign omnipotence, and displace the uncertain future with the spector of a horrific but familiar past?

ON BEHALF OF *NONDIFFERENTIAL* DIAGNOSIS: WE ARE MORE THE SAME THAN WE ARE DIFFERENT

We must include people who have experienced extraordinary difficulties among those clients who are to learn how to be happy. Survivorhood, cathartic grieving, getting "healed" miscast the therapeutic project. Do not be distracted by the extraordinariness of a client's extreme difficulties. Each is to be helped in achieving the universal goal.

A client should not be prejudged (diagnosed), based on the difficulties he has experienced, as meriting treatments that are diversionary from life's spiritual purpose: deepening the ability to give and receive love and know happiness. He should not be put onto a specialized subtended tract that aims short of the universal goal.

"Specialists" are therapists who are undistracted from the universal goal by the extraordinary difficulties they specialize in. Someone who specializes in working with schizophrenia is not distracted by the eccentricities peculiar to this diagnosis and brings happiness, hopefulness, and expanded skillfulness to such clients, essentially, just like with any other clients.

Someone who specializes in abused adult-children is not distracted by the extreme difficulties experienced by such clients. For, if the client is not helped in going forward into life's greatest opportunities, he can more easily fall backward. The opportunities will likely always be more subtle than the catastrophics of the dramatic past, yet this subtlety and its innocence of hope must be understood as more dramatically alluring than the overtly dramatic horrors.

COHERENCE HAS ITS LIMITATIONS

Because a story designed and written by an author must be coherent for us to follow its themes and plot, do we assume that a person's life has "themes" and a "plot" and is as coherent as a book? The therapist's idiom, "I see this theme in your life," could be exchanged for, "Apply this theme to the events of your life." (What themes are therapists taught to use with clients? What themes are never mentioned?)

Just because we have read many stories of people's lives, fictions or biographies, these are still only books. Consider all that is left out of any book. All that description, billions of words. Who is to choose and how can anyone say, "This is *the* story of his life"?

When more events of one's life are added into the story, the consequences are more than merely additive; often the impact significantly alters the life story and the sense of the protagonist-self. And there is always more that can be added in, most of which we do not know about now. Where does this information exist before we find out about it?

A story cannot be too incoherent—or we won't recognize it as a "good story." If rewriting doesn't end, as new events relentlessly keep occurring, there will be no final story. But what if one's real life is composed of events so mosaiclike, so minced together, that it is too incoherent to be a "good story" narrative? How would a therapist deal with such lives? Indeed, how does the therapist function when each new event can suggest an altered significance to the whole mosaic of past events?

"God works in mysterious ways": ways that are not only perhaps incoherent, but invisible to us. All that we are left with is a feeling of the suspense of life as the penumbra of the Infinite.

For we cannot say where thoughts come from, or what they were before they were the thoughts they now are. Try to trace a thought you have to its origin before it just now became a thought. Thus Heidegger speaks of "the horizon of being."

A therapist earns her living by interpreting the client's life as a coherent narrative to explain why the client is the way he is. In this language-livelihood game, she does not earn when she cannot or does not explain, and if the client stops explaining his life, why would he stay in such a therapy?

If therapists ignore the soteriological resources (scorning them as problematic superego introjects or as "dependency inducers"), they cannot help patients develop those abilities. They lay fallow. The etiological search of pointing out and grieving what went wrong and feeling how it went wrong ensues as the austere cure. Without much access to the soteriological sentiments, therapists become primarily "analytic empathizers," and loyal to its austerity. Buddhist psychoanalyst, Mark Epstein describes a response to an adult patient who,

> [sees herself as] a five-year-old girl . . . hiding behind a huge billboard proclaiming all of her achievements. Her fantasy was of being rescued from behind the billboard. But, mindful of Winnicott's injunctions, I asked her *only* [my emphasis of the esteemed austerity of method] how it felt to be noticed in such a good hiding place. (Epstein 1995, p. 38)

The therapist cannot thank her for sharing her loneliness and hope with him, or help her to receive his admiration for her courageous honesty. Yet, if so, can he then praise (redeem) her achievements and receive gratefully the nourishment of her thanks and help her export these new abilities/poignancies of receiving and giving into the rest of her impermanent life, thus lessening her faultering overreliance on achievement narcissism? The psychoanalytic austerity gives rise to the proud "only" and its knowing and playful (and thus very nourishing) hide-and-seek "finding" of her.

Consider the assertion: A lived life may be too incoherent to be made into a readily coherent life story. An event may have more factors than reported, or noticed, by those involved. New events occur and change the outcome of a week ago. A long list of themes might lead to ostensibly contradictory themes. But "contradictions" only emerge when we are looking at the list through a binary contrast, logic lens. Without this lens, this way of looking, we just have the list. Sometimes we use this lens and other times we might ask a client for contradictory stories.

2, 4, 6, 8, 10, . . . What is the next number? The answer I am going to give helps us look at this sequence in a new way. The answer is, I don't know yet. I must wait and am willing to wait and see what you write next. The answer is, It will be the next number you write. Knowing as watching, not as generalizing from what has already happened. But, even in watching, will t we t be t aware t of t impermanence and the new moment during which t the next number is written?

But, over and over I see clinicians creating "coherent, noncontradictory narratives": Thus, what drops out of their clinically adduced life stories are the inconsistencies: and in most therapies this usually means "the good, inspiring times," which are incompatible with the special etiological history story being spun. 12 always must follow 2,4,6,8,10. Thus 14,16,18 *must* be next, right (to prove the existence of the *pattern*)? All the odd numbers drop out, as generalization knowing overcomes watching-waiting knowing.

"History" goes in a direction other than it would if the power of apology-forgiveness were strong. Apology or forgiveness can seem like they come out of nowhere, that they are inconsistent with one's anger and disappointment of a moment ago.

Coherence of narrative is everything if one wants to be convincing. A client says, "I *can't* apologize!" which does not necessarily mean that he is *unable* or even unwilling to apologize. Consider that it can mean that within his narrative, it would be inconsistent to his role as the protagonist-victim in his etiological "history" to apologize for anything. And within his therapist's healing narrative, urges to apologize or forgive will first be suspected as "flights to the light" or repressions of yet more buried rage requiring perhaps months or years of working through. Try apology and forgiveness with the anger coming out too. This is soteriological "working through."

When perpetrators are willing and available to come to sessions, their visible and expressed shame and contrition can foster a forgiveness in the abused. Thus, unforgiveness is not simply a matter of repressed affect, but of the need for sufficiently expressed (by the abuser) and then let-in (by the abused) contrition. This "sufficiency" is a function of the abused venting his feelings and watching his perpetrator wince in empathic shame and contrition. In the end (over the course of weeks or months), sorrow, anguish, relief, admiration, forgiveness, and apology have been exchanged. Here is the basis for a deep "Alternative Dispute Resolution" process: The unusually high soteriological aim *helps* make it work. The lack of a high enough aim—mere compromise, or punitivity—is the problem. Something greater than the dispute must lure the disputants: noble soteriological goals do just that.

The power of forgiveness to dissolve anger and create reconciliation and health will always confound conventional sensibilities. Thus, *soteriology* carries the definition of "sciences of healing," as well as "ways of redemption." The anger-processing therapist will always need to inspect for his own covert (countertransferential) vengefulness against perpetrators as animating his interest in sustaining his client's anger phase. Without a clear image of the beauty of the possible mutual reconciliation, the therapist can hardly convey to anyone (including herself) why anyone would want to even come to such a session. With a sense of the beauty, a facilitating grace comes.

Forgiveness as healing the cause of pain, not the effect: Jack Schwarz, a man with documented extraordinary endurance of physical pain, discovered his powers as a teenager in Germany when, as a young Jew, he was arrested by the Gestapo and was being whipped by a German soldier. All that Schwarz could think of was how sad it was that this soldier had to be beating him, that it must be horrible for the soldier. The bloody welts rose on Schwarz's back and would immediately heal after each blow. The guard could not bear this miracle and released Schwarz.

VENGEFUL INFLATION OF "ANGER": A MORE MODEST DEFINITION

I am wondering if situations in which anger is typically reported can be described more accurately with other words such that a peculiarity of the emotion "anger" is laid bare: that its unique function is as a weapon, that is, as a kind of aggressive instrument ("claw" or "hiss"?) whose jobs include self-defense or protection via threat, avenging, securing objectives by force (intimidation, taking), endowing oneself with a sense of dominance or security, or as a kind of emotional-erotic sport or martial game (as in sadomasochism, the multifarious and perverse enjoyments of pain and anguish).

Look more carefully at client situations where therapists use the term *anger* (or "that pisses me off") to ascribe meaning to a client's behavior/feeling-state and see if *frustration, defeatedness, alarmed warning, disappointment,* or *sheer passion* might be words that grasp more of the full context of the event at hand than the word *anger* does.

See how using aptly (to the fuller context) one of these other words with clients depolarizes people who are in conflict. Practically and semantically, we become convinced that such context-accurate naming has merit, for the conflict found some of its footing in the rambling effects of a mere linguistic inaccuracy.

This is an intervention not best evaluated by the criticism, "you are avoiding the anger with that intervention!" The emotion of anger becomes obsolete if we see the matter as better described as frustration producing, disappointment producing, and so on. This is the curious relationship between the cognitive, conviction-sense that accompanies a certain word-label for a certain event ("Yes! *That* is the right word for this event!"), and the emotion-sense that goes along with that word-label. This is not the same thing as looking for "another emotion beneath the anger."

In many cases, the word *anger* is misused in conventional therapy, which has led to its overuse. At this late date in the mass training of the populace by popular psychology in the misuse of the term *anger* a reeducation in the accurate, limited usage of the term is in order. Likewise, an expanding of the client's vocabulary of emotional descriptors is also in order.

I am taking a stand on a definition of *honesty* or *truthfulness* as being the use of the correct terms to describe accurately a situation. Thus, a "full enough" sense of the situation is the critical factor—how much we "understand" the (extenuating) circumstances. (Understanding more of the circumstances can, of course, reveal either a more or a less horrendous situation.)

I am not using honesty to mean "whatever I actually felt" (or, more precisely, what I reported *in words* [chosen from my perhaps limited emotion-descriptor vocabulary] as my feeling, in response to a particular therapist's inquiry)—although this is a common operational definition used by many clinicians.

Thus, the mental (naming) and the emotional (feeling) mesh together, ending the humanistic psychology biased, iatrogenic mandate to "get into your feelings and out of your head." As soon as we speak or think in words we are using our heads.

The matter now is, What is a full enough sense of a situation? Full enough for what? Here moral principles such as peace, justice, vengeance, mercifulness can enter the picture. For example, what about the guidance to respond to animosity with kindness? Is this moral guidance to be written off as "mere repressiveness" of affect? Pathologized as "trying to be nice"?

These are problems that must be faced by any therapist who chooses to be "spiritually oriented."

What remains to be discerned is when is the term *anger* the accurate term? With therapists being the "authorities" on such matters, it behooves us to review the emotion vocabulary they use. Would you agree that *anger, fear, grief, sadness* are their most commonly used terms? But is this due to their underexploration and underinclusion of many other emotion terms? And what the masses don't learn from the experts drops out of the popular emotion vocabulary pool, while the terms the emotions experts dwell upon bloat up.

But adding a new term to the clinical vocabulary is more than a sheer expansion of terms, for the whole distribution economy of emotional meanings across all emotions also changes. That is, the "amount" of any particular emotional event covered by each term on the short list shrinks somewhat as the new terms constituting the long list parse out emotional nuances and convert them into full-fledged emotions with their own distinct term.

Add *frustration* to the short list and what *anger* (currently) refers to shrinks. The difference of the effects fostered by choosing the one term or the other becomes apparent, particularly if anger is a weapon while frustration is not.

In emotionality, nuance emotions provide important information to the therapist and client that the dominant emotion cannot. We live in the adjectives and adverbs, and the subadjectives and subadverbs of intonation, body language, and blushes. And beneath all this is the flickering glow of innocence and other mysteries requiring special terms including the phrase "a poignancy not at all easily put into a few words."

A spiritually oriented therapist will need to grapple with this matter of near-ineffability, just as theologians have grappled with it. For example, *not* putting something into words might at times be better for a client than him and/or his therapist putting something into words. But when to do which?

If I don't say I am angry but say I am frustrated, some will say I have chosen the softer term. They say I am repressing the anger, trying to "make it nice." They encourage me to "let it out, to feel the anger" and even "get in touch with the buried rage." What are they trying to champion? That I am entitled to use the word *anger* and thus to feel anger, my anger; and others are entitled to their anger and we should accept each other's anger, that is, not squelch them. We learn to be accepting (softer) toward anger. We don't have to be perfect and act unperturbed when we really feel irritated or enraged. Once we get it out, we aren't so angry as before, we relax and feel safer because we have affirmed our rights and human feelings.

But what about clients who stay angry or bitter? And what if the original situation could justify using the emotion descriptor, *disappointment* more than the descriptor *anger*? Certainly, incompetence in forgiveness or apology can engender undue vengefulness and degrees of anger.

See if the word *anger* is being used to instigate motivation to change. "You must be angry about that!" inducing in the client an "I ain't gonna take it anymore!" Why not use the phrase "You are really longing to make it better" inducing in the client "I am going to turn my whole life around, from this very moment!"

Sometimes it's a matter of just raising one's voice emphatically and awakeningly and not "anger" at all: "I WANT IT TODAY!"

Can therapy manufacture anger by discussions that stimulate those glandular secretions that correspond to anger, just as a pornographic movie can stimulate sex-glandular secretions? Does viewing a lot of pornographic movies "release" or *evoke* hormonally based sex desire? Will seeing many such movies finally "release" *all* the sex desire in the viewer, or just the same amount as was evocatively stimulated by the images? Is the therapist helping the client to *release* "buried" anger or is he *provoking* anger?

Consider emotional catharsis therapies as forms of exercise that might not merely "release repressed emotions" but might also foster the development of specific neuroendocrinal modes of human embodiment, the conventional psychology mode of (emotional) embodiment, which corresponds to the conventional psychotherapy emotion vocabulary. (A soteriological body?)

Within a spiritual or soteriological emotion body, the value of anger is no longer absolute—there is no fixed quantum to be released, for forgiveness emotionalities dissolve anger and develop their own neuroendocrinal mode of human embodiment. Let us call this the embodiment of the soul's emotionality. (Would Christ have taught us anything about spiritual life if He had raged while being crucified, instead of forgave?) (See chapter 2, note 10.)

The body informed by the powers of soul is a different body than that of conventional psychology.

We could say that we no longer have to feel hopeless that we will not get to express anger (brandish a protective or vengeful weapon). Anger can be a kind of hopeful hopelessness. Thus, the *Oxford English Dictionary* distinguishes between passive, troubled, irritated anger, and active, indignant, vengeful, hostile anger. We think anger is "worse" than it is, so we hide it. We get angry and it's okay. We stop hiding anger, we voice it more and our relationships have more emotional breadth to them.

But, is anger a "bad" emotion?—some have asked. Well, we don't get angry when *wonderful* things happen to us, do we? Violence often comes from anger. Thus, I can easily see why someone would say that anger is a bad emotion she would prefer not to feel. I can admire her idealism. But let's also be sure *anger* is among the right words and feelings for the situation. (And before we go on: what *is* anger, anyway? How does it rest upon *whose interpretation* of the situation is to reign?) If so, then I can help this person to express her anger. She expresses her anger, and the situation changes. She might feel relieved, then apologetic, for her expressed anger does not happen in a vacuum: She looks at the recipient of her anger and sees his fear or tears and feels avenged, sorry, afraid, tender.

Something doesn't go our way and we say we "get angry." Isn't it more accurate to say that we have experienced the limitation of our mastery of a certain situation when things don't go our way? Does not anger—yelling, demanding, storming about—typically give us a merely reactive sense of adrenalized power at times of hypopotency? And when other people are thrown by our anger, we feel even more powerful. And when we no longer care about proprieties or politeness—"I don't give a flying shit!"—we feel a kind of pseudo-omnipotence. This "anger" is better termed as a "flight from feeling nonomnipotent."

This cover for hypopotency imparted by such anger causes many further problems and we are left with a new powerlessness: We *have to be* ("get") angry, either habitually via glandular secretion habits, or as a quick fix to feel powerful. Our adrenal and other glands begin to secrete and we call the earliest sensations thereof "anger." We develop a narrative that helps sustain our anger by justifying it.

"I should not get angry." Here a moral principle of "be forebearing" or "be compassionate" or "anger is wrong" has entered the narrative. Or

Questioning Words—Reviving Time 73

perhaps this a cognitive guidance that if I understood more of the situation, if I grasped enough factors and nuances, I would not get angered at all.

Justifiable anger, justifiable homicide, here a reasonable principle has entered the narrative. The context justifies anger for the average, reasonable person. We need as well a sense of justifiable disappointment or frustration. Yet, for some people disappointment will feel "weak" compared to anger. They may prefer to feel angry rather than to feel disappointed—that is, "weak." They may prefer to "be intimidating" rather than to voice a kind of nonomnipotent preference for nondisappointing outcomes.

Rules active in language games that (aim to) govern anger or rules that skillfully provoke it. Vengeance, sadism, masochism, domination, and humiliation: a kind of eroticism: the rule-making powers of logos hone their edge in the taunt of mystery: that which dares us by what (outside some propriety) of it remains yet concealed (by civility/by the known). The mysterious edge of life and death, "chicken," bloodlusts, and *Who's Afraid of Virginia Woolf?* emotional chess games. "Can't you handle my rage?"

Perhaps there can be too much trying to understand a situation via proper naming and examining, as indicated by what signs? That I am frequently irritable, but never angry or disappointed. That I am passively aggressive, hurting myself with the anger that should be directed at others. That I am unable or unwilling to forgive.

But consider the character of Dostoyevsky's Prince Mishkin and Melville's Billy Budd: endless understanding, a kind of innocence, as a plighted gift. The oft-misunderstood spirituality of martyrdom, mercy, innocent anger, and passive resistance are all forms of life that a spiritual psychotherapy must fathom.

When our glands first secrete or are about to secrete and then don't, what emotion terms do we have to describe this sequalae? "I almost felt like I was going to have an emotion." (Recall that the "fully releasing" genital orgasm was the clinical model for all other "emotional catharsis." Thus, "almost feelings" are not merely indescript, they are axiomatically incomplete self-deprivations. If there are "suppressed feelings," mightn't there also be feelings we should call "complete, vague feelings"?

In kundalini yoga there are numerous descriptor terms for subtle, sublimative hormonal emotionalities including *rasa* (juice of life), *amrita* (nectar of eternal impermanence), *auras* (glow of virtue), *virya* (essence of virtue), *kundalini* (glow of ultimate development), and many others. Like Eskimo vocabularies that discern numerous shades of white, these yogic terms portend a broadening of our conventional psychological world.

Forbearance in yoga becomes *tapas*, a physio-spiritual alchemical heat whereby breath, movement, and concentration can deconstruct or "transmute" the glandular substrates of anger (for example), into those of anguish and forgiveness. We think transmute means "stifle," but what if it means *transmute*?

When, at a certain time, we choose the word *anger*—or *compassion, forbearance, fear*, or *hope*—we make those sensations at that time into samples for future reference. And merely naming a certain emotion ("I'm getting angry") has certain next causative emotional effects, both in my body and in other people's bodies who hear me.

Exercising forbearance is a positive way of denoting what "containing" an emotion denotes in a strained, negative way. "*Express* forbearance," not "contain anger," nor "witness it without acting it out." Forebearance is a longstanding positive characterological trait that is typically mispathologized in conventional psychotherapy as being a "repression of feeling." The term itself has dropped out of the clinical vocabulary and out of the definition of the matured self. Thus the concept of repression has also bloated up. The whole (currently inflated) economy of meaning of our emotional vocabulary could be brought into greater balance by rehonoring forebearance.

"I have a *right* to my anger." Here the political liberational passion of "rights" with innuendos of "Give me liberty or give me death!" perhaps echoing in the background, graft this anger expression onto entitlements for free speech (rights to bear arms?), yet overlooked is whether *anger* is the accurate word in each instance. Correct grammar and usage might precede political rights in matters of free speech, as well as free emotionality. And, certainly, we must not confuse unlimited license to do something with freedom. There also can be freedom in not acting.

And since emotions and their vocabularies exist in an economy of distributed meanings and even an interconnected "ecology" of protocols and interactive responses, we must view any changes in our use of the term *anger*, with the many other economic redistributions of emotional meaning I have been suggesting. For, as gratitude, apology, and forgiveness are enhanced and put into greater usage, the sense of hopeless futility (or simple nonomnipotence), which can drive us to frustrated misuses of "I have a right to my anger," also diminishes. And if anger is far more of a kind of weapon, while these other sentiments are far less so, then the consequences, at first subtle, could ramify.

In the contemporary judiciary interest in "alternative dispute resolution," *soterio*-logic proves to be just such an alternative method. This spiritual jurisprudence is comprised of the subtleties of inarticulate contritions and apology, "trapped in the souls" of the adversaries, needing authoritative admiration and encouragement to come forth.

For at this soul-characterological level of relatedness (instead of the plaintiff-defendant relatedness of litigation), there comes a turning point where it can feel better to apologize and to forgive, to admit shame or guilt or to admit contributions to one another's shames and guilts, than it does to fight to "get off" or beat each other. In shifting the fundamental narrative of justice, another form of life emerges.

The soteriological mediator wields the various soteriological powers explicitly aiming so high as to gradually inspire the adversaries to aim for these same (previously unthinkable) heights of achievable mutual respect, admiration, concern, and even love, without fear of the consequences: the one might apologize and the other might forgive. This becomes the turning point: It becomes more shameful and embarrassing to persist as adversaries berating each other than it is both inspiring and frightening to forgive and generate a sense of the soul's unconditional power to live beyond eye for an eye or the street smarts of "beating a rap."

And, as in the paradoxical soterio-*logic*, the more hopeless a situation seems at the beginning, the more inspiring is the mere attempt at meeting—the more deserving the parties are of admiration—even if they are court ordered. And it is the unfolding of this inspiration further and further, nuance by nuance, that makes such turnabouts possible, yet always subject to the weatherings of impermanence.

Thus, a kind of commitment emerges between the parties to see the resolution through, as if in the unsuspecting mystery of their own characterological maturations. Each sees how certain words and perceptions keep the soteriological alive and growing, or not, and how to help (by saying this, asking this, admiring apologizing, forgiving) each other to keep it alive, for their sakes, and for the sake of the exterior community and its collective hopes and faiths, of which we are all guardians. Perhaps this is what people seek in court, it's just not there, so they think they are seeking what the courts keep offering.

The soteriological way may look soft and unreal in the eyes of the cynically grim realist, yet it is only a disbelief in its powers that makes it seem so. For, to grasp these powers after years of fighting only renders a deeper shudder of remorseful recognition: It could have all been otherwise; instead of the fighting, there could have been many comings-together. The ideal proves far more real—even if it is subtle—than the grim reality, which now appears like an enacted nightmare from which one has awakened.

And any sadomasochistic enjoyment of the fighting, the surging hormonal joys of "You ruined my whole fucking life!" and "What a fucking asshole!" decryings will also become apparent. The whole sordid tangle of verbal adaptations to a life estranged from the soul stands forth. For behind the glare of hostility—in vivid contrast to it—in a muted, sullen glow in those same eyes is dashed-hope-now-being-stirred from its cynicisms, its "justice."

Inside the bitter scoff, at the end of its haughty exhalation is always withered hope, and in the withered, stale gape of that expired breath is the dormant seed for another hope and another breath, and another hope. And I have used the image of that very last exhaled mortal breath, after which there comes no other, to awaken soteriological powers in those whose hopelessness has blinded them to their own potential magnanimity.

Learning when to apply new emotion terms is very difficult because we do not yet have a sample sensation/credible image for the term and we may be committed to other protocols and terms we are (over)using. Consider the problem, which may be more elusive than initially meets the eye, of coining a (changeable) "standard feeling of anger" (or "protocol of justice") to be able to call "anger" or ("resolution of the matter"). As Wittgenstein notes:

> There is *one* thing of which one can say neither that it is one metre long, nor that it is not one metre long, and that is the standard metre in Paris.—But this is, of course, not to ascribe any extraordinary property to it, but only to mark its peculiar role in the language-game of measuring with a metre-rule. . . .
> This sample is an instrument of the language . . . not something that is represented, but is a means of representation. . . . And to say "if it did not *exist*, it could have no name" is to say as much and as little

as: if this thing did not exist, we could not use it in our language-game.—What looks as if it *had* to exist, is part of the language. It is a paradigm in our language-game, something with which comparison is made. (Wittgenstein 1968, p. 24)

This name, "anger" (or "resolution"), like all other names, is part of a talk that goes on and on. What the name refers *to*: Try to find "it" without the aid of language traditions and we find ourselves in a zen koan, listening for sounds of one hand clapping. Is it that, because anger is loud (or penalties are clear), we feel more certain about it as a standard feeling (that must not be denied) than subtler feelings (reconciliation protocols) that exist, but whose names are rarely employed? Yet subtle and dramatic feelings are equally drawn from "standard metre" samples within the shiftable semantic economies of language games.

"It was a happy time, but you seem angry. What *else* was happening ... and what else, and what else ... okay, *now* we've found why you are so angry." Is it that we did not stop until we found something irritating (we always find what we look for in the last place we look, because then we stop looking, and we seem mostly to find what we look *for*), and have missed the important lesson of teaching the client about "feeling happy," as if he did not, in this case, know how to use the word *happy*, to "feel" happy?

"Let's find out if you are happy. What might you be happy about, well, what else, what else, what else. . . . Ah, there, see you were happy (proud, admiring, apologetic) all along."

In kundalini yoga, *pranotthana* (intensified life energy) involves roaring, stretching, outcrying, rapid breathing, and moments of bodily and mental stillness. In a culture without kundalini yoga—its vocabulary and encouraged practices—(or some other transpersonal expressivism), anger, sobbing, competitive activities, or sex may be among the very few nameable outlets for impassioned expression. Again, the set of names delimits a form of life and a mode of human neuro-glandular embodiment, breath, and movement.

Yet, all the while, nonviolent anger that seems invariably to happen is just part of our human reactivity. And my reactivity or misreactivity can engender yours. It's nothing, he's just blowing off steam. "To hell with me?! I wasn't angry before, but now, well, to hell with you too!" But then what happens? Will we go on to reconcile and share life's greater opportunities, or express more anger and perhaps break asunder? Let's not get distracted: Getting better at the former is the goal.

How slippery between "an interpretation" and "an excuse for" and then "a justification for." How slippery between "a search for understanding what happened" and "a search for vengeance." How slippery the edge between frustration, then anger, then vengefulness and new hostility. And it is those whom we love the most that we invest the most hope in, who can thereby possibily provoke our greatest disappointment. And then what, and then what?

If I'm angry at you, then you might be afraid of my potential violence, even if my anger is based in my own misunderstanding and would dissipate if I knew more. But now I'm angry and so you're afraid, which really enrages me, which frightens you more.

From one misunderstanding to another these exchanged, misnamed emotions generate each other into a bulky but unreasonable tragic virtuality. Can the therapist pull one thread and unravel the whole tangle? "You were frustrated by him, not angered, don't you see?" "You don't know what will happen next, it is uncertainty and not fear that you are experiencing."

SELF, FOR THE SAKE OF WHAT? AND SHARED RADIANCE

We must repeatedly ask, What is this intervention for? The conventionalist answer: to restore a sense of self. But what is this "sense of self" supposed to make possible? What is it for the sake of? Our answer: to be confident enough to participate in the world and thus to rewardingly give and receive. Don't stop asking until you get beyond theoretical constructs to goals like "optimism" or "happiness."

Only for those who have been really happy does it become clear that this is an ultimate goal. Other emotions have their place, but the concept of well-being would seem to give special importance to the goal of abiding happiness. And if for some reason I am not happy, I don't want to lose my bearings.

The *self* is more of a verb than a noun, for life and people-in-time are more verblike than nounlike. (In Sanskrit, *kriya* means "verb" or "yogic maturational movement." Here also *ananda-maya kosha*, "bliss body," is also the causal or most-alive body, which survives the death of the mind and flesh bodies. As Marshall McLuhan once stated: "I seem to be a verb.")

Pleas to put things into one's own words can exaggerate the importance of the self-owning (choosing) of words. It's what the *saying* of the words—whomever they belong (sic) to—*is for*, what the saying foments into the next social moment, that is the crux. Thus, at times, I speak for clients or give them words to speak, like throwing them a rope. I thank and admire clients for their willingness, trust, and interdependence in the therapeutic project.

Like "emotional needs," this "ownable self" seems to borrow connotations from capitalistic economics with an emphasis on buying and selling, rather than sharing, stewarding, or what Thich Nhat Hanh calls "inter-being."

All these metaphors of "self-structures" (boundaries, defensive mechanisms, ego structures, self-object constructs) can disguise the fluidity and uncertainty of being a mortal with a veneer of machinerylike solidity, that is also depicted as utterly fragile.

(Conventional) transpersonal therapists alarmed at Buddhist talk of "no self" or yogic "transcendental unity" will say "First you must develop an ego/self before you can transcend it." Better to avoid these semantic difficulties by dropping the terms *ego* or *self* and to speak instead of the importance of social competencies to be developed. We might too consider the phrase, "First develop *superego-soul* sentiments, then you will have a characterological basis from which to grow toward transcendental consciousness." For thousands of years such has been the maturational guidance of numerous spiritual traditions. ("First develop character, then transcend it": The phrase is spiritually ludicrous, denoting that the contrast, "preegoic/transegoic" is based on a shallow contrivance of subjectivity, "egoism" [sans conscience], whose psychoanalytic bolstering is mainly what presses us to take it seriously.)

INSIGHT, ANALOGY MAKING, AND NO CONSTANT SELF

Watch to see if analogy making is being granted the status of an "insight." Even so, perhaps it is the client's blushing awakening into the now as he says, smiling with his eureka, "What I am doing now is analogous to what I did then!" that has the crucial therapeutic value, while one's insight is a mere catalyst. Or he is enjoying the sheer language play of making a clever analogy. Isn't it what happens next (not the intervention itself) that validates any intervention? And the shared eye contact of this blushing awakening might be a most crucial next event, whatever the insight, to focus on.

"Having an insight" denotes a linguistic skill in making convincing analogies (metaphors, similes) or interpretations. At some point this skill must give way to other actions involving new skills. Please note that the "insight" of insight meditation (*vipassana*) is not an astute analogy or interpretation but a release from analyzing and interpreting into sheer experienced impermanence, *anicca* and *anatta* (no constant self).

UNCERTAINTY, EROS, AND MYSTERY

From uncertainty to fear to danger. I can get named as "frightening" to someone when I am merely "uncertain" to him. And if each human is a kind of divine mystery, then perhaps it is awesomeness that we feel across from one another, always. (Xenophobia: fear [not awe] as a [mis?]response to the unfamiliar.) Consider a transpersonal vocabulary of consciousness studies whose central term is not awareness but *awe*.

Is it desire or "the awesome allure of mystery" that draws us closer? And the temporal mystery is always the wonder/awe/uncertainty of: "what comes next, t next, t next?" Is sexual pleasure an intense "feeling of mystery"? Next moment, next moment, next. Desires as ways/protocols to handle the mystery.

Spiritually oriented therapists might need to contend with an "alluring mysteriousness," an "awesomeness" of the human (and inescapably gendered) encounter that is more elusive and undetermined than the term *sexual* can grasp; more undetermined than the (currently overdetermined?) terms *male*, *female*, *heterosexual*, or *homosexual* can grasp.

In the case of the hermaphrodite in *Herculine Barbin*, Foucault revealed the human tragedy that emerged from a merely deficient erotic vocabulary whose only two legitimate word choices (*male* or *female*) force from an inscrutible mystery a singular naming that must thereby be lived.

> Brought up as a poor and deserving girl in a milieu that was almost exclusively feminine and strongly religious, Herculine Barbin . . . was finally recognized as being "truly" a young man. Obliged to make a legal change of sex after judicial proceedings and a modification of his civil status, he was incapable of adapting himself to his new identity and ultimately committed suicide. (Foucault 1980, p. xi)

Here is the linguistic tragedy: The form of life demanded by the binary rule of a certain language game pressed a more elusive mystery of the body to death. There was no place mapped out by the words of nasceant medical psychology for Barbin to live in, and no medico-legal allowance to live the life of a name that her body did not fit exactly enough, according to the arbiters of the names. Deficient clinical vocabularies can have dire consequences.

More primordial than the oedipal metaphor is the compelling mystery of gender itself. Gender as mystery encircling the origins and future of all incarnation and romantic loves. The human participation, life by life, minute by minute, in the whorl of the endless mystery.

What kind of body is it that contains kundalini-shakti: an inner Mother-force? a pubescent spine, heart, tongue, and pineal?

Get in touch with your masculinity, your femininity, your gayness, your self. Is it really so simple? What is this search for the right gender sense for the sake of, and what is *that* for the sake of?

TEMPORALITY, UNCERTAINTY, AND NAMING BODILY EXPERIENCES

Are we preoccupied with historical explanations because we do not look at the potency of the unknown future, its uncertainty, its possibilities, its apparent perpetuity? A psychotherapy of the present-future will address emotions of suspense, wonder, hope, daring, longing, yearning, dread, mortality, rebirth, telos (guiding purpose). A psychotherapy of the past (which is what conventional psychotherapy is) dwells in nostalgia, concludedness, old beginnings, pattern similarities, precedent searching, less mature stages, less experienced stages.

Dare we to have hopes? And which hopes will we choose to consider, dare, and then endeavor—come what may—and then what? And then what again and again and again? And, moreover: Is there justice in life? Divine intervention or at least inspirations? Such are the spiritual questions and vissicitudes of human freedom, choice, uncertainty, spiritual indeterminacy, impermanence, and limitation.

In conventional psychotherapy, the economy of temporality is skewed. Just as in how adding terms to the emotion vocabulary forces a redistribution of valenced meanings among the previous short list of terms, so will the placing of more attention on the present-future force a (relative) shrinking of the significance of the past in clinical explanation.

"Repeated fearfulness," for example, is not merely a pattern from the past, but can be (phrased as) an utterly novel reaction to the uncertain future as "repeated uncertainty" or "awe."

With its numerous unmapped (in the West) bodily developmental stages, kundalini yoga will vastly expand the psychological sense of the future, and thus alter the temporal economy of past-present-future time frames. Imagine the impact on our sense of the developmental future if we could look forward to a life-enhancing, identity-transforming "spinal puberty," which can occur between the ages of forty and fifty.

Freud used the archeological dig as his prototype for the psychotherapist's role in uncovering precedents to explain patient symptoms. Consider using as a prototype the rock-climbing guide who must be alert in the present and able to guide his patient step by step, should he become stuck at a certain point, in going forward. That events flow forward and not backward suggests that the latter prototype is generally preferable to the former.

Or consider the white-water canoeist whose location is constantly changing and whose every previous experience must come to serving the negotiation of each current moment's bend and jolt. He must focus on the suddenly emergent pathway through all other potential hazards or dangers which, although significant, must remain peripheral to the swerving *way* that unfolds before him.

Constructing a coherent narrative "from" the past to explain a current difficulty does not necessarily teach the client how to solve his difficulty. Knowing what frightened you of the water at age five does not yet teach you how to swim, nor is it clear that the precedent be understood in order for you to be coaxed into the water. (Sometimes, the beauty and described potential joyfulness of the water will themselves be alluring enough.) Even if a clinical interpretation works (correlates with symptom relief), this does not prove the interpreted trauma as cause of the "problem." Like it or not, suggestion permeates "the work."

Verifiable certainty is both greatly desired and hard to come by. Certain clinical aphorisms/metaphors lower the standards for something to be certain beyond the need for verifiability. Many bodywork therapists tell each other, their trainees, and clients that "the body never lies": infallible, absolute certainty. What do you make of this?

"If I think x happened, then it probably did," is another guidance of some popular clinicians. If I am willing to utter a certain sentence, then what the sentence purports probably happened. Some clinicians merge First Amendment rights with issues of esteem and veracity, asserting that clients "deserve to be believed." Understood: Yes. Empathized with: Certainly. But believed? Shouldn't the criteria here include cross verifications?[4] (Believed *versions*—within *what* form of life?)

When the Freudian sexual hermeneutic was in vogue, body psychotherapy sought the "orgasmic body." Predictably, with the sexual-orgasmic hermeneutic now replaced by the object-relations "wound history" hermeneutic, the body psychotherapists have developed the "wound-storing body."

How do we verify the meaning of a sensation? Where is the standard of samples with which to compare a particular sensation so as to say, "Yes, this tension is anger toward Father!"? Is it merely in the bodyworker's decoding abilities (what he was taught), which are delimited by his emotion vocabulary and his stockpile of clinical explanations? Fitting the catchy, untested claim that "the body never lies" into the rest of conventional psychology makes the final amalgam even more of a dogma, rather than a set of working hypotheses.

Nostalgia can be mislabeled "the beginning of depression"—especially since the term *nostalgia* is rarely found in clinical vocabularies. "Looking into the past" has, in psychotherapy, come to mean "finding out the truth of one's current problems." Looking into the past creates nostalgia. Nostalgia can be mislabeled "the beginning of depression"—especially since the term, "nostalgia" is rarely found in clinical vocabularies. The client looks into the past and feels something "down" and, with his therapist, considers he has found a hidden depression. The word *nostalgia* is never mentioned, only the now-revealed, once-hidden *depression*.

This is one way that circular iatrogenic conundrums can be engendered in conventional psychotherapy by not including the phenomenology of impermanence as the substrate of human experience. Not including the unreduceable phenomenology of "mysterious uncertainty" (allure, suspense, awe, excited trepidation) creates other special hermeneutical problems. What if there is "a lot more" that we do not know than what we do know, and perhaps more uncertainty about the latter than we would prefer?

That the client might be misnaming impermanence as "hopelessness"— *that* possibility is not in the vocabulary that therapists consult when wondering about "client hopelessness." If the client doesn't know about such factors (have them in his mastered vocabulary), then both will be forced to find a psychodynamic reason for this present hopelessness. "Why *do* you feel hopeless?"

Family history explanations and/or ontological explanations?

An insightful interpretation can give us a good feeling that lasts for a certain amount of time. The limited duration of that feeling is a property of how all experiences pass away. The feeling of "a passing-away good feeling" is wistful. Soon it will feel nostalgic. Later, it can be mislabeled "the beginning of depression." This is another way that circular iatrogenic conundrums can be engendered in conventional psychotherapy.

"Bearing impermanence," the core enlightenment of Buddhism, must be part of the psychotherapeutic project. The spiritually oriented therapist must be practiced in the bearing of impermanence, as his life passes in those fifty-minute elapses, entrusted by a stranger with some of the greatest of the latter's hopes.

If we say, "He knows it 'more deeply'" we only mean that we now expect this (so-called) deeper knowing to sooner (than before) flow forward into the future as a kind of confidence into new behaviors, including new speech acts such as declarations of happiness, forgiveness, apology, or gratitude.

Getting more deeply into one's soul is to enter the deep present where the mystery of perpetual existence (Nietzsche's "eternal recurrence") blooms anew, anew, anew. Soul *is* this mystery given a human name. Its cosmic infinitude contracts to a sense of optimism or a longing for, when we narrow our focus for some particular action.

In keeping with the spirituality of devotion and faith, we must also inquire for a translation of "a deeper pain" to "a deeper longing for." Here, again pain is to be understood poetically as yearning, and the deeper one goes into this pain, the more into the ek-stasis of temporal impermanence one uncovers—not mere forgotten histories—for impermanence is the fundamental forgotten history into which we try to awaken. Yet this is an unbroken temporal flow, unbroken by any distraction of any eventualities. Thus, dauntingly, the eternality of real time looms.

AVOIDING "MASOCHISTOGENESIS"

In making analogies that are rewordings of a client's original statements, the therapist is in the position to enhance or diminish the significance of the client's reports by his choice of adjectives, adverbs, verbs, nouns, and metaphors.

What is termed "vulnerability," a delicate emotional availability, would often be better termed "openness," since this eliminates the unnecessary maudlin-victimistic nuance of the former term of being, more specifically, weak and susceptible to attack. In the heat of difficulties, one resents having been open, and now calls it "vulnerability," and the enhanced sense of weakness inherent to the word conspires with the new narrative that now speaks of how "bad" that previously "good" relationship now is.

"I feel attacked" is usually better termed, "I feel afraid" or perhaps, "criticized," or "insulted." Attacking is more associated with physical mugging. Some conventional therapies linguistically escalate the matter of (merely) being criticized even further and rename it using explicitly violent metaphors such as "getting beat up," "wounded" or "violated."

Clients should be listened to as if they were not only reporting *how they felt* or *what actually happened*, or what kind of a person someone else *is*, but also as if they are showing you what words they choose to use to answer your questions or to recount an event. What might they be trying to *do* with these particular word choices? Client reports can be heard as new actions—speech actions—not mere reports.

If vengeance as a response to injury is a primordial (spiritual) psychopathology, then telling one's "wound history" must be heard with an ear attuned to vengefulness through the telling. In such (vengefully catharted) narratives, totalistic exaggerations quite possibly abound. Perhaps parents are characterized as invariantly and totalistically wounding of the client as a retaliatory act, shaming them in absentia before the empathic gaze of the therapist. Parents are depicted as "utterly unpredictable," "utterly uncomprehending [of the client's struggles]," "relentless disparag[ers]"; their communications are "a nagging, screaming, fusilade," with childhood itself being "like waiting for a Nazi siren to go off" (from case history in Stolorow 1987, pp. 58–60).

Situations of disappointment can be exaggerated and distorted by inappropriately calling them "betrayals" or "abandonments." "When you didn't show up on time, *it* brought up all my abandonment stuff." Look at this "it" that therapists have taught clients to justify using the word *abandonment*. Is having to wait for someone only a time to worry about oneself?

Can we think of "it" as a time of missing, praying that the other is okay? Is it even fair or accurate to ourselves to take "anxious waiting" and beef it up into a "feeling of abandonment" and then consider ourselves to be in an infantlike powerlessness? When is it (in)accurate for therapists to support such verbal escalations and embed them in an infancy ontology of primordial and utterly powerless "abandonment anxiety"?

If the client is taught how to miss, endure uncertainty, and appreciate longing and impermanence, there might be fewer occasions for a legitimate hermeneutics of abandonment anxiety. (The term *abandonment* itself should be reserved for situations of being left without explanation at an orphanage, being deserted, usually forever).

And if the client of such a conventional therapy is driven to tears by the escalating word choices and the kind of memories they *depict*, and says, "It's good to get the tears out!" will client and therapist take this to be an end in itself? Or will other perspectives be considered, ones which would not provoke tears of abandonment but those of concern for others, and the understanding of perhaps complex circumstances that surround even the most horrific malevolences. Such expansions on the part of the client in his "feelings for," which now include more of the world, help to embed his experience as a being-in-the-world, instead of as the more isolated individuated ego with "*his* feelings" of conventional psychotherapy.

"Anxiety" names a response to the unknown or uncertain. Qualifying anxiety as being about abandonment is an effort to reduce this uncertainty by positing what it *might* be about. The certainty of this abandonment interpretation is itself drawn from the mother-infant totem—that psychoanalytic ground the mere touch of which is enough in those circles to certify a matter without further question. Thus, we see that it is a conviction about psychoanalysis the adult client is being given as a kind of narrative certainty. No doubt most any intervention carries the conviction of its assumptions into the client's life. Let us just try to be clear about it.

Much therapeutic work is thus required to help some clients use the English language more accurately than our potentially sadomasochistogenic conventional psychological vocabulary has foisted onto them. Hope-dashing disappointments are to be termed, simply, disappointments and *not* "enraging betrayals." Now apology and forgiveness can do its work where, in the linguistically hyped-up version, only ventilations of anger seem possible and even seem to be the only therapeutic course of action.

UNACKNOWLEDGED HEALTH, REPRESSED JOY

Clinicians are trained to assume that when people are really honest they will tell you how frustrated and angry they really are. That being "really honest" might entail disclosures of unspoken joy, hope, and gratitude has become unthinkable.

"Feeling seen" is a skill that we need to develop through the course of bearing shyness, pride, embarrassment, and having the readiness to thank those who have seen us for caring to take the time and artfulness to put us into words, with their own joy in so doing: the joy of giving and receiving. We must then become competent at "being the source of another's delight."

In a conversational lull, the client and therapist are not merely waiting for the next thing to come up. They are experiencing the wordless phenomenology of the unknown: suspense, shyness, uncertainty, trembling trust, visual wordless alluring-and-shying eye contact, doubt, suspicion, hope.

SUSPICION AS INQUIRY

I have never heard of a therapist saying to a client, without a trace of psychopathological suspicion, "I wonder why you are so courageous/kind/happy/sensitive." It may be impossible to do so, for the questioning seems inherently imbued with suspiciousness.

"I wonder what that *means?*" queries the therapist. He thinks he could not possibly be inducing a mood of suspicion, and certainly not a mood of unsettling eeriness or the macabre. He thinks he is involved in no more than a curious, empathic exploration. But what if it is such moods that are induced? What kind of data will be educed?

APOLOGY AND FORGIVENESS

During apology and forgiveness, admiration is also engendered, for each partner sees the courage it takes to deescalate, and to apologize and forgive. The apologizer's courage to do so suddenly makes him admirable in the eyes of the apology recipient—as much as (gradually) forgivable. The recipient's courage to seek a reconciliation, as difficult and risky as it might be, makes him admirable.

It is as if there are two parallel universes: one of utterly convinced hopelessness, anger, and wounds, and another, a breath away, holding our greatest hopes and warmest feelings. It is the possibility that they *are only a breath away from one another* (that we might grant validity to such a hopeful metaphor) that can become *so troubling* as to force us to imagine it and believe it to be, and thus to act, *otherwise*. Then, the hope really seems to be far away. And all this semblance is constructed by certain metaphors being granted credibility, and however hemmed in we are by our ineptitude with the soteriological powers.

The soteriological approach corrects for conventional psychotherapy's potentially iatrogenic vocabulary of "wounds to be healed," and the like. The middle syllable, so*terios*, is the fulcrum for change and transformation. A brief etymology is thus: From old English *theoh* and Germanic *theuham* (thigh, or swollen part of leg) and from Latin, *tumere*, to swell (as in tumor, tumescence, to be swollen with pride, a wound, *or with increased strength after a struggle*). The difference between injured swelling and strengthening swelling is the crux of the matter.

What I find here is a point of transformative significance in response to a "traumatic" or a "shocking" or "painful" experience. I use quotation marks to indicate that at this point in the event at hand, *one does not know* how to apply the categories of "good" or "bad" to the experience. One is beyond the logic of the ordinary pleasure principle.

This prater-linguistic condition, which is not even yet one of ambiguity, is part of the merciful or grace-laden domain. Here, forgiveness and letting be can reduce the negative impact of any difficulty to a bare minimum while also catalyzing spiritual/characterological maturations. Here is the martial artist's skillfully surrendered, self-protective fall. Here the romantic *spirit* enters the tragedy, beyond reasonableness.

Here the same event can become a heartful reconciliation rather than an embittered grudge. Here is where the logic of "an eye for an eye" is displaced by the boldly awesome, "love thine enemies"—not as a moralistic command, but as a perceived, natural, and too-true feeling of compassion. Here is the magic of religion and sublimative hormonal alchemies, while just outside in another kind of hormonally infused flesh, the hot and attractive stirrings of vengeance churn: "I *like* vengeance better than forgiveness! I *want* the son-of-a-bitch to suffer!"

GIVING AND RECEIVING

Upon gaining hard-won abilities to receive (to appreciate the awkward charm of his own blushing gratitudes), the long-deprived client begins to intuit flickers of care that lived hidden and crusted over in his parents' ineptness with sharing.

> When my cousin got caught for drugs my Father yelled at me, "If I ever catch you becoming an addict I swear to God I will feed you a poisoned meatball. And if they catch me and send me to the electric chair, I will die a happy man because I will have cleansed my conscience by ridding the world of the scourge I brought into it." (client quoted in Stolorow et al. 1987, p. 62, to which the therapist gives the standard "empathic acknowledgement")

But consider the following soteriological response:

> THERAPIST. Do you hear his tortured logic: To protect you from drugs, he would be willing to be executed for killing you and even for the sin of bringing you into his inept care, which he feels too guilty to admit, so he blames you. But if someone could have helped him to be a better dad he would have done that. Who wouldn't?
>
> CLIENT. I would have thought you were taking his side, except by now I see that there are no real sides. My poor fucked-up Dad, we both (tears) really missed out on something beautiful, didn't we?

"I know you love me more than I am able to let in"—it is the rare client who will say this. Certainly, the conventional therapy discourse does not encourage such admissions. Yet, letting in love that seems too good to be true is "a bear."

We must also consider that I can love another "more than I usually let on to you or to myself that I do." There is a great deal of uncertainty in life, and variability from hour to hour. There is a lot I do not know, and *how much* I don't know is even more unknown to me.

When I realize that there is even more to know than I already do, do I then wonder if all my current certainties must now be considered as provisional?

Therapy often focuses on "big emotions" like rage and grief and has scant familiarity with subtle emotions like shyness, bashfulness, or quavering hopefulness, which are no less dramatic or significant. The same session can go in very different ways depending on what is made of these subtle emotions, and thus over time, the client's life and relationships. Here is where the substeps and sub-substeps of progress flicker and live just enough to be finessed into further progress or missed, leading to failure or impasse in such a way that a therapist will not know the opportunity that has been missed. What is missed is *missed*.

Consider a phenomenology of giving and receiving, however subtle: the various pink, bluish, silvery, blushing prides and shaded, glowing shynesses around any embarrassed hopes to be liked; the I-dare-you-to-make-me-happy eye glimmerings behind any scowl; the beguiling, breath-halting, and beckoning sense of things too good to be true, by degrees, won over to the romanticism of unverifable grounds to be hopeful.

The potency of thanking one's benefactor and watching one's thanks be absorbed nourishingly, blushingly, by him; the developing of "the moment of reception" into a "sense of confidence" and then into "declarations of new intentions," and then carrying forth such intentions and intimacy skills into other outside relationships (or to bring significant others into future sessions to learn these ways); adjusting to missing people more deeply without resentment or anger; for some time, feeling equal to greater involvement in life (having children, visiting estranged family members, seeking parttime employment, etc.).

Consider a therapeutic course to help clients gain this skillfulness: It involves (a) subtle meditative tracking of evanescent nonverbal emotive expressions; (b) giving compliments while tracking the client's moment-to-moment receptivity; and (c) prescribed therapist phrasings and guidances that can encourage continued receptivity within the fundamental challenge of impermanence. (The challenge is to the dream state of pseudo-nonimpermanence or resented impermanence); the translation of feelings of receiving compliments into expressions of gratitude; blossoming of gratitude into senses of confidence, and then into declarations of intent, and then into new actions.

We must map out the subtle increments of progress—of mercurial happiness—within impermanence and be able to guide clients through these steps. The increments are the momentary pinkish, shaded blushes seen for a moment longer: the flush of embodied elan vital, the palpable radiance of the soul washing through and infusing us. Thoughts thought in such moments are of a different world, thus the world we perceive or live in at any time is a matter of the ensouled state of our body at the time.

Perhaps because Freud and Reich derogated (semipathologized) sublimation and inflated the significance of desire and orgasm, we now have this under appreciation of the subtle blushing emotions lauded by poets for centuries. Indeed, Freud went on to deprive blushing of its intrinsic meaning and charms by distorting its integrity via genitalizing homologization calling it a (mere) displaced "erection of the head." (Yes blushing is an erotic phenomenon, but let us place eros itself within a fundamental context of bodily mysteries no longer anchored to the genitalia.)

ATTAINING THERAPEUTIC GOALS

The mere continuity of a perhaps varying sense of happiness is (intrinsically) a worthwhile goal. Continuity can be created by merely talking about a success for a longer time, unpacking the details and the further details. Where were the details before the therapist asked about them? How does a memory become more nourishing by a detailed unpacking of its subtler beauties? How very mutable are "remembered events"!: "What did you like about that and that?" and "Why did you like that and that and that?"

Therapy, the making of a client's life to be happier, more caring, and more mature is not an analytic project; it is a phenomenal project. It is like fanning a spark of quavering hope into an ember of willingness and then into a flickering flame of confidence, and then into a growing flame of enthusiasm, and then into a substantially warm and glowing fire recognizable as such by oneself and others as happiness, optimism, gratitude, and a matured capacity to deal with difficulties.

Regardless of the "developmental past," the wood for this fire building is always serviceable. That is, the therapist can find sparks to fan to ember, flicker, and flame, for where there is life, so there is already spark. And perhaps even in death.

There once was a horse breeder in ancient China whose talents in bringing forth the finest colts were legendary. When the local villagers learned that Lao Ling was coming out of retirement in his seventieth year to venture into the wilds to find a stallion to breed but one more champion with his mare Sun-sun, they all felt excitement.

But when, after many days in the wilds, he brought back the swayback, lump-kneed, dazed old horse on the end of the rope he held, smiling gleefully at each neighbor—when that happened, the villagers rolled their eyes, "He is too old, he has lost his judgment, there will be no new champion."

Yet one year later, when Lao Ling brought out the colt of this horse, all were aghast at its perfection. Indeed, never before had they seen such excellence in a horse. Lao Ling responded to their doubting questions saying, "Yes the old stallion was swayback, lump-kneed, and dazed.... But, did you see the proud and spirited *tail*!! It was from this tail that I recognized the real stallion, and have bred this fine new colt needing to know no more than the tail to see the colt already in his father, the swayback. Ha, Ha Ha."

THE SELF AS LOCUS OF SHEER HOPE: GIVING AND RECEIVING AS THERAPY

Hope is what brings people together. Thus we *are* each other's hope and engender each other's hope. Intimacy is a matter of the degree of hope being shared by people and ranges from casual friendships to lifelong partnerings. The clinical relationship is also based on such mutual hope.

An individual is essentially a locus of oscillating hope and not a mere structure of "selfhood." The latter terminology is already a rigidifying distortion and a departure from living temporality.

To give one's hopefulness to another is an act of entrustment. The client gives/entrusts his hopefulness to the therapist. The therapist is the recipient. He gives back to the client admiration and thanks for the client giving/entrusting him with this hope.

In *receiving* the therapist's appreciation, the client learns that he is a *resource* and not a mere "taker." When he believes the therapist, or grants the therapist credibility, his receiving from the therapist immediately also becomes an act of giving to the therapist. He has given credibility to the therapist, which makes t the t therapist t feel t worthwhile and helpful.

This is all pointed out by the therapist. What more potent way for the client to learn of his beneficial effect on others than through witnessing it on his therapist as the latter describes these effects to him? The shift proves fundamental: The client is now an undeniable source of goodness. His glow of pride says it clearly. And the therapist's own glow only adds further veification, health, and warmth.

The client is not expected to be competent in knowing about these subtle acts of giving and receiving that are happening. And it is not the client's job to make the therapist feel worthwhile. It is, however, the therapist's hired job to educate the client as to the subtleties of this giving and receiving that is taking place between them and to guide him forward experientially.

But how else can a client learn of the potency of his actions or personal qualities in therapy unless the therapist tells him, with full affect, of his admiration or gratitude for such actions or qualities? Such interventions also foster client independence (not dependence as is imagined by conventionalists) by instilling in the client a sense of worth and potency in the world. The analytic spell deters us from wondering about this.

To receive another's hopefulness—as the therapist receives the client's hopefulness—is an honor. The recipient (the therapist) feels gratitude and inspiration. The giver (the client) receives the recipient's gratitude for being entrusted with his hope. The giver experiences the joy of giving this hope. The greater the hope, the more that feels possible, including enduring great obstacles with resilience.

Each is both a giver and a receiver of hope. Each feels the gratitude of giving and of receiving. Each gives and receives gratitude of having received the other's hope. Each can state feelings of being threatened/burdened/daunted/inspired (choose your word carefully) by this entrustment of hope.

Many times it seems to me that clients "get better" largely through consistent heartfelt communications of gratitude and admiration. The therapist keeps asking for details, "What about that did you appreciate, can you describe a few details?" As they learn to export such exchanges into other relationships, their lives get better.

Pop psychology can mispathologize "giving." Dissatisfied "givers" often need to learn how more fully to receive the appreciation due them, not how to be less giving. Those who receive from the giver must be taught how to express thanks to the giver as well. The giver must also be made aware of what he is receiving from others. This goes as well for so-called caretakers and certain codependents.

Someone receives a compliment and wonders what it means. In other words, he shifts out of the mode of receiving and steps off to the side and judges, doubts, and adopts a stance of suspicion. These stances and moods shrink one's ability to receive. Receiving less, they mistakenly believe the other has given them less than they actually have been given.

Since receiving invariably awakens us, and awakening is always heralded by awe, wonder, shyness, and uncertainty, there is the possibility of misconstruing/misnaming "receiving" or "awakening" as being "awkward" or "uncomfortable" or "fearsome" or "suspicious." The therapist must not be fooled if the client uses such words nor abide by the conventional maxim of "following the client's process." He must instead name the moods more accurately as "gratitude," "awe," "uncertainty," "shyness," and so on. He must educate the client regarding the phenomenology of awakening at times of receiving compliments.

Even then, the awe of receiving is invariably daunting, for the awakening thus provoked is to glimmers of the infinite. Thus, soteriological sentiments extend from mundane politeness to the depths of mystical enlightenments.

One can be suspicious of his own ability to receive, to think he is receiving less than he actually is. But this self-doubt can lead to wondering if he is receiving more than he thinks.

Wonder if you are receiving *more* than you currently know/believe/grant as real. The spiritually oriented therapist must wonder how nourishing the cosmos might actually be.

There is also the witnessing of the impact of the other receiving one's gratitude. In couples or family therapy, the one will often cry grateful tears when he receives the gratitude of his spouse or family member. Such tears can be mislabeled as "pain" by the therapist or client and in such mislabeling can slip from gratitude into sorrow if one's mind gets distracted from the present and suddenly misassociates with some archaic memory of loss.

But why *that* particular memory from the past? This question can take the therapy away from the task of coming more into the present matter of receiving: looking at each other, responding to the glimmers of shy interactivity.

Conventional therapists pursue the (mis)association and its (irrelevant) saddening context, thus (unwittingly) losing the positive import of the contemporary event of giving. They have only one word to name tearful events—*sadness*—and don't discern tears of poignantly appreciative reception. They say, "You look sad" and the experience of poignant appreciation is lost and the client is instead plunged by the expert-therapist into neighboring feelings of sadness and grief, the only tearful emotions in the conventionalist's scant vocabulary. No one notices the loss, and the (masochistic, iatrogenic) appreciation of tearful catharses persists unquestioned.

People usually look away in a shy blush when receiving a compliment and thus don't see their benefactor anymore. They need to be taught to keep taking in and to keep looking at their benefactor.

As in meditative concentration, the therapist must carefully protect the present tears from such mindless distractions by keeping the client's temporal frame of reference in the here-now, where hopeful life now fragilely emerges. He has greeted gratitude with gratitude. Each sees the impact his gratitude is having upon the other. Perhaps each can begin to merge into the one deep Gratitude which melts individuality into a flux of sharing and impermanence. Here the goals of "differentiation" or "individuation" are supplemented by the mystical participations in the all—what the eighteenth-century German theologian, Friedrich Schleiermacher (1958 [1799]) called "absolute dependence."

> [A]long side of the contracting endeavor for something definite and complete, [in spirituality there is an] expansive soaring in the Whole and Inexhaustible. In this way he [the spiritually attuned individual] restores the balance and harmony of his nature. . . . (p. 87)
>
> [T]he essence of the religious emotions consists in the feeling of an absolute dependence. (p. 106)

THE IDEAL POSSIBILITY, MISSED, IS ALIVE SUBTLY AT ALL TIMES

Problems can alienate couples/family members from one another, leaving each pessimistic and without access to one another. By first invigorating the "ideal" relationship, rather than dealing with problems first, energy and motivation emerge to deal with specific problems second. Each is now flushed with an experience of the "light that is at the end of the tunnel," with feelings of "what it is all for": *the blushing exchanges of love and optimism.* People who were at odds become more clearly resources to one another. Because the partners now have each other as resources, while before each was the enemy, the problems now seem smaller and more resolvable.

The fundamental problem for troubled couples/families is that their problems leave them *missing* one another and *missing* the hopefulness and enjoyment of one another. This "missing" is simultaneously the problem and the route back to union.

Conventional clients and therapists can misperceive (misname) the phenomena of (let's call it) "missing" as being mere pain or hurt. But in yoga this missing is called viyoga, "union during *apparent* separation." It is seen as mystical union. From "resented disappointment" to "shared missing" is the knottedness of misfirings to be untangled into the bond of hope and love that (re)connects people, as loci of hope, in mutual relatedness.

> THERAPIST. Look at all your family members. Consider they each miss you as much as you miss them. Feel the one big wishing of your family. You're just not that different from one another. Look.

Missing must not be allowed to dip into the masochism of self-righteous anger, suspicion, or self-pity. We must learn how to *sustain* sheer missing, which is the crux of devotion and the core of all devotional spiritualities. When the missed one returns, she is greeted with welcoming and not with the anger of "Where the hell were you!? I felt abandoned!" Then together they can *share* missing, viyoga, and feel just as missed by the other as we missed him.

In a couples session the wife complains about her husband's work schedule. I introduce the viyogic sense of missing to replace the mood of frustration and she agrees she is "missing him," something he can more easily relate to. He then says, "And I miss you too!" Instead of a fight about what he does wrong, they are learning *how to miss one another*.

In the same session, we talk about the valor of each of their professional lives (junior college coach and nurse) to such an extent that both come to tears in their pride in one another. Both feel more appreciated for their contributions to the community via career than ever before. I speak of all the kids helped by the coach, giving them a chance, going out on a limb, instead of cutting them from the team; the effect on their growing self-esteem and then on their families. I speak of her careful helping of her patients to move a finger a half inch more today, and a quarter inch more tomorrow, of hopelessness converting into hope because of her years of training.

I have them look at each other as I speak, inviting each to speak of their own pride in one another. I thank them for what they do and for allowing me to show it to them. "We are in a living community," I say. Being-in-the-world has been rehabilitated, and not just "giving the wife a cathartic experience in venting her frustrations about her husband" followed by efforts to change him. Why? Because I am seeing being-in-the-world and not "trapped individuals."

Now missing has been augmented with tonalities of pride, respect, and admiration that I tell them also makes their children feel pride and respect for them. The lateness of the husband's coming home from work is no longer merely a problem but a shared pride. Now he *wants* to come home as quickly as possible. Indeed, it is a *different home* that he now comes home to, the ideal home that was buried under this couple's "bad marriage" narrative.

The ironic twist is often a trustworthy guide toward our goal, not the etiological logic of diagnostic explanation. Irony shows the goal as strangely hidden in and as the problem.

An outsider—a therapist, an elder, a teacher—can sometimes do for a family what it cannot do for itself. The impossible becomes possible, the hopeless becomes hopeful in such trust.

The therapist must understand various ideal hopes in such common projects as being a husband, wife, mother, father, son, daughter, worker, artist, or neighbor. Whitman's "A Song of Occupations" is relevant, as is Confucian formalism. Birth, death, weddings, home seeking, job seeking, partner seeking, and the like, must be understood as filled with valor, daring, courage, uncertainty, enjoyment. One becomes confident by being inspired, far more than through analysis of the reasons why one feels insecure.

The spiritually oriented therapist must be able to discern many nuances of the poetic-romantic phenomena of missing. With this expansive romantic vocabulary, he can avoid mispathologizing experiences of missing via misuse of transferential hermeneutics. He can avoid the overused term of the conventionalist, *abandonment*, and the even more insidious concept of *abandonment anxiety* when regarding situations of missing.

When a client is late to a session, the waiting therapist should sustain her missing of the client and be able to greet him with such missing instead of, as the conventionalist is trained, to subject him to an inquiry regarding "what it means," the "resistance" or the "acting out." First take a stand on the existential ground of mortality of being glad to know the client is alive. Then we can explore how the experience of missing the time can be shared nonsuspiciously as a missing of contact and what we might have accomplished. Such exegesis on the phenomena of missing reveals a heartfelt relatedness that provides an authentic allure to being on time.

When the punctuality endures in a spirit of appreciated temporal respect, the whole developmental-failure explanation for the lateness—where does it go? It goes into the bin of unnecessary causal explanations. It goes into the museum of psychoanalytic memorabilia.

The phenomena of missing are both ignored and proscribed by conventionalists, thus its therapeutic value has not been explored. Even with repeated lateness, the existential ground of mortality should be held fast by the therapist. Further explorations should proceed later. (How strange to believe I *have to* say this.)

Experienced clients will not believe that the therapist really missed him. They will need more exegesis to flesh out the existential ground of mortality that all beings share. How else can a client learn how to feel missed without guilt if the therapist doesn't at such times miss him or help him to feel missed without guilt? How can he then export this ability into his greater life?

This awakening can even disrupt the passive-aggressive vengeful reactivities whereby clients act out via lateness. "My god, we are just two people," the astonished client remarks, "How petty to use lateness to get attention or to get back at someone."

Conventionalists misconstrue that for a therapist to miss her client puts the focus on the therapist's feelings—as if the missing were not *about* the client or were a burden to the client. Consider instead that the client needs to learn how to be missed and to share being missed.

The greater we value someone, the more we might miss them when they are late or away. Therapy should discern that such missing is a form of love and not abandonment anxiety. Borderline difficulties known as "clinging-distancing behavior" can benefit from cultivating the *ability* to miss someone. Missing/waiting often accentuates the sense of time passing and thereby both impermanence and mortality. One feels a suspensefulness in the temporalized uncertainty of wonderings, hopefulness, dread.

Current problems can be deconstructed into various existential issues: impermanence and finitude (commitment, sharing, time and money problems), uncertainty (decision making and the problematics of awakening into the indeterminacy of present-future time), will-to-power (addiction problems), forgiveness, apology, and resilience of the soul (self-esteem, the abused/abuser), loneliness (psychosis).

Thus various issues and problems become dignified as "philosophical-spiritual problems," rather than being "wounds" or "patterns" or "transference neuroses" to be healed or analyzed. True to the existentialist tradition, philosophy becomes an emotional and not just an intellectual matter.

Demands are often invitations restated with frustration, and long-developed masochistic pseudopleasure. PATIENT: "What's the matter with you? Why don't you spend time with me?!" THERAPIST: "Do you hear the invitation, covered over by frustration? Can you recover the invitation?"

SHADOW OF TIME

Like the shadow creeping across the sundial, the soteriological shadow carries all events into an unknown and constant ending(s). The shadow here is not a composite of avoided or repressed emotions, but is the composite of mortal limitations and finitudes. Rather than being merely what we "don't examine," this shadow is the fact that we *can't* look at everything and no matter how much we learn, mature, and enlighten, it will be the penumbra of mystery that yet surrounds us.

Shadow emotions such as jealousy, greed, envy, or hostility can transmute to appreciation, admiration, or protectivity when the constricting pressures of finitude or missing and longing are made bearable enough. The generosity-fomenting poignancy of "life is too short for that" can transmute these shadow emotions into light emotions, a transmutation that occurs at the edge of time, in the heart of our collective impermanence. Strange how a neighboring temporal poignancy (of desperate selfishness) will foment the jealousy, greed, envy, or hostility.

Or consider that these shadow emotions also have a shadow behind them, the shadow's shadow of light: the soul's unrelenting glow of love and hope, hidden behind fears of being "mushy" or "corny" or "all milk and cookies." As Whitman once stated, "I did not know I had so much goodness in me."

Perhaps the clinical fascination with the shadow has some basis in the appeal of the lurid, and even in the hautiness of going into "dark" matters that timid others won't go into. Such shadow exploration (some of which is no doubt helpful) is therefore prone to melodramatics and self-indulgence that can actually help the explorer to distractedly evade the existential shadow his own mortality more quietly casts as his lifetime (and all others') relentlessly slips away. t,t,t,t,t

Conventional therapists critique various forms of client gratification because its "cure" is temporary. They say we must instead explore the shadow to deepen the cure or at least to be able to see the (inevitable) return of our "darker nature." But everything is temporary, and evanescent temporality is our challenge. The soteriological challenge is that a life of ever-deepening gratitudes will inevitably come to an end, and such an ever-deepening life will invariably terminate on the very best day of one's life—the "worst day to have to leave life." This forshadowed ultimacy gives steady soteriological progress its ontological shadow: Even inexhaustive love is nonomnipotent across from relentless impermanence and the limits of the body.

SYMBOLS, THE UNCONSCIOUS, AND THE NARRATIVE AS CONTRIVANCES

The psychoanalytic term *the unconscious* is often used to expand the concept of *intentionality* to include things we would otherwise consider un- or nonintended in ourselves or in other people. The term thus serves us to attribute intentionality, "unconscious intentionality," to slips of the tongue, dreams, and to all sorts of actions.

The term becomes a kind of license for therapists (or others) to attribute intentionality, desiring, fearsomeness—almost without limitation—to their clients' actions. One feels the enjoyable and mysterious theatrics of being a sleuth in search of the "Real Intention."

Let's use the term *the unconscious* to refer to the *phenomenology of mystery itself*: the sense that there is more to know than we *can* or *do know*. Thus awe, dread, humility, uncertainty, allure, and wonder pertain: that which reveals *something* of what otherwise remains concealed. A special beauty of the concept of "essential mystery" and its surrounding phenomenology is generated by brooking no compromise: After all is said, a sense of mystery remains, and when well said, an even more profound mystery. Even a blade of grass is spellbinding, as Whitman noted.

Yet, the conventional therapist treats the unconscious as merely another puzzle for the conscious mind to solve.

That which is unconscious to the conscious mind, its limit, the mysterious and uncertain, might be known as and by reverence. "I am moved by your entrusting and sharing of your dream with me, for it is of the inmost privacy of your experience"—such is more than enough therapeutic response to the client's dream. Let deciphering be freed of the cryptic: Just ask the client to consider x, y, z, but not as a reading of the meaning of the dream as a message from the unconscious.

> The result of Freud's discovery is indeed to lock us into a predetermined possibility, which now appears to be the only one that merits attention: we can no longer see the dream without the need to find a Freudian meaning in it, convinced that it must have one. (Bouveresse 1995, p. 111)

A sense of eeriness accrues as the client is given interpretations by her therapist that there is *something* hidden in there. Since we lack a sense of Primordial Mystery that is inherent to (something called) the Unconscious, the sense of hiddenness is assumed to be a covering over of something quite nonmysterious and eventually understandable by the conscious mind, using its discursive and logical methods. In the conventional hermeneutic, we never can encounter The Awesome Mystery: the endless time sense in which our life takes place.

Consider the mystery of the unconscious to be essential and primordial, not a narrative to unravel. When we feel increasingly spellbound, humbled, awed, and silenced, then we are knowing the "unconscious" more fully. Here, possible extrasensory perceptions or psychic/intuitive or precognitive powers are part of the mystery. Who can say for sure?

"In dreams, all the characters are part of you." This is a common Jungian hermeneutic device. It aims to give a referential function to dream characters. "They" are (parts of) "you." But from the other direction the device is also an operational definition of what a "you" is: It is something that can be identified with images of other people that appear in one's own dream. But we must stop for a moment and ask: What kind of "you" is fostered by such dream-bound procedures (in the context of many other Jungian, Freudian, etc., devices)?

The conventional therapist may seem like a kind of magician. Yet his powers are merely based upon the license he has been given by his predecessors to see hidden motivations far beyond what all other people, by conventions of normality, allow themselves.

> The principle of mythologization lies in our need to find someone or something responsible for everything that happens; so when an action is performed "unconsciously" and therefore cannot be attributed to the conscious subject, we are tempted to look for another author, which it is difficult not to conceive as a conscious agent perfectly aware of what it's doing, though the person concerned is not. However much the psychoanalyst might be tempted to believe, according to Wittgenstein, that they have discovered conscious thoughts which are unconscious, we can suspect them of believing they have discovered a conscious agent, and indeed it could scarcely be more conscious (the unconscious), which is not exactly conscious. (Bouveresse 1995, p. 34)

A therapist believes her back became injured in a car accident because she "unconsciously desired" to be hurt exactly there in her lower back. All other factors—the slippery road, the drunk driver, seat-belt position, the poor lighting—were either irrelevant or seen by her as fulfilling her unconscious desire to hurt exactly her lower back. What do you make of this?

Uncertainty or unfathomability is not made more intelligible by inventing a home for it in coining the term *the unconscious*. This is just a word game—call it statistical inference, unconscious, or what you will, it remains just as uncertain. But now on top of it, we have this play of words or images. In the context of Mystery, even "soteriological impermanence" is a kind of word play.

Thus, I resort to t t t t t t t: pointing to the unending reemergence and passing: The Mystery (Us) Who now, now, now, Reads and Is. For, as Whitman hints at in "Whoever You Are Holding Me Now in Hand," there is a Place of Union that could be overlooked where we are, to an unsuspected depth, already intimately One. Consider the "*I*" and the "*You*" in his poem to be forgotten disguises for this *Oneness* of author and reader (of you and I, too).

> Whoever *you* are holding *me* now in hand,
> Without one thing all will be useless,
> *I* give *you* fair warning before *you* attempt *me* further,
> *I* am not what *you* supposed, but far different, . . .
> The way is suspicious, the results uncertain, perhaps
>   destructive,
> *You* would have to give up all else, *I* alone would
>   expect to be *your* sole and exclusive standard,
> *Your* noviate would even then be long and exhausting,
> The whole past theory of *your* life and all conformity
>   to the lives around *you* would have to be
>   abandon'd, . . .

> (For in any roof'd room of a house *I* emerge not, nor in
> company,
> And in libraries *I* lie as one dumb, a gawk, or unborn,
> or dead.)
> But just possibly *with you on a high hill*, first
> watching lest any person for miles around
> approach unawares, . . .
> And thus *touching you would I* silently sleep and be
> carried *eternally*. . . .
> For it is not what *I* have put into it that *I* have
> written this book, . . .
> For all is useless without that which *you* may guess *at*
> many times and not hit, that which *I* hinted *at*.
> (Whitman 1958 [1891–92], p. 114) (my emphases added)

The linguistic/interpretive methods of the conscious mind include logic, analogy, linear causality, word:phenomenon correspondence, thematics, cultural custom, and idiom. As we go further into the unconscious mind, we might need to leave these methods (which are part and parcel of the conscious mind itself) behind.

Entering more into the *un*conscious could mean and require leaving behind, more and more, the methods of language. What if the rendering of verbal interpretations or definitions from nonverbal symbols are to be left behind as well? And even the *idea* of the "symbol" as *something* that *stands for* something else must be left behind. The *un*conscious could be far more *un*like the conscious mind than the conscious mind would like to think. Even images "from the unconscious" (if we want to situate images this way) would seem to deserve protection from too-easy decipherings by the language of the conscious mind. Perhaps "seeing is forgetting the name of the thing one sees" (Weschler 1982).

Perhaps "making the unconscious conscious" is a matter of leaving its images and dramatics to evaporate into sustained, distractionless clarity. One enters what Heidegger called the *deinotaton*, the overpowering power whose silence overpowers the word methods of the conscious mind; what Rilke called "the uninterrupted news that grows out of silence." The "hinted at."

Mandalas (or *yantras*) are not devised primarily as symbols for something else, any more than a hammer is primarily a symbol of power. These things are tools to be used primarily to achieve specified ends. The mandala is to watchfully stare at until conscious consciousness reverentially grows more conscious.

Some are pictures of eyes-closed visual phenomena that are held to occur during meditation, where meditation is considered to be not a spiritual "practice" but an endogenously arising "postgenital puberty" of the mind itself. Some mandalas may depict artifacts of the rods, cones, and fovea centralis retinal structures undergoing their own postgenital puberty. As watching *MTV* helps gestate modern teenaged puberty, so do mandalas help gestate these puberties. In this context, we could say mandalas *correlate with* yogic stages, but there is still a danger of missing the point of these so-different puberties.

For, studying a mandala to decipher its "symbolic (semantic) meaning" can defeat its very purpose: to facilitate the postgenital puberty of the conscious mind as it outgrows (transcends) the constrictive grip of the genital puberty, dualistic intellect which *subjectively* studies/tries to figure out various *objects*.[5]

Compare such academic study with the teenager who reads in some library about "the facts of life" as a literature scholar would, laboring to discern the recurrent metaphors used by the author, their etymological origins and political referencings, yet never once stops—awestruck—to marvel at the profundity of his own, now-unfolding genital puberty, which the text only points *to*.

Suddenly, trying to discern symbolic meanings of yogic artifacts seems like measuring the shadows in the proverbial Platonic cave, while something more alive passes by in the brilliance outside. And the chains which aim our heads into the dim light? Are they not the proudly forged hermeneutical methods and aims of psychoanalysis, its offshoots, and the academic modes they helped spawn?

Consider, too, *mantras* as the nonsemantic sounds of labor that bear the ensouled body toward further postgenital maturations.

In kundalini yoga, mantras involve transformations of the functions of the hypoglossal-cerebrospinal anatomy completely unknown in Western developmental physiology. Imagine a spoken "language" the articulation of which is a means to fix the tongue tip to specific neural sensitivities located variously on the hard and soft palates or to engender "onomoto-somatically" specific "developmental quiverings" in the spinal cord. Body language, not as a reservoir of stored memories but as a sensory field of endogenous maturations now developing into the future.

Let us replace conscious/unconscious with a binary contrast where both sides are conscious: extroversion/introversion. Here what is aimed at with the term *the unconscious* (the "inner world" of interpreted dreams, unsuspected intentions, synchronistically caused events, precognitive intuitions, forgotten, suppressed or repressed motivations) is embedded within a linguistic continuum that begins with the listed parentheticals. But this inward awareness gradually enters more and more wordless realms of meditative consciousness. There it encounters maturational processes that aim into a developmental future far more vast than the conventionalists have so far imagined.

Thus, the Freudian and Jungian "unconscious(es)"—dreams, slips of the tongue, and so on—are the foyer to this consciousness of introversion, which might better be called "the precincts of the ineffable," or outer lips of the mind-as-womb to the long-maturing, ensouled body.

As Wittgenstein noted philosophically, "Whereof one cannot speak, thereof one must be silent." The silence here, however, comes after the Wittgensteinian silence of intellectual honesty and humility. This gasped silence is of awe and wonder: the hushed reverence in witnessing the incessant, continuing gestation of one's own ensouled body, and that of others. In considering such developmental possibilities, the preoccupations with the past of conventional psychology seem even more limited.

Thus, codes of "symbolic interpretation"—*the* archetypes, *the* symbols of death, of phallus, of parents, and so on—should include the disclaimer that all stock interpretations of yogic artifacts must be weighed against any future discoveries about the meaning or purpose of these artifacts and the yogic processes *to* which they relate.

For example, the yogic *linga*, understood via Freudian hermeneutics as a phallic symbol, reveals its esoteric meaning via etymology, for linga is the *lingual* tongue and not necessarily the penis. Furthermore, most esoterically, the linga is *a picture* (not a *symbol* for something else) of the tongue of a yogi attaining a specific maturational stage and has nothing to do with sex or fertility in any conventional sense, as we will see in chapter 3. How far astray can we go with our Western codes of interpretation in misguided decodings of cross-cultural artifacts, and in decoding the content of our own unconscious minds or collective mind? If this maturational stage is ontogenetic, as yoga purports, then mightn't we conjecture that Western dream analysts may have been misinterpreting long-dreamed objects, at least on some occasions?

As religious artifacts are seen as if they *are* what they are, and no longer what they *stand for*, they typically become objects of worship—actual gods—and *not* (mere) symbols *for* gods. Those who do not glimpse the deity itself (not its idol or symbol) and throw their arms up in delight are left outside.

Those who do go further within look back and now see that the concept of the symbol is an academic contrivance or analytic lens used by the scholar who (merely) studies religions and cultures. Should he become a "believer," he loses his distance, his reflective objectivity, and enters the realm where there are no idols or symbols—there are only living stone gods and breathing bronze goddesses.[6]

> The secondary sense [of a word] is not a "metaphorical" sense. If I say "for me the vowel *e* is yellow" I do not mean "yellow" in a metaphorical sense—for I could not express what I want to say in any other way than by means of the idea "yellow." (Wittgenstein 1968, p. 216)

I quote Wittgenstein here to provide some perspective on the use of the concept of *metaphor*, which is often heard/used in conventional therapies in such a way as to bolster the impact of an interpretation. In this interpretive query, "Is this dream a *metaphor* for your faltering marriage?" *metaphor* should merely consolidate the difficulties and equate this marriage with a certain dream. The dream is merely *another way* of construing the difficulties of the marriage.

Be aware of how this metaphor can be heard *as if* it reveals a deeper discovered truth hidden from wakeful consciousness: the "hidden truth" of how truly faltering this marriage *is*.

Thus, wakefulness can be construed as an obstruction to emotional truth that dreams (and dream therapists), sleuthlike, get through. Therapists and clients should be watchful for such construed reversals of ordinary definitions, particularly regarding "dream truths."

SIMILARITY AND TEMPORALITY

Where is the future?—We mustn't think of the future as existing anywhere. What we can imagine as "the future" is not *the* future, this is still the realm of imagination. We can make blueprints for a building and then take the next ten months to build it from the blueprint, but we cannot make a blueprint of the future because future time is something that happens *when* it happens. What am I pointing to as "an experience of the future"? I don't quite know. My next breath? Aren't these words kind of blueprints that guide my eyes toward what is to show up next? I want to point to future time only, what keeps being *next*.

Clinicians use concepts of patterns and cycles to deal more with similarity than with temporality. They emphasize *what* seems to reappear more than the graceful flow or drift of time which *cycles*. Grammatically, consider *patterns* or *cycles* as action verbs, more than as noun things.

The troubled past is of little value as a fund of generalizations from which to understand this newness with its awe (not fear), with its uncertainty (not doubt), with its sense of possibility (not resentful entitlement) and longings (hidden in any complaint). Conventional therapy can misassociate the difficulties inherent to newness with past difficulties. If there is one thing that characterizes newness, it is that generalizations from the past can be among the least relevant descriptors to name its distinctiveness. Learning a next step forward, not how one has failed in the past in similar situations, is the priority.

Only as a convenience do we say of things that they are the same from moment to moment. At some point in becoming more aware of impermanence it is confusing to keep speaking that way. Then it feels more accurate to say that "Nothing is the same age from moment to moment, therefore nothing stays as it was."

I have defined "the same" in deference to time passage and not in deference to the concept of similarity or the logic of identity, which might ignore time passage. Can there be something that does not age? Even the immortal body reported in yogic texts ages as its youthfulness reemerges, again and again.

Analogy is a logical category, not an existential one. No thing or event *is* an analog to another, except we apply such a comparative grid to it. Psychoanalysts and their followers use their stockpile of analogies (oedipal relationships, ego structures, "like it was with your mother") to forge connections between different events in a patient's life, at times shaping events with the clinical vocabulary themselves so that they will appear as persuasive analogs to one another.

Such interpretations rob the patient of a sense of the novelty of each event and of future events. "You have married someone like your father/mother!" (Implying your marriage will be like your parents' or like your relationship was with your mother/father.) Even if similarities exist and the analogy proves helpful in some ways, the novelty of *these* never-happened-before "versions" can easily get lost, presence gets easily lost.

What distinguishes one similar event from another will often be subtle. The new time in which this version occurs is subtle. Putting detailed, subtle perceptions into words, haikulike, can make the mundane ring with poignant impermanence: "And how I loved seeing his shoes strewn all over the floor each morning."

OBLIVION AND LETTING PASS

A lesson to learn about the past is that it is over, it has slipped into oblivion (*oubliez*: to slip from the mind in the passage of time, a sensitivity grasped aesthetically by the French Impressionists, and philosophically by Bergson).

Perhaps it is our fear of oblivion—that all events recede into concealment—that motivates us into overusing the capacity to remember. Thus clinging or "attachment" is a common barrier to enlightenment. Combined with vengeance: "I ain't forgetting!"

Like the word *death*, the word *oblivion* has a frightening connotation of utter destruction. Yet both are merely names for the unknown. Oblivion is the name of "where" events go when they slip from one's current sentience. If there is "repression," there is also "clinging" and "fabricating" as if to avert time passed's inevitable slippage into oblivion. Memory as memorial.

How consciousness is tripartitioned into "current awareness" or "perception," "memory," and "expectant fantasy," and how the economy of time gets tripartitioned into "my past," "my fleeting present," and "my future" is *at stake*. My experienced temporal dimensionalities and narrated lifetime is *at stake*.

The unfamiliar, a kind of forward-alluring mystery and not something from the past, could be our primary focus. The living God: YHWH, "That Which IS IS IS IS. . . . "

From what clincial vocabulary will "forms of life" be made?

> As an epoch comes to an end, its principle withers away. The principle of an epoch gives it cohesion, a coherence which, for a time, holds

unchallenged. At the end of an epoch, however, it becomes possible to question such coherence. In withering away, the supreme referent of an age becomes problematic. As long as its economy dominates, and as long as its order disposes the paths that life and thought follow, one speaks otherwise than when its hold loosens, giving way to the establishment of a new order. . . . The justificatory reason of an epoch has its time: it establishes itself, reigns, and eventually founders. . . . Ultimate reasons are unquestionable, but only temporarily so. (Schurmann 1987, p. 25)

CLIENT. You keep seeing me as this really good person and I notice that I am not so interested in my deep dark secrets.

THERAPIST. Yes, that's true, yet certainly you can bring up what you are thinking of as your dark secrets. But the secret that I ask you to consider as, at times, the darkest and deepest secret, the secret of all secrets, is what a beautiful human being you are. And, if you look around when you know this, you will see everybody else in this same way, even though they might be acting otherwise, as if their beauty is hidden from them too.

CHAPTER 2

Revenge against Impermanence: Temporal-Spiritual Psychopathology

In this chapter we explore another sort of etiology in which the sufferings of the past become entangled with more generic difficulties with time and language. This etiology is an admixture of (1) the reverberations of the troubling events, (2) the spiritual challenges relentless impermanence always bequests us, (3) the limitations of popularized psychoanalytic "healing narratives" with their overly deterministic developmental schemas and weakened soteriological powers, and (4) other linguistic ambiguities. Altogether and in the extreme, a kind of "past" can come to such preeminence that living presence turns against itself via the suicidal narrative, gesture, and act.

THE UNDERLYING IMPERMANENCE

All events, including this one, take place in time and thus are subject to the phenomenology of the temporal. Words just now enunciated recede into silence and the past as new words are sounded in each present moment.

A smile peaks in delight and then relaxes into pleasantness, then shyness. Glimmers of various feelings—anger, hopefulness, affection—spark in their own evanescent moment and then pass, giving way to some more obvious and preponderant mood.

This too shall pass. In addition to what everything is and does, everything also passes. In addition to our reactions to what everything is and does, we also are always reacting to the temporal fact that all events, conversations, and actions slip away and are supplanted by something new that will also slip away. Even our own reactions slip away and this slippage can make us feel strangely powerless.

THE INNOCENCE OF IMPERMANENCE GROWS PROBLEMATIC

As we age and age (that is, as we slip away while also relentlessly slipping into, into, into an uncertain future), the accretions of years of reacting to this slippage can persuade us that we are victims of something (*sic*), something lingering and elusive, perhaps malevolent. *Something* that has "caused" this slippage and remains as the (etiological) impetus for future problems.

Something that has "caused" us to leave our innocent beginnings and seedlike hopes, "causes" this path of our lives to happen, strewn with the otherness of other people and the unpredictableness of events all, now, in various stages of being over (with each new generation feeling it sooner and more intensely than the last, as rising teen suicide statistics denote). Through the anthropomorphic lens of causal-deterministic reasoning, time passage appears to have grown thin hands that reach tragically into human lives.

THE INNOCENCE OF IMPERMANENCE IS OBSCURED BY A RETROSPECTIVE SEARCH FOR EXPLANATIONS

The search for a "convicted feeling of certainty" concerning why this slippage happens or has happened to us (as if it might be prevented in the future) typically runs shallow and we settle into a blaming of (assigning tragic causality with a passion equivalent to our escalating sense of victimization) each other for what otherwise are merely the consequences of impermanence itself. As if (we hope) there was someone who could be held (with vengeful vigor, not just hope) responsible for the ways of time, someone who should have prepared or protected us (with adequate safety, information, resources): our parents, leaders, spouse, children, the gods, some "them." We might even vengefully blame our aging selves. For vengeance marks the divergence from soteriological time into evermore severe circularities.[1]

THE LIMITATIONS OF THIS RETROSPECTIVE SEARCH ARE APPROACHED . . .

The profundity and sheer mystery of our situation is lost in such dispirited inquiries. Adulthood seems too late, another irretrievable fall from innocence, if not a sacking. Thus now emerges the current therapeutic ruse: "Seek in the past for your inner child!"—a last, desperately hopeful metaphor for some refuge from impermanence by a culture of Nietzsche's "last men."

> The earth has become small, and on it hops the last man, who makes everything small. . . . One is clever and knows everything that has ever happened: so there is no end of derision. (Nietzsche 1970 [1882–83], p. 129–30)

AND CURVE INTO A CUL DE SAC OF THEIR OWN MAKING

And even if we have come to understand some past event that explains a few aspects of current matters, even that explanation and its eureka pass away, leaving the analytic machinery to whir on, looking for something, something yet eluding us, to explain this "residual feeling of inner emptiness," an unsafe feeling or depression, a fear of commitment, an original woundedness with the threatening sense that if we don't keep looking, something as yet denied or repressed (in ourselves or in others) might overpower us someday or, the unthinkable, might overpower us (as it has all who have preceded us) even if we do explain it: "'Formerly, all the world was mad,' say the most refined [last men], and they blink" (ibid., p. 130).

As the search for precedent explanations more and more displaces the mystery of constantly passing-rearising presence—as our hope for improving our future lot—a spiraling circularity takes over the search for those becoming lost (from t sheer t impermanence) in retrospective time. Cut off (or seemingly so) from soteriological time and with all answers seeming to be in the past, time passage feels evermore like a desperate urgency, if not a "too late." Past events are considered as evermore causally determining or structuring of the present, even who and what we are.

IMPERMANENCE IS MISSED AND THE SUBTLE POIGNANCY OF ITS GRACE NOW SEEMS NARROW AND SEVERE

In this constrained sense of impermanence and its obscured soteriological powers, the sublime *poignancy* of inescapable time passage darkens. A veneer of its mercurial subtlety contorts in the grip of the searcher *into* a severe exactitude to be named: invariant developmental "needs" or "dire consequences." Poignancy and awe (their hormonal correlates) of the endless passing recoil (transmute) into a narrowed and passionate concern for dangers, traumas, salvation. What was once the condemnation explanation of The Fall or "coming from bad blood" contorts into the etiological explanation of the more sorrowful troubled childhood.

THE SEVERITY OF THE SEARCH GROWS EVERMORE EMPASSIONED HOPING TO TRUE ONE'S COURSE ALONG SOME NARROW PATH

An inquisitorial self-regard (the so-called superego) precipitates out of the soteriological flow, along with its precarious, queried ego. In the

West, this passionate inquiry has taken two external forms: Haunting us on the one side, Jonathan Edwards, in a long line of introspective predecessors, deified this shuddering investigative passion of the precarious sinner facing an exacting moral determination:

> O sinner! Consider the fearful danger you are in: 'tis a great furnace of wrath, a wide and bottomless pit, full of the fire of wrath, that you are held over in the hand of that God . . . you hang by a slender thread. (Edwards, "Sinners in the Hands of an Angry God," 1733, in Bradley, Beatty, and Long 1967, p. 65)

From another psychological side and in reaction to the harshness of the former, the passion of inquiry becomes a caring pity, a searching cleansed of wrath yet still conjuring a fragile self, but this time in the pathos of less exacting yet fully deterministic developmental needs where one's hellish fall (or dropping) from grace, too, is "forever":

> [There are] babies who have been significantly "let down" once or in a pattern of environmental failures (related to the psychopathologic state of the mother or mother-substitute). These babies carry with them the experience of unthinkable or archaic anxiety. They know what it is to be in a state of acute confusion or the agony of disintegration. They know what it is to be dropped, to fall forever, or to become split into psycho-somatic disunion. (Winnicott 1989, p. 260)

Along this narrative trajectory of inward concern for righteousness/mental health, I locate two closely related products of this caring but suspicious concern: the precarious adult sinner and the precarious innocent infant (or adult-child), both drawn forth by a peculiarly slender and inexorable kind of Time. Thus, as the soteriological spirit gets inscribed more and more as the letter of some law, sheer mortal impermanence becomes miscast as a precariousness before that law, whether a moralistic or a psychodevelopmental law. The word overcomes the spirit of its own message and the deeply nourishing poignancy of soteriological time grows anorexic.

IMPERMANENCE AND THE SOTERIOLOGICAL SENTIMENTS GROW DISTANT; TRAGIC NARRATIVES EMERGE AND PROLIFERATE AS THE SEARCH CONTINUES

And, since ours has become a linguistic, dialoguing consciousness, a story-to-tell is fashioned, a painful history of the present as, somehow, the (fallen) past reverberating still. In the echoing remembrance of this story again and again into the openness of the present (What would a t "history" t of t impermanence t look t like? Could there even be such a thing?), a dramatic sense of tragedy can breed a forgone, fated world where past abuses (we are told) engender invariant issues and patterns, which unremittingly consume more and more of the present lives of those who are becoming hopeless. With their explanations already languaged in that most questionable rhetoric of pop psychology, many enter the analytic domains of professional psychotherapy.

Abandoned, betrayed, shame bound, a mere survivor of . . . , healing from emotional primal wounds, inexcusably denying one's rage, burdened with original pain, emotionally incested by toxic parents, filled with unmet needs, in search of a hurt, inner child—such is the melodramatic vernacular of pop psychology.

THE "HEALING" NARRATIVES PRODUCE THEIR IATROGENIC SIDE EFFECTS

Thus, also, the complexity, subtle ambiguities, and wavering uncertainties and nobilities of family life (even heinously abusive family life) and individual maturation can be lost in dispirited oversimplifications. Looking backward for the full meaning of the present and blinded by allegorical reductionisms, our psychotherapeutic narratives have become snared in the Joycean nightmare of history from which it had hoped to awaken us.

OVERVIEW OF SUBTLE TEMPORAL-LINGUISTIC FACTORS IN THE CLINICAL SETTING

The Fifty-Minute Protocol

Temporality enters into psychotherapy in visible and barely visible ways. The fourteenth minute of the hour gives way to the fourteenth and one second, and two and three. The therapy hour begins at 6:00 P.M., and sunset occurs gradually during the hour and finally at some point, say 6:48 P.M., a kind of nostalgia fills the dusk air of the session. Finally, each session, with oftentimes metered precision, ends.

The whole tradition of clinical note keeping, often performed with more concern for clinical bureaucracy and legal liabilities than for sheer therapeutic interests, creates another snapshot narrative the therapist reviews again and again, reifing the past and aligning all future therapy with a singular retrospective. Some schools teach that the opening words of the first session, or the initial phone call, set the whole course.

Patient and therapist both age during the hour, each leaving behind his youth evermore for the uncertainties of the future and wearing-down process of aging and eventual death. The patient spends his hard-earned hourly wages as recompense for an hour of the therapist's diligent skill, as they both literally spend some of their lives with one another.

Hermeneutic References Are Anchored in "The Past" . . .

Relying on the hermeneutic of interpreting the recent past, the present, and the likely future through reference to analog precedent "first traumas" in the long past (typically, childhood), psychotherapy can over-engender feelings of nostalgia and retrospective melancholy. On some occasions, the back-and-forth, back-and-forth method foments subtle, time-fractured "multiple personality" phenomenology—reports of which once increased as rapidly as these clinical methods spread.[2]

and the Search for the Explanatory Traumas Begins

Week after week, client and therapist "go back" to find out what happened in some distant "ago," facing the therapist's pointed query of possibly "denying something" if nothing severe is found. And since therapy is a hermeneutical project, the more severe a remembered event, the better, for such can be used to explain even more of the client's present difficulties.

The Singular Direction of the Cure Augers Onward, Committedly

Such therapies search for a deeper shame or an earlier trauma that will end the repression and dissociation from how much worse a wounding one really received than one's currently defended state will admit. Yet, even when true and helpful, these searches often do not know when to stop. The challenges of the present-future, the continual arising of further possibilities, and of impermanence itself are lost to the sustained retrospective gaze and its inherent melancholia, perhaps for years and years.[3]

The Search for Certainty Quietly Preempts Spiritual Freedom

As Dostoyevsky's Grand Inquisitor chides, an ever-renewing spiritual freedom can seem like an overwhelming burden for the already suffering individual, and not a merciful lightening of all such burdens. Consider Dostoyevsky's "You" (Christ) being addressed here by the cynical Inquisitor as the soteriological promise of undetermined, eternal impermanence Personified:

> Instead of taking possession of men's freedom, You increased it, and burdened the spiritual kingdom of mankind forever with its sufferings. You wanted man's free love. You wanted him to follow You freely,

enticed and captured by You. In the place of the rigid ancient law, man was hereafter to decide for himself with free heart what is good and what is evil, having only Your image before him as his guide. But did You not think he would at last dispute and reject even Your image and Your truth, if he were oppressed with the fearful burden of free choice? They will cry aloud at last that the truth is not in You, for they could not have been left in greater confusion and suffering than You have caused, laying upon them so many cares and unanswerable problems. (Dostoyevsky 1960 [1880], p. 129)

Innocent Wistfulness Gets Coopted in the Clinical Narrative

Such freedom and its merciful love often proves too elusive, as the Inquisitor predicted. Instead, the relentless slippage of innocent time passage provides a constant supply of wistful ("vague and enigmatic," as the Inquisitor notes) feelings that can be escalated linguistically (a loss is renamed an "abandonment," a "violation" and then a "betrayal," while abuses become "original wounds," "primal pain," or "soul murderings") and projected forward into a predictive fear (as a misnamed anticipation or sheer uncertainty) of further depression or abuse. Perhaps as endless as time itself.

Thus, a fortified (hormonally) and familiar dread foments, seemingly capable of permeating the newness of each new moment (and something new and unfamiliar can only happen in a *felt-as-new* moment) for as long as there can be future time. Dread thus sustained commingles with the ominous feel of eternity itself. Together we name them: doom.[4]

Familiarity Gets Confused with Certainty

Over time, the sheer *familiarity* of this singularly repeated dread is hardened into the illusion of a hopeless *certainty* (or is further enhanced into obsessions or delusions). In the spirit of revenge, the wholly temporal self wields vigilantly this repeating, hardening, and sustaining into a simulacrum of immortality, a travesty of Nietzsche's eternal recurrence. The revulsion against temporality and the resistence to Becoming approaches metaphysical depths.

Condensations of "Pain" Build from Grammatical Contractions and the Logic of the Inferred Extreme

Thus, finally, these difficulties with impermanence can enter the eerily dangerous and extreme clinical position of talking about suicide, that is, the languaging of ending an utterly familiar, summative "it" or recurrent "is" (personal life as regularly repeated dread of yet another hopeless moment) in some "near" or "distant" future time.[5] Destiny wielded as a narrative: suicidal ideation, notes, plans, and available gestures or means become the instrumentalization of death, of taking time into one's own hands.

Cognitive Certainty Merges with Temporal Conclusivity

The life story collapses into a singular, abysmal, *cognitive* sense of certainty ("it" is most *certainly* bad), merged with a *temporal* sense of conclusivity (time for improvement has most certainly *concluded*). Although *cognitive certainty* (I am convinced of x, and that is *that*) and *temporal conclusivity* (yesterday is *over*) are concepts of very different measures, they get merged together and can prove to be persuasive ultimately.

Certainty, Conclusivity, Grammatic Contractions, Consistency, and the Logic of the Inferred Extreme

In a matter of words—with "it" = all knowable substantives and "is" = all temporal processing, contracted into a singularly dense "it's"—"It's all over" serves as the summarizing, defeated totalization. In a morbidly perverse sense, suicidal language—"What's the use; I feel like killing myself, like ending it all"—feels logically and semantically consistent with how unwaveringly *convincing* irresolute pastness is. Some certainty, definitiveness, and *results*, at last.

Player and Language Game Reverse Their Priorities— To End the Game and Its Form of Life, the Player *Must Go*

So convincing are these composite mergers that the one who lives can become *convinced* to kill himself as a consequence. "It" is the logical thing that (therefore) *must* be done. Those who declare war often subscribe to a similarly "inexorable" logic of doing what must be done. The poignancy of our shared condition gets obscured in such self-steeling severity.[6]

The Inconceivability of a "Death End" Is Surmounted: Life as Hopeless, End as Solution, Death as Hope

As *being* or "is" becomes the container for all that is unbearable or hopelessly over, with clockwork precision another alternative "somewhere else" begins to come to life: The temporo-spatialized notion of an elsewhere that comes after, called "death," begins turning about in one's mind as a meaningful sentence/possibility. Death names something that seems to be both demanded by and is a way out of this life story into some timeless, storyless is-not elsewhere place. (The fights for peace, racial purity, honor, *lebensraum*, or other drum-beats into the instrumentalization of death as warfare.)

The Mutable Immortality of Hope

At such moments, a marbleization of repeated themes—thwarted vengeance, lurking shamefulness, mournful remembrance—preempts any phenomenological sense of fluctuating meanings and emotionality, that is, the sense of diverse possibilities and unpredictable change *out* of life: the repeated, dire narrative preempts the present-futureness (the t "life" t) out t of t life. But this is a sleight-of-hand illusion, for the essential meaning of life-as-unfolding t openness, as other t and other t and other t and other . . . possibilities—that is, hope—does not truly vanish but consolidates into a singular dark hope via psycholinguistic manipulation.

For there comes a turning point in this psycholinguistic shell game where hope is no longer granted as being possible within the word shell labeled "life." Thus, suicidal language becomes thinkable or realistic. Its dark vocabulary becomes persuasive as if to show a way of expressing something or taking, finally, *real* action: a metaphorical way out, in extremis.

Yet, as suicidal language becomes thinkable, hope—no matter how subtle and insubstantial—transmigrates like the Hindu *atman* to hinted-at realms verifiable (or not) only upon getting there. Hinted at by innuendo or one's final boldness, it will soon or then ("soon," "then": sleepy whisperings of sheer inference) be found hiding, perhaps desperately and motionless, under the shell labeled "death" or, more precisely, "the (idea of) THE VERY NEXT MOMENT after the suicide has been completed."

Thus, the suicidal narrative represents a paradoxical turning away from the hopeless past—and is therefore hopeful—toward a lifeless concept of the future whose only entrance is an act of violence—and is therefore tragic.

If one thinks that all hope has died, suicide, as a chosen (albeit desperate) act, becomes a varyingly dramatic burst of living willfulness into this idea of that next nonmoment moment. It is the thought-act of the taking of one's life. But taking it where? To where most societies (language games) conceive of the opposite of life as resting—in death.

Unthinkable Uncertainties within Suicidal Death

The word-idea *death* signifies where one will be (or not-be) in the next moment after the suicidal act has fully burst. But if suicide turns out to be an indeterminably echoing hell, what worse eventuality could there ever be? If the next moment lived would have awakened one to the grace of impermanence beyond all narratives, what more tragic irony could there ever be?

Death *as a Word Assumed to Contrast with* Life

Death conceived of as *not this*, as *not being here*, is the assumption that makes suicidal talk logical, and even morbidly and perversely merciful, to the suicidal patient. Suicide represents here the end of time, at least as we (try or have learned how to try to) know it, as, we hope, the end of all time-passage problems.

If Time is the problem, then perhaps Not-time will be the solution. The at first oscillating and later more desperately razor-edged path to this morbid extreme is guided by the evermore unswerving linearity of bare logic, itself a severe device of coherence: Logic becomes the superego's persuasive steel.

The inversion of valences of the common duality of life and death is complete: Life holds the dreaded feelings of unchanging overness and is therefore hopeless or dead; thus, not-life in logical fashion can seem more and more to be the only tenable cache for change, for relief from temporality and hope, or for a coup de grace of a long-standing narrative of martyring revenge or shrinking shamefulness.

Over and over again, at dawn, while eating or walking or waiting in lines, one listens to the inwardly mentalized sentence, "There is only one thing left to do. I should just kill myself."

Lure of Mystery Enters the Suicidal Narrative, Drawing the Author-Protagonist toward the Greying Climax

Thus, one's last hope (and suicide is always among the last of hopes) thickens into the plot line of this mysterious tragedy, compelling the patient through these days like so many pages toward that final word on that final page t,t,t. And, as in any mystery tale, it is the anticipated terminating ending itself that draws the reader on and on and it alone will climax in him as the action that has all along been building.

Whoever contemplates suicide finds himself in such a morbid mystery, where the most hidden and unknown of allurements, beneath all the tragic events of one's frustrating and oppressive lifestory, is the terminus of death itself. Of course, the mounting eroticism of this alluring compulsion cannot be ignored. For what is eroticism but the beckoning scent of our own impermanence?

In Summary

Thus, the phenomenology of temporality (the incessant slipping-away sense of time passage as a familiarity, then as a hopelessness, a dreaded certainty repeated, a basic identity sense and a forgone conclusivity) merges with:

1. the inexorable mechanics of binary logic (if t is bad, then not-t is good),
2. energizing narrative themes such as shame-being-disclosed, vengefulness-being-aroused, or painful-secrets-being-told,
3. analytic "cause seeking" escalates into encouraged cathartic discharges of rage or grief in a therapeutic quest for etiological certainties, entrusted disclosures, and unenmeshing emotional releases, supported by:
   a. the current masochistogenic pop-psychology vocabulary, e.g., "reclaiming one's inner child wounded by toxic parents,"
   b. an ironic circularity whereby well-intended, diagnostic generalizations (self-help check lists, identified causes or developmental failures from the past) can iatrogenically curve in upon themselves, loading the client with answers that come to feel like more problems,
   c. the marginalization of good childhood experiences in the construction of the clinical family history,
   d. the linguistic condensations of meaning in the contraction "it's" (so bad) and other such grammatic subtleties,
   e. the sustained retrospective psychoanalytic hermeneutic and its melancholy gaze,
   f. the hypnotic and concretizing powers of repeated phrasings;
4. the structural allure of story narratives, particularly the "tragic mystery," where a peculiar compulsion draws the listener uncertainly onward from dark origins (in a dysfunctional family) to an ordained end (the predictable syndromes), as well as
5. the hidden allure of the mystery of death itself and
6. the perhaps infinitesimal essence of hope that yet resides in any willful or intended act, however brief and suddenly executed—even a fatal one.

THE SUBTLETIES OF IMPERMANENCE AS SHOWS OF FREEDOM

Yet, there is another way out beyond the misconstrued problematics of time passage, the search for all meaning in the "psychoanalytic past," the, at times, morbidly predetermining powers of logic (or *etio*-logic) and sadomasochism-prone pop terminologies. It lies in a therapist's sharpened perception of emotions that live in very brief time spans, a focus on the "almost freedom" or "unjustified mercy" that impermanence bequeaths us in the evanescence of each most immediate moment before it has been appropriated by the narrative story line of the "burgeoning past."

When singular clinical observations approach the limits of unaided temporal-perceptive discrimination (through an almost meditative regard for the patient), the burgeoning past narrative phenomenally dissolves, reemerges, and dissolves into the unlanguaged indeterminacy of the most immediate impermanent moment. "Newness" is revealed.

Event-perception sequelae approaching .15 seconds can be discerned ("small delta-t"). Ephemeral and pregnantly meaningful flutters and tensions of the eyelashes beckon, repel, and beckon. Slight and rapid changes in moisture and viscosity on the surface of the eyes invite, hope, beckon, receive, and guard. A nearly inaudible warble of complex microemotional innuendoes are heard, such as "resentfully hopeful scorning charm," or "longingly hateful ever-ready playfulness"—what jazzist Charlie Parker called "the notes within the notes."

Thus, the "living protagonist" is seen aesthetically to emerge from his story, which is like awakening from the ideational dream world of a past history into the vivid present where, all along, the past less and less exists. "The past" is needed with less and less therapeutic urgency to serve as a hermeneutical basis to derive the meaning—the raison d'etre—of the present and the hoped-for cure.

As the remembered past is less invested with revenge or developmental significance, what might be called the mercifulness of the present penetrates those memories with unreasonable forgiveness and, as yet, unthinkable forgetting. One lives, as Rilke noted, more unshieldedly: "In the end it is our unshieldedness on which we depend."

SPIRITUAL TIME AND SPIRITUAL FREEDOM

This transformation from rage/grief/hopelessness/vengeance to forgiveness proves difficult, not because a significant amount of processing of these feelings is prerequisite, but precisely because nothing of the kind is necessary.

The affront to our sensibilities is that so subtle and pervasively benign a power as graceful, forgiving impermanence should (beyond justice or explanations) be equal to our most grievous violations. Even the Grand Inquisitor is silenced . . .

> When the Inquisitor stopped speaking he waited some time for his prisoner to answer him. His silence weighed down upon him. He saw that the prisoner had listened intently and calmly all the time, looking gently in his face and evidently not wishing to reply. The old man longed for Him to say something, however bitter and terrible. But He sud-

denly approaches the old man in silence and softly kisses him on his bloodless aged lips. That was His whole answer. The old man shudders. Something trembles at the edge of his lips. (Dostoyevsky 1960, p. 139)

Where something trembles, the fixity of any explanatory narrative or diagnosis succumbs to a spiritual temporality. Another phenomenal world emerges during such subtle observations, a world seeming to have its own semantics and therapeutic possibilities, including momentary renewals of self-confidence and felt connection with others; the liberating aspects of paradox, indeterminacy, and humor; the remarkable intimacy that comes from sharing desperate thoughts and spent mortality, the emergence of such unverifiable spiritual sentiments as "some faith in . . . ," "a little respect for . . . ," or "a glimmer of love for. . . . "

Thus, we must consider the swaying healing force in the courageous Winnicott's physical holding of his client (and his widely adopted clinical metaphor of the "holding environment") to be mutually trusting adult-to-adult kindness, *not* the hypothesized interpretation and sincere charade of "early infancy reparenting."

> The detail I have chosen for description has to do with the absolute need [sic] this patient had, from time to time, to be in contact with me. . . .
>
> A variety of intimacies were tried out, chiefly those that belong to infant feeding and management. There were violent episodes. Eventually it came about that she and I were together with her head in my hands.
>
> Without deliberate action on the part of either of us there developed a rocking rhythm. The rhythm was rather a rapid one, about 70 per minute (c.f. heartbeat), and I had to do some work to adapt to this rate. Nevertheless, there we were with *mutuality* expressed in terms of a slight but persistent rocking movement. We were *communicating* with each other without words. This was taking place at a level of development that did not require the patient to have maturity in advance of that which she found herself possessing in the regression to dependence of the phase of her analysis.
>
> This experience, often repeated, was crucial to the therapy, and the violence that had led up to it was only now seen to be a preparation and a complex test of the analyst's capacity to meet the various communicating techniques of early infancy. (Winnicott 1989, p. 258)

And the possibility that this graceful head-rocking kindness is analogous to yogic and other spiritually developmental movements proper to adulthood must also be considered (see p. 153).

Thus, the clinician must follow the Heideggerian challenge to "think being temporally," to experience the patient and himself as fluctuating temporal realities. He must be open to Quinean linguistics where language is understood as, finally, referentially indeterminant. He and his patient might even find a little peace and quiet in the Quinean categorical disclaimer, "The inscrutability of reference is not the inscrutability of a fact. There is no fact of the matter."

The ontological or perhaps theological giving of this release from pastness, the *mercy* itself, renders one's efforts to secure this freedom vestigial. Without reference to a deity, inexplicable evanescence becomes the merciful healer; with such a reference, we enter the theological psychology of spontaneous forgiveness, grace, innocence, and transcendence.

In either case, we enter the problematics of inexplicable and ineffable mercy as something too good to be true—the single most powerful ambiguity of feeling or cognition, which thus serves as gatekeeper to any further sustaining and enduring of the here-now awakening and its inevitable passage.

Here patient and therapist risk coming so far out of the narrative past as to experience each other as merely two currently temporal persons (grasped shallowly by the pop term, *vulnerability*) with roles and transferential/countertransferential hermeneutics molted off to the sides.

Furthermore, the attitude of the observer at small delta-t levels of observation becomes ever more critical in its effect on and assessment of the observed. A meditative and responsive *appreciation* (no mere mirroring) of the patient, his presence—free even of compassion or empathy, which at subtle levels can be somewhat condescending—seems most promising. Within the sparkle of the patient's eye, or perhaps in the sparkle of the sparkle, something freely captivating lives that requires no specialized compassion.

Subtle beauty as the inexplicable aesthetic mystery of sheer presence draws us into the world of undetermined possibility that, for the depressed or passively vengeful patient, may be construed as too weak to combat his depression—yet, maybe this soteriological world of compliments, gratitude, apology, forgiveness, play, longing, shyness, poignancy, and awe is adequate.

Let us now consider some of these factors in the clinical setting of individual therapy with the becoming-hopeless patient.

TEMPORALITY AND HOPELESSNESS IN THERAPY

The Past Enters Language While, All the Same, Time Passes

When a depressed patient expresses hopelessness, the very expression of the words instantly fades away into silence. The sense of his own words fading away is heard and felt by the (depressed) patient as "more" melancholy. His voice trails off into a sad whisper. New words enunciated by the therapist emerge into the present moment, purporting a response to the now faded-away words of the patient.

The newness (a sense of newness heightened through an even slight encouragement like "Good morning, and how are you today?") of the therapist's words can try the hopeless patient with their ring of currentness in a moment whose unobtainable contemporaneity seems to discount his hopelessness about the past; a contemporaneity that appears as an impossible goal for the patient to reach, that only accentuates his feeling of weakness. (This feeling of weakness? It is his humiliating inability to not slip away with each passing moment, to not "progress.")

For, in temporal reality, the therapist's words or even his response of silence cannot occur in the moments in which the client enunciated his hopelessness. Thus, the alternating and sequential structure of verbal dialoging can also perpetuate for the patient a sense of well-being as unobtainable, as existing only in the "other chair."

The present (read "the therapist"), it seems, cannot enter that which is past; by definition the present (or the therapist) comes when the past is over—for the depressed patient, "hopelessly" over. Therapy always comes when it is "too late."

The revenge against the "It was," as an entire temporal-phenomenological category, has already set in. The patient fee and the meter-ticking hour offer more grounds to resent the spending of time in therapy, becoming over, for what?

> *It* was really bad back then with my family. I can't believe I put up with *it* for so long and I told no one. *It* just seems to have gotten worse since then, even though I had forgotten about *it* all until recently. Now I see how *it* has handicapped my entire adult life. And my parents? They are both dead. There is nothing that anyone can do about *it* now.

The summative *it* that typically enters the therapeutic dialog is the effigy of temporality signifying remembered past injuries, inadequacies, and angers—in short, the now-shared story of the patient's entire hopeless past. This shorthand *it* condenses perhaps individually manageable events into a tumorous accretion of implacable hopelessness. Further, in the analytic approach, mainly more pain is to be found in each unpacked event.

Through the grammatic contraction of the *it* and the temporal *is* into the *it's*, we have a linguistic amalgam of exceedingly dense potency. All the pain of the past, the *it*, has been melded into the open *is*, which is taken over completely by those residual negative sentiments.

The *is* of the sheer now becomes, almost surreptitiously through the grammatic contraction, the subservient bearer of the painful *it*. The opportunities of current time are nearly totally displaced by the *it* of the past. This is no trivial event. For, when *else* is something not of the past going to happen, except in the possibilities provided us in current-time events?

Furthermore, the patient saying "*It's* hopeless" loses more ground than if he had said "*It is* hopeless." We hear the incremental difference somewhat, merely in the extra energy and verbiage (the extra commitment) required in the three-word sentence and in the preservation of the *is* as separate from the *it*. The two-word version with its collapsing contraction, bespeaks of yet more futility and resignation.

The quiet passing of current time liminally recreates *it* over and over again for someone so sensitized and so suffering. The pain of past traumas and the sense of sorrowful memories seem to echo in the tonalities of every contemporary ending.

Every therapy session's ending—from the forty-fifth to the forty-sixth, forty-seventh minute and thirty seconds, forty-eighth minute t,t,t,t,—with its phenomenology of anxious anticipation, the shame of feeling dependent on the therapist, bracings to leave and hopes that, finally, one won't have to go, reaches an unspoken crescendo of, "Let's get *it* over with, I can't bear the last few seconds t,t,t,t—no, please let me stay—how shameful to even ask—you don't care about me, *really*—what a horrible thought, I'm sorry. Yes, yes, I'm going. No, yes ttttt." flip-flopping ("micro-splitting") innumerable times within increasingly briefer and briefer time spans (resembling the emotional sequelae which likely precede many suicidal acts), simple delta-t (time passing) become unbearable.

Thus therapy itself, particularly the closing minutes, recreates and intensifies the very feelings the patient is trying to delete from his life. Yet, within this admixture of tug-and-pull feelings is the crux of therapeutic hopefulness in the form of ambiguous microemotions: the "forward-longing to stay and the correlate sinking shame of even *wanting to*" or "the vengeful, hateful sinking shame of appreciating a present someone for *possibly*—ttt—impossibly seeming to appreciate you, for whom you have nothing but past heartache (and the dirty hourly whore fee) to leave behind."

The therapist might even feel drawn by this oscillating hopefulness/hopelessness as the session ends and be tempted to manipulate the situation by extending the hour to comfort the patient (and himself). Yet, the compassion of stretching out the ending an extra five or ten minutes is rapidly converted into more of *it*—that is, a tortuous burden—"You have given me so much, this is more than I deserve" or, "The longer I stay, the harder it is to leave. I don't want to leave," which enters such tortuous therapeutic circular splits as,

Revenge against Impermanence 127

> How can I contemplate suicide when I want *to stay* here so badly, so badly that I can't bear this pain of leaving and therefore I should just end *it* by killing myself, or devalue you [the good future] so that I won't want to stay [stay in the daunting, fleeting impermanence] so badly, you heartless bastard [of relentless impermanence] who is too good [too mercifully renewing in each new, open moment] for me.

Derailed from the poignant truing powers of the soteriological sentiments, time turns circularly into and against itself. The derailed soteriological powers, now atrophied into the severity of the moral "ought" and set within the well-intended syndromatic determinism of the clinical narrative, begins to drive living time into and against itself: "I *should* just end *it*. . . ."

Masochistic Opportunities: Revenge against the "Too Good To Be True"

Over against this composite *it* (the problems, the fucked-upness, the abuses, the expense, the amorphous stuff), the very *presence* of the therapist makes vivid the fact that a helpful enough person was not there in the past.

Current presence accentuates past absence, reparenting efforts accentuate original ill-parenting, the hope of the present adds insult to the injury of the past. To (mercifully) avoid getting one's hopes up, the blank check of the present moment is self-protectively filled in each moment with the word *void*—that is, hopeless negativity—before *it* might be recognized poignantly as an opportunity that is "more than I could've ever hoped for."

The expression of frustration and revenge finds a foothold in this dashing of hopefulness—a dashing that feels masochistically good to the patient. Through the transference (for those who see life psychoanalytically) of course, such passive-aggressively dashed hopefulness hurts the therapist qua past abuser and is thus a more outward expression of vengeful anger and quite possibly sadistic pleasure: "I'll show them/you how bad they hurt me."

Perhaps this is just a stage toward finding healthier satisfactions, where getting revenge provides a (sadistic) delight that the patient thought he would never get, that itself was held as too good to be true. Here, the catharses of rage invigorate the client's will to live with unleashed passions, for a while.

In any event, these first glimmers of hope are invariably greeted with a "too good to be true," seminegating gratitude. Any moments of closeness between therapist and client, or rises in hopefulness, are squeezed through a "Yes, but how long will *it* last?" temporal masochism providing a first rush of pleasure in the subtle and fleeting feeling of hope and a second, more perverse pleasure that coincides with the temporal passage of the first: the pang of pleasure-disappointment of confirmational knowing as in, "I *knew it* wouldn't last. (See, you can't help!/See how bad it was!/Take that, you louse! What do I care!)"

This aspect of masochistically twisted pleasure in the cynical certainty of getting disappointed once again is less a response to any painful events of the past and more a sorrowful response to the innocent phenomenology of time passage. Moments of progress, too, slip away and the poignant pang of what is no one's fault is escalated from disappointment to hurt to blame to the higher dramatics of the inquisitory accusations: "This *isn't* fair (of God-therapist-parents-Time)!"

Since the possibility of getting better in therapy defines the beginning of its ending, each moment of progress implies that final session. Within the heated passions and based in the ethic of nonfraternizing with expatients, helping the patient get better is like kicking him out of the therapist's life forever. Progress mercilessly aims the patient toward the final forty-ninth minute and thirty, twenty, ten seconds of the inevitable last session, as if he were attending to his own formalized rejection, his own demideath (in the form of termination) foretold.[7]

And in our culture, a legacy of violence, punitivity, and revulsion covers over the mystery called death. Thus parents, in the inescapable grip of their aging, will accusingly plead for a moment of relief from their children, "You will be the death of me yet"—parents who once endured similar sentiments as children from their (deceased) parents.

Indeed, at this time, one hears the counteraccusation of "abandonment" leveled (sometimes by therapists helping to reclaim their patients' inner child) at a parent who has merely died—as if a last bit of sadomasochistic etiologization might be squeezed from the parental grave, "as if the shame of it must outlive him" (Kafka 1970, p. 229).

The Egoic Narratives Take Responsibility for Time Passage

During the therapy sessions the following wonder occurs: "Since we are trying now, maybe someone could have done something about *it* then. I could have had a good childhood!" The sense of "trying" emerges and more and more permeates the air of therapy.

The interpretations, extra sessions, emergency phone calls, and the time and money spent are evidence that people are trying and are thus agents of change. "Trying leads to then-deserved results" is the belief implied in all efforts. Yet, in chronic conditions, again and again results do not persist; as if anything but impermanence *did* persist.

Thus the awakening to impermanence stalls at the most feared of prospects: (1) that, endlessly, nothing lasts; (2) that present, uncertain possibilities abound; (3) that the gratifications of vengefulness will wither into a shameful sense of cowardly collapse (or feared denial of more rage) *before* the warmth of an attempted forgiveness can bestow its enobling blessing; (4) that during that collapse, one feels foolish or weak and then too shy to put down one's vengeful power/raison d'etre and become instead forgiving (and this feared [yet beautiful] shyness is the final crux that can transform many child-custody battles, suicidalities, or near divorces into coparenting alliances, personal redemptions, or reconciliations); (5) thus the urge to give it up and go back to the stinging familiarities of woundedness and vengefulness; (6) that client and therapist are merely two mortals sharing what they can. And so another ironic obstacle accrues.

The sense of agency surreptitiously merges with temporality. The sense of trying—which slips away, reemerges, and slips away again and again—is construed as evidence that therapy seems not to be working and engenders a sense of obligation and responsibility or, more accurately, failing responsibility. Thus, forgiveness and the new world it would foment slip undetectedly away. For, in many therapies, forgiveness is nearly always "premature," if even a held-out possibility.[8]

The *it*—the hopeless feelings associated with time passage, the memories of past traumas and unsuccessful therapeutic efforts—is now laden with the groan of effort. The ontological passage of time now seems to have oarsmen who are very tired, for their rowing is in the endless currents of impermanence.

The patient's depression can make use of this as well. (Note the personification of depression, which often has a life of its own by now in the thoughts of therapist and patient.) He feels that he is responsible: He unwittingly (and impossibly) begins taking the blame for the inevitable phenomenology of time passage, along with the impossibility (via his "inadequacy") of any specifically identified events of progress to not slip away: "*It's* my fault *I'm* still not getting better. I should have known because everything *I* touch goes bad."

Identifying conclusively with this illusory sense of causing the ever-familiar feeling of time passing away can imbue the patient with a convicted sense of terminal hopelessness. One is the (ir)responsibility itself, as and for that which is always and ontologically beyond one's control. He becomes the powerless sinner in the hands of a too-exacting developmental narrative.

Like a Moebius loop, this sense of being (ir)responsible only feeds back into the depression; no matter what side of an issue one begins with, one returns to a trapped circularity. "*I've* been coming for a year now, but what's the use. *I'll* always be the one who was abused. Who will want me once they find out about my past? *It* feels even worse to have a few hours of happiness, *it* feels like a water torture."

This is the completion of hopelessness in time. Just as the causal determinism of ego developmental theory implies that one *is* what happened to him, so does the patient construe himself Moebiuslike as hopelessly responsible, destined to perpetuate the twistedly circular *it* of what was that still, still is. And as narrative cures strain, medications appear appropriate.

For neuro-endocrine secretions are precipitates of the rhythms of impermanence; thus we can even have *bio*-chemical interventions which lighten the burdensomeness of the past. In terms of his own powers and waning confidence in his talk therapist (and the therapist's own confidence), the patient feels doomed, sentenced, destined to remain with "*it*" without end. (And as each medication fails, then what? And if medications, referrals, supervisions, and hospitals were already tried and have failed, *now* what?)

Just as the incarcerated felon "does time" (according to the doctrine of penitentiaries), becomes the time done, and is measured by his time served, so do patient and therapist become the wear of time itself. "When is *this* going to be over? How long can *I* go on like *this*? One more session like that and *I've* had *it*."

The Microlinguistic Subtleties of "To Be" or "Not To Be"

Here we also encounter a world of subtle semantic nuances and innuendoes and affective inflections based in the ambiguity of the word *is* within its infinitive form *to be* and the denouement tones within any past-tense verb. I discussed some of these factors when we explored the density of meaning in the contraction *it's*. Grasping these fleeting innuendos also induces the meditative regard that can become an exodus from the deserts of retrospective time into that of sheer promise: the ontological "is" of living-now, shared impermanence.

The verb *to be* holds ultimate significance in analyzing the language of hopelessness, just as it is at the heart of Hamlet's "To be or not to be. . . . " Its variable meanings, usages, and ambiguity also foster temporal problems for the hopeless patient and can imply the suicidal solution as well. Thus, we must take a closer look into these subtleties and ambiguities.

This word *is* can be used as a copula, a passive name-to-name equater; as a tense signifier, and as indicating a sheer condition and other subtleties of being, proving or verifying, and doing. *Is* grants credibility and fosters certainty merely through its mundane simplicity, that is, through its *missed complexity*. When inflected with innuendos, the word can be made to taunt us with the incomparable expanse of its reign.

In the sentence "The past (trauma) is what is over," the first *is* connects what is over with the name *past*. It is as neutral as an equals sign as in "The past = what is over." The past "does" nothing via this first *is*. Things and events, in a positivistic sense, "simply are" or "were" as named. To the hopeless patient, this *is* feels utterly impotent.

The first *is* could also be construed as an infinitive condition of sustained being in which there are particular things, like "the book is, God is." In this sense, there is a phenomenon called "the past," and it just heretofore is.

More specifically, we could say that the past exists as a sustained temporal condition that holds all the "whats" that are "over"; thus, the "past is" is a kind of eternal dustbin. We hear a subtle ring of obdurate fatalism when the is-ness of past events is depicted as a standing condition.

As a sustained condition, all past events—all that was—*still* exist as the past. The hopeless patient finds this "is" to be the beginning of a possible sentence of life imprisonment. For the reign of *is* goes on and on and on. Does *what was* never end? The *was* leaks into Being itself, not so much as a projection, but as the continuity of the incomparable range of *is* which now sways the ever more deterministic narrative. We become sinners in the hands of an angry god, or syndromes in the skein of a deterministic etiology.

Skew *is* and all else torques. The being of the world, the three-dimensional *is*, can then seem to stare back at the depressed patient with an accusing countenance and "psychotic" features emerge such as hallucination, paranoia, or nightmares. Fueled by sadomasochistic affect (relentless temporal passage overtorqued into a dominating severity and its strange hormonal brews), the innuendoes of *is* offer psycholinguistic slippage in which these apparitions breed: Hell becomes its name.

The second *is* in the sentence "The past is what is over" functions as a verb to the specifier-subject *what* and its predicate *over* and gives it a tense in the present. What is over, or what was, *is* now and forever forward over, not later. The matter is certain, proven, conclusively, truly over. Or at least it *sounds* this way, when you say the sentence and the *is* this way. Yet, ironically, the ring of this certainty goes on forever carrying with it, yes, that's right: the past.

But, strictly, the "what" is the only thing that, in a subject sense, is "over," for the "what" refers to the events that pass, which constitute, inactively and through sheer temporality, (merely) something over that we call "the past." From this narrative past, there is another way out of suicidality:

My abuse made me so ashamed I thought I must kill myself to get out of this world. I'd kill my abuser, but things would only get worse. Then it all came together: these were all events that were passing and lived in the worded accounts of those events and its ramifications. *My life*, the one I thought about taking, however, became incredibly vivid in its separateness from that whole tangle and what it all supposedly meant. Sobbing, I felt extricated from the tangle and felt the sad tragedy, like in Truffault's *The 400 Blows* of innocent errors compiling onto one another. Suicide or homocide seemed only possible when lost to that innocence. The story and events of the past no longer ruled my life, they were just tragic conditions that could beget more tragedies, perhaps forever. Even my abuser was merely someone enacting the stories she was entangled in.

This pervasive was-is-will-be skew, when grasped as such, provides a soteriological way out that mystics and no few capitally condemned or fatally ill persons find. Perhaps all find it in the silent moments of dying, lending a final sense of pardon and tragic contradiction to the death that is by one's own hand.

Yet, within the narrative world deprived of such soteriological grace, there is one more deeper turn toward hell possible: The severe conceptual lord of all determinisms can enter the was-is-will-be: embodied fatalism: "I was destined to suffer, I have bad blood, it's genetic." Racisms, genocides, damnation, and various genetic theories of psychiatric disease or sociopathic behavior can also be found here. Yet, who knows *that* much?

The Circularities of Vengefulness

In a world where truth, justice, success, and happiness are hard to come by, suffering can become a quasi-morally invigorating raison d'etre: The harrowing past becomes the unjust truth to be told and retold, lived and relived. A search for justice, always so easily entangled in vengeance and punitivity, can foment. Thus, there are the convoluted phenomena of law enforcers becoming abusers; or Pogo's "we" becoming "them": the crazed mob; or the abused becoming perpetrators themselves or falling into real or imagined further victimizations, or, at best, entering a martyred, group identity of continuous "survivorhood." Like the cycles of war, these perpetuations ring with a strangely circular temporal disorder that Nietzsche called "the revulsion against 'It was.'"[9]

The telling and retelling of the truth of his past abuses to his therapist can be like the patient's day in court. Catharsis takes on more vindicative sentiments in this search for justice. The sadomasochistic enjoyment of the effect one's anguished story might have on compassionate others is the patient's emotional escalation and intensified involvement with what was previously only being caused by him. The patient seems to be "really getting into his feelings," yet, as if to say, "Let my disabling, intractable depression remind you of how shamefully you treated me and be proof commensurate to your inhumanity. Let the costs of treatment, emotional, financial and durational, weigh on you and the worse, the better!"

In this mode of wrathful bitterness, nothing simply "is," but is-with-a-vengeance. "Is" becomes an auguring "izzzzz." One patient hates the plant in my office because it grows. It reminds him of the stolen life he both vengefully hates and wants. He is envious that I water the plant and competes to become drier than it. The plant izzzzzz and he fights back by picking the leaves off, by insisting that I starve it by closing the shades, as he starves his body by barely eating.

Vengeance Exhausts, Yet Time Persists so
"The Last Thing To Do" Comes to Mind

Finally (for some few), there is only one thing left to talk about that matches the feeling of the closure of time and the convincing certainty of one's narrative. Having failed as a vengeful plaintiff in securing release through catharses and his therapist's empathic interventions, he becomes the sullen condemned, sentencing judge, and euthanasiac executioner: Suicidal language (or perhaps hypochondriacal or annihilation fears) enters the dialogue. "It will be *better* if I kill myself. *It* will be over then." Beneath utter powerlessness, a murky, feigned omnipotence begins to swell.

The pills, razors, guns, and hoses become necessary, fetishistic properties as these tools of mortal consequence grotesquely distort the subtle eroticism of impermanence with exaggerated potencies. In a protracted period of suicidality/self-mutilation, much of this dark fascination can emerge.

But when the patient tells the therapist instead of secretly suiciding, he also creates an audience who is listening to these words. Perhaps the patient is trying to safeguard himself by alerting the therapist to prevent his suicide. That is a practical interpretation of this communication. As far as I have seen, the less it seems to matter to the patient whether the therapist is listening or not, the more dangerously morbid the suicidal disclosure. He is also expressing subtle hopefulness about some fantasied future, but the hopefulness is so distant that it belongs on the "other side," that is, death.

The therapist might try to extract the subtle essence of hopefulness from the patient's suicidal talking, yet doing so without disturbing the suicidal image, for that is what is currently (albeit perversely) holding the hopefulness. The no-harm contract is one strategy. The involuntary commitment is another. In addition, at small delta-t, various other less formalistic interventions become visible.

Innuendoes of future hope and empowerment lay nearly invisible in the grey dusk of the patient's thoughts and images. Pills, for example, might be related ambiguously to seeds; a certain characteristic shared look as reflecting wistfully the now nearly dashed, once hopeful mood of certain moments from various past sessions; a razor as a face too sad to cry; death as one's loyal, dark comfort.

Suicidal utterances, often confessional in tone, are thus often equivalent to giving one's inmost-held fear and last hope to another. As the inmost of intimacies, suicidal disclosures can be received with a somber appreciation. THERAPIST: "I feel that you are entrusting me with the most sorrowful and private of your thoughts and fears."

Yet, it is not only what is said but the perceptive regard of tracking and responding to various glimmering emotions and waverings of utterance, a sort of mercurial "micromirroring," wherein various fluctuating ambiguities and a kind of elusive "mystery" seem to live.

Interventions of further subtlety—the way the therapist opens the door to his office as the prelude to "beginning," the way the payment check is reached for and received at the end of the hour—which are attuned to the subtlety of impermanence can be protective adjuncts to the no-harm contract and the extra sessions. For suicidality, as an ultimacy and as a morbid hopefulness, ironically also quickens the sense of impermanence that has for so long been lost in retrospective time. It is as if these are the last precious moments, a preciousness that can invalidate suicidality by rising out of the narrative trance.

For, within such subtleties of gesture or phrasings lives a shifting nuance of indeterminacy that, sensed one way, allures with the morbid denouement of a waning hopelessness. Yet sensed another way, allures with the *maybe* of a suggestive hopefulness. And so allured, so we become, slip away, and become, again and again.

THE MICROEMOTIONAL WORLD WITHIN HOPELESSNESS

As the therapist observes her client at small delta-t levels, mercurial impermanence becomes more palpable aesthetically, and its ontological hermeneutic emerges as more fundamental than any: developmental-stages templates; genetic-biochemical equivalencies; psychoanalytic, Jungian, or recovery semiotics; object-relations structural blueprints; family history exegeticals; past emotional wound-trauma diarials; or *DSM* grand lexicons.

Impermanence is more fundamental because it helps explain all other cartographies and hermeneutics of human happenings. Indeed, silently it carries them all forth and silently it withers the moments in which they are invoked and never the reverse.

In the nuanced transience of the more Proustian details—an off-guard, mutually caught look of surprise, the clean scent of rain-washed streets outside, the passing of the carefully shielded struck match that lights the other's cigarette, the shade of the other's sweater at noon—the poignant innuendoes of impermanence can displace the hermeneutics of family history, transference reenactments, or developmental-stage incompletions. Why? because, in those moments they are *more alive*.

Furthermore, such vivid but subtle immediacies can prove more germane to therapeutic ends than astute musings based in the latter hermeneutics: the moment as an end in itself, the individuals as ends in themselves to one another in a moment that, like the look, the scent, the glowing match flame and shadow, passes.

Then retrospectively, from such poignant innocences, perhaps even the fragile yet everlasting hope *within* the dashed hope *beneath* every abusing parent's (spouse's, one's own) new failure to refrain (or failure to act) will be remembered and granted. The lips tremble apologetically, however lifeless, and the redemption of what could have been begins to raise its downcast gaze.

Perhaps the innocence of it all will be known and granted as "what happened" succumbs to what (if the truth be told) all parties most long to have happened. As temporal conclusivity, cognitive certainty, and memory-as-the-unforgiven succumb to soteriological time: Life's too short; There, but for the grace of God, go I; I now confess. For the most-hoped-for lives in the "withins" and the "beneaths": *this* is the inmost buried Secret.

In those moments, the intolerable mercy of the human spirit transcends its own self-justifications or "developmental derailments." Here is birth and rebirth anew. The past as a standing, frozen condition thaws and comes alive. The masks of history are put down and the players step forth, redeemed outside all narratives and their nightmarish plays.[10]

Certainly vengeance, as the revulsion against the "It was," collapses during those moments when, via some subtle phenomenon visible at small delta-t, evanescent presence is granted. (Listen, hear how vengeance drives the false plot of every unhappy history, for, beyond the reach of gods, it drives a wedge this way then that way into time itself.)

The past, as a carried-forth set of hopes dashed (developmental wounds), becomes momentarily obsolete as an otherwise chronic way of securing explanations (units of temporary certainty) for one's most current experience. Without a basis, the revulsion withers and the "unperformed condition"—grace—of forgiveness, reigns for a while. Soteriological time unfurls.

The posttraumatics remit, thus chronicity erodes. Traits associated with vengefulness—rage, primitive splitting, passive aggression, obsessiveness, entitlement, self-pity, grandiosity, and inferiority—relent, and thus the concretizing concept of "personality disorder" is temporarily obsolete as a way to catalogue the client's condition. Indeed, on the world scale such occasional witherings of vengeance during some natural disaster redirect the otherwise dour course of geopolitical history toward shared humanitarian involvement, at least for that while.

As the gratifications of shared presence displace the (settled-for-in-bad-faith) sadomasochistic gratifications of vengefulness, a new problem becomes palpable: the "eroticism," that is, the *enigmatic allure*, of shared impermanence (not sex desire, as we have been taught to name it.) The undulating senses of urgency, suspense, and calm; expectant indeterminacy and the circadian rhythms of longing and its fatigue; the arising of hopes that permeate the limbs as a reaching to hold onto something or someone stationary; the many poignant separations and reunions; the images of dwelling with one another "forever."

For, what is any eroticism except that which allures us mysteriously by seeming to both slip away from us while also beckoning us anew: the eroticism of impermanence, the impetus for all other more derivative eroticisms. A violent borderline patient slowly traces with her index finger the dark surgings and vanishings in the veins of my left hand and, inexplicably, after years of doing so, slashes her wrists no more.

The past-referencing transferential/countertransferential hermeneutic, with its Oedipal-seductive innuendo, has always been excessively backward and overdetermined: the worst of the *scientia sexualis*. Isn't "transference" merely distancing jargon for "carried-forth nuances of hope"? Such was the transference of Breuer's first patient with her pseudopregnancy—her "hope of a hope" to stave off impermanence by conceiving and bearing new hope—and such has been the case between every patient and therapist, ever since.

Perhaps what Heidegger called "presencing presence," or two "mortals" sharing some of their lives together aware of being and time simultaneously, is the crux. To think being *and* time, that was his "most difficult challenge."

Shy, proud, grateful, shamefully petty, or embarrassed blushes; glancings directly at and then—with delight, spite, or shyness—quickly away; shared uncertainty and unknowing-of-the-interpretation-for, shared innocence, breached aloneness. Shared not as "insights" or interpretations but existentially, as mortal truths common to both: a sharing of The Fear, The Hope, The Uncertainty, The Sorrow, The Joy, The Wonder, in these passing moments.

For no word is really one's own, but is part of the moment's play in language games no longer so severe as logic or "developmental determinants from the past" decree. Thus Wittgenstein used a semideterminant "playing" as the grand metaphor for all language-communication games:

> We can easily imagine people amusing themselves in a field by playing with a ball so as to start various existing games, but playing many without finishing them and in between throwing the ball aimlessly into the air. (Wittgenstein 1968 [1945], p. 39)

And echoing Nietzsche a half century earlier, referring to the play of impermanence itself:

> Verily, Zarathustra had a goal; he threw his ball: now you, my friends, are the heirs of my goal; to you I throw my golden ball. More than anything, I like to see you, my friends, throwing the golden ball. And so I still linger a little on the earth: forgive me that. (Nietzsche 1970 [1883], p. 186)

Such is the intimate *ars erotica* that replaces the Freudian scientia sexualis in the clinical dialogue and relationship. Its goal? An awakening to "what calls most for thinking": a flickering glimpse of the soul, the *jiva*, anatta, I-Thou, suchness—the heart of it all—and what that provokes: the shy awe of shared impermanence, the beginning of the eternal sense. Here is the Dionysian revel, the perpetual dance of Shiva, the endless return tttttt.

Shyness Is the Dawning of the Impermanent Self

In this phenomenology of impermanence, that most innocent of feelings, shyness—and its pink nuance of embarrassment; azures of an alluring coyness; silvers of overdelight; rosy, long-hoped-for acceptance; frothy gleams of pride; brazen yet trepid curiosity; and, once purged of popular pejorations, the dark folds of shame—is the wavering eminence of the now concealing, now revealing soul and serves as emotional gatekeeper for all greater being-in-the-world.[11]

Look carefully. All self-assertive processes of individuation are consecrated by a shyness. Indeed, without this revealing-concealing penumbra (ambiguously mislabeled as "vulnerability" or the "inner child"), our innocence withers and individuation leaves character for caricatures of an over-bold strength.

The therapist must be masterful in shyness, admiring it in herself and others, thus she is a midwife to the soul's further embodiment, what

Reich saw as "orgone," the blue-tinged glow of life itself. And the fleeting emotional sequelae within shyness? They are the seeds of "the ideal" and the "most hoped for" in each new moment, yet to be brought further into sustained, shared expression. Yet to be made, haikulike, into a narrative history *of* impermanence.

Predictably and with inhibiting clinical consequences, Freud imagined blushing to be a mild erection of the head. But perhaps blushing and all other manner of interpersonal disquietings quicken the self-sense in its impermanence, not as a triggering of an instinctive drive or a displaced libido, nor signifying a need to shore up one's structural boundaries, but as soteriological epiphanies: "Please, forgive me my wonderment at the alluring mystery that you and I are, in our inexplicable coming forth and passing."

And the "good little boy" in *Beyond the Pleasure Principle* is not learning to renounce instinctive and immediate gratifications when he plays his "throwing away" game.

> This good little boy had an occasional disturbing habit of taking small objects he got hold of and throwing them away from him into a corner, under the bed, and so on, so that hunting for his toys and picking them up was often quite a business. As he did this, he gave vent to a loud, long drawn out "o-o-o-o-," accompanied by an expression of interest and satisfaction. His mother and the writer of the present account were agreed in thinking that this was not mere interjection but represented the German word for "gone." I eventually realized it was a game and that the only use he made of any of his toys was to play "gone" with them. One day I made an observation which confirmed my view. The child had a wooden reel with a piece of string tied round it. It never occurred to him to pull it along the floor behind him, for instance, and play at its being a carriage. What he did was to hold the reel by the string and very skillfully throw it over the edge of his curtained cot, so that it disappeared into it, at the same time uttering his expressive "o-o-o-o-." He then pulled the reel out of the cot again by its string and hailed its reappearance with a joyful da ["there"]. This, then, was the complete game—disappearance and return. . . . It was related to the child's great cultural achievement—the instinctual [*sic*] renunciation (i.e., the renunciation of instinctual satisfaction) which he had made in allowing his mother to go away without protesting. (Freud, *SE* 18, pp. 14–15; quoted in Richardson 1988, p. 105)

He is in the throes of the cycles of shyness, where toys are animistic playmates that peek as he peeks and hide as he hides, a game that goes on, essentially unmodified, all the rest of our lives. Thus, the numberless tonalities of shyness and ecstatic "looking" that infants, in their innocence, manifest.

In this game and the hypothesized infantile desire [*sic*] it provokes,

Lacan conjectured "the child is born into language" (1977, p. 103, quoted in Richardson 1988, p. 105). Verbal and ineffable plays (*jouissance*) with shyness constitute the glimmering waves by which we engage with the alluring mystery/impermanence again and again, in these passing moments.

But who will believe that the subtleties of impermanence can reign for very long?

CHAPTER 3

Maturation of the Ensouled Body: Kundalini Yoga and the Far Reaches of Human Development

INTRODUCTION

Thus far our soul psychotherapy has drawn from universal spiritual principles of gratitude, forgiveness, poignant impermanence, and the like, while remaining largely within the precincts of conventional developmental theory. In this chapter I broaden our scope more toward the body by delving into the farther reaches of human development as is becoming known in the West under the heading of kundalini ("coiled Creatress," "human ultimacy in potentia" emanating from the spine's sacral base) yoga.

What we will find is a well-mapped developmental continuum beginning with the most ordinary of the soteriological sentiments and then accelerating into degrees of awe and gratitude which mature the ensouled body to an untold depth. And, it will be in the context of this unaccounted-for bodily depth that the entire range of human functioning—normal, psychotic, or saintly—can be seen as an ongoing spiritual development.

We will be considering developmental phenomena at the nexus of soma and soul associated with kundalini "awakening" largely unknown to conventional psychology or Western religions (yet echoing there too) and little discussed, except in the most esoteric interpretations of yogic praxis and texts. We look to this yoga because its energetics have nourished human hopefulness for at least five thousand years, since the hoary origins of shamanism. And, as we shall see, kundalini yoga sheds a most interesting light on our topics of temporality, the constraints of narrative truth, and spiritually informed psychotherapy and psychopathology, so-called spiritual emergence.

That thousands of bodily postures, expressive movements and utterances, characterological cultivations, breathing patterns, and degrees of concentration could constitute a "spirituality" clearly leaves kundalini yoga and its cognates (e.g., taoist yoga and sacred dance) unique among spiritual traditions. Yes, various traditions speak of the body as the temple of the soul and that the "kingdom is within." But yoga goes on to assert *how* the body's very movements, sensations, and breath *can become* deeper and deeper prayers within this temple. As prayer, as hungers to know the eternal, the ensouled body stretches in numerous ways and comes to embody perhaps the greatest of all human hopes.

Thus, kundalini yoga, as do the origins of Christianity, reminds us that truth is an incarnation, a logos become flesh, and not a text. It is just that in kundalini yoga (particularly in the subdivision of *hatha yoga*), more attention has been devoted to the nerve, gland, and cellular level of such physical-spiritual aphorisms. According to this yoga, the body bows itself into greater maturation in eighty-four thousand movements, none of which should be considered mere stretching exercises.

The vastness of our subject, however, must not obscure how nearby—as close as certain inmost sensations—the beginning of the path of yoga is. Certainly, whenever great admiration, reverence, contrition, forgiveness, or the poignancy of discerned impermanence (the yamas and niyamas, the yogic correlates to the soteriological sentiments) course through us, some measure of this soul-embodying maturation quickens, giving our character spiritual-physical "backbone," giving our awareness a greater feel *for* things.

But how much further this quickening fructifies throughout the body via the neuroendocrinal maturations of bodily poses and "delight gestures" (*asanas* and *mudras*), the vital *spiritus* spark (breath cultivations of *pranayama*), and the mind (maturations of attentiveness of *pratyahara, dharana, dhyana,* and *samadhi* stages of meditation) is the unique concern of this yoga. And this further developmental expanse proves to be both consistent with and radically transformative of conventional psychological theories.

For, via adult developmental processes described in this yoga and almost grasped, yet with obvious condescension, in Freud's notion of "sublimation," spiritually matured identities can become as embodied, challenging, and empowering as teenaged puberty is for the twelve to eighteen year old. Thus, I am proposing that kundalini yoga (and its cross-tradition similars), traces a series of endogenous, overlapping (for growth does not emerge in discrete stages, thus many a rub), developmental maturations that each deserve to be termed an "awakening," the shivering spinal quickening merely being the first to enter Western parlance. Indeed, in their practical and metaphoric associations with sexual transformations via the range of *tantric* ("spirit-matter weaving" that minces differences and thus deals with many a rub), bhakti ("ecstatic devotion," whose soteriological warmth loves one through the rubs), and other psychophysical manifestations, I am willing to go substantially further in bringing these profundities into more words.

Given the radical *degree* of change in identity sense, and newly emergent body/mind arousals and internal secretions consequent to kundalini awakening, we must consider whether we are encountering what deserves to be termed not merely awakenings, but full-fledged *puberties*, unaccounted-for *postgenital* puberties. For such are the constituent transformations of the body and psyche that define the maturations of a puberty—*any* puberty—and far exceeding what the less comprehensive term *awakening* entails.

And as we shall see, viewing yogic awakenings as puberties helps resolve various dilemmas in transpersonal developmental theory, particularly regarding the relationships between sexuality and spirituality, and between the ego (what Freud explicitly called the "genital primacy" ego) and the Self (or Buddhist no-self or soteriological soul). For, in the long and challenging "prepubescence" that follows genital puberty, and particularly in midlife—with its wonderments about a true identity and any purpose to life beyond personal survival, wealth, and sexual pleasure—spirituality deepens or, for some, is born for the first time. Thus, the concerns of the adolescent of sex, career, affiliation, and identity are often replicated at another level of sophistication, from midlife on.

Simply stated, my perspective is that all manner of religions, spiritualities, shamanisms, and mystical paths constitute the splendorous phenomenology of unnamed-as-such postgenital puberties and the long, daunting arc of their prepubescences. The view of spirituality as the emergence of historical saints or saviors and their teachings must be put into this bodily developmental context, if we are to get beneath the diversity of sectarian "faiths" to some ontologically common transpersonal and body-inclusive ground.

The psychoanalytic reduction of spirituality to the ambiguous product of sublimation must certainly be questioned if spirituality is to be seen as rooted naturally in the body. The Jungian view of a purely psychically transformative alchemy underappreciates the role of the body and must also be referred to deeper endogenous roots if spirituality is to escape the terminology of "processes" and "techniques." Even the yogic and meditative "practices" must be rescued from such superficial enframements. Spirituality is a natural, body-positive aspect of human development, not a derivative of sexuality, a set of techniques, practices, or doctrinal beliefs. However radical the bodily phenomena of kundalini may seem at first, they provide us with a way to substantiate such a claim. And, although transpersonalist Michael Washburn concludes in *Transpersonal Psychology in Psychoanalytic Perspective* that:

> *No one knows* [my emphasis] for sure why the first half of this journey [egoic maturity] is completed by almost everyone and the second half [ego transcendence and spiritual-power embodiment] by only a few.... The path of transcendence may be a path that is still "under construction." It may, that is, represent the future of the species, a future into which only a minority of individuals have ventured. (Washburn 1994, p. 318)

a quick sampling of those commonly believed to have walked the "second half" of this path including: Buddha, Christ, Socrates, Eckhart, John of the Cross, Theresa of Avila, Hildegarde Bingham, Rumi, Lao Tzu, Mirabai, Patanjali, Ramana Maharsi, Ramakrishna, Irina Tweedie, Dalai Lama, Shri Aurobindo, and The Mother, reveals one commonality: they have each achieved a transformed sexuality, a "postgenital puberty," as I term it.

But try to move full maturity much beyond the ground of the fifth and final psychoanalytic stage of genital puberty, as many transpersonalists do, and psychoanalysis (and the vast majority of all people) warns we walk onto thin air. Extend the physical ground synthetically, and the chemical mysticisms of McKenna, Leary, and the shamanic and yogic alchemists take root, perhaps even Prozac. Make of them what you will. Consider yoga (or, for example, tai chi) as merely healthy exercises lacking in developmental import, and much is lost. If seen as credibly endogenous, however, the vast range of kundalini yoga bodily phenomena reveals the gradually steepening physical *ground* of the more spiritual stages of development, thus finishing the "construction" of Washburn's path and adding flesh to the more meditative spiritualities and archetypal psychologies that have underwritten the transpersonalist's advances thus far.[1]

Furthermore, if these slow-developing yogic maturations are *innate*, yet unaccounted for, the consequences could radiate throughout our current model of the developmental span and its entire hermeneutic economy, and not just pertain to some eccentric transpersonal level. As I have stated, when a correction or an addition is made to the psychological vocabulary, a global correction of imports must be considered.

And it is the context of the slow, developmental press of these postgenital puberties, far short of the rare "full awakenings," that helps us to see various psychological dilemmas and pathologies as difficult spiritual epiphanies of the magnitude that assail the teenager's entrance into genital puberty. For the *import* of a lifelong developmentalism intensifies radically and with unsuspected degrees of hopefulness with the addition of a "sixth through fourteenth" stage of kundalini psychosexual maturation. Imagine the auspicious feeling of knowing that at ages forty-five, fifty-five, and seventy you could undergo a burst of maturational transformations on par with adolescence (Oh no!), but with the benefit of previous wisdom and experience, yet still requiring a mapping of the changes entailed (Um, okay). In such a long-extending developmentalism, the preoccupations of conventional psychotherapeutics on "the past" appear even more quaint and truncated.

Other consequent and pervasive changes in cognition—what epistemic knowing is even *for* and its convergence with feeling and the flesh—are more relevant to the limitations of narrative and language as a semiotic resource, as already raised by postmodernism, meditators, and mystics of all times. For, as we shall see, during the kundalini maturations, the articulating tongue and larynx also undergo a dramatic puberty, known as khecari mudra ("eternal-space dancer delight gesture").

Likewise, the narrator-ego self outgrows his genital primacy, desire-based, subject-object immaturities during the puberties of the mind (known as *unmani mudra*: "no-mind mind delight gesture") popularly called the "stages of meditation." At those points, a new identity forces itself upon the meditator who now states he "is and is not" there. Consider such language contortions as analogous to the teenager who also claims he is and is not the same kid you remember him to be, and who also claims along with his teenaged contemporaries to be very much "in the now," and with younger children idolizing him longingly. Puberties change us-as-narrators so much that they make us talk funny. Or, we could say that *language* is itself a developmental phenomenon, a changeable artifact reflective of each point in our spiritual maturation, not merely *a way* of recording and conveying consentual meanings. When people start talking strangely like this: "You one with-it dude" or "You no-self Self," suspect a kind of puberty.

And, in some mysterious way, speaking differently (and moving ["gimme five"] differently) furthers the maturational process itself. During the long preadolescence before khecari mudra, the pure, emotive sonics of certain utterances serve as developmental "laborings" of the "birthing" of these puberties. Known as anahata-nada, "endogenously arising utterance" (and heard in numerous world religions as "speaking in tongues," the Hebraic nigune, the Islamic "call to prayer") they further flesh out the emotional, cognitive, and linguistic changes of these postgenital puberties.

Such spiritual-emotional utterances exceed the grasp of conventional "cathartic" release of repressed past affects, for these are the forward-yearning birth pangs of more fully entering the Now. The living Flesh endogenously become Spoken Words: the NOW of a certain moment held in the instantaneous *florish* of a zen calligraphy; God as the shouts of children echoing down Joycean cobbled streets.

Entering Now is forever forward. It is more of an awakening to an endless beginning than to a conclusive arrival. And, as it is said, "pride [of attainment and the first of the "sins"] cometh before the fall." During puberties, everything one believes or was told by authority becomes questionable and better answers or ways of putting things are sought. Thus, any puberty also quickens in us a heightened sense of responsibility, to the extreme point of the saint, *bodhisattva*, or savior whose maturation causes her to feel responsible for the universal family; as Buber put it, to the "dreadful point" of loving everyone, dreadful because of the endless, unrestrictedness of this matured love so merged into eternal time. Thus, from the prepubescent side, each *new* puberty also foments a fear of not being equal to the very sense of responsibility that is just now emerging in us, or perhaps foments a brash overestimation of oneself, or torturous oscillations from one extreme to the other.

And, perhaps, as Gopi Krishna, author of numerous popular books on this subject maintains, kundalini, as the puberty of the soul identity, is on an evolutionary temporal scale, a scale that, as Aurobindo, Nietzsche, Teilhard, Neumann, Gebser, Wilber, and others described, is far more of a spiritual nature than mere Darwinian adaptive evolutionism (and its widespread metanarratives and the eery eugenic technologies they still spawn) would permit. Yet, even within Darwinism, sociobiologist Donald Symons conjectured the following regarding the origins of how genital puberty sexuality was first decoupled from fertility cycles for early homo sapiens:

> If one views the matter in terms of ultimate causation, and assumes that permanent group-living is adaptive for some reason, then, all other things being equal, selection [Darwinian natural selection] can be expected to favor the most economical of the available mechanisms that results in permanent sociality. One possible mechanism is for a formerly episodic reward to become permanent, but in terms of time, energy, and risk this seems to be a very expensive solution if the reward is sexual activity. It is [would have been, but still *is?*] much more economical [from a biological perspective] to alter the reward mechanism of the brain itself, so that the sight, sound, or smell of familiar conspecifics [members of the same species] come to be experienced as pleasurable. (Symons 1979, p. 102)

For, as we shall see, certain potentials of the hypothalamus, the Symonsian "reward mechanism of the brain," are the loci of several yogic puberties, while many tantric and communal practicings of the "experienced pleasurable" perceptions of one another are both catalysts and consequences of such awakenings. Poignancy lives moment to moment, even on the epochal scale.

Perhaps even kundalini yoga itself is wrested from its own indigenous tangle of competing views which have come to depicting it too as a system of mere techniques, more than as awesome phenomena of Nature (or "Supernature," for those who prefer superlative, but confusing differentiations) that they are. For, in spiritually preoccupied India (and various other mysticisms), the descent further into the body has held mixed interest, with the recent exception of Shri Aurobindo and the Mother's image of both descending and ascending developmental forces, and the nondualistic yogis whose esoteric interpretations I now approach.

RECOVERING THE DIONYSIAN-ENDOGENOUS YOGA

In order to view yoga and meditation as just as endogenous to our development (and as awesome) as gestation once was, as taking one's first postumbilical breath, as adolescent puberty, we must deconstruct the overformalized pedagogical edifices that have grown around it. Both indigenously over the ages, and in their translation and importation into the West, the "innately arising" (*sahaja*), panentheistic, dionysian origins of *yoga* and meditation have been shaped and overshaped into apollonian pedagogical constructs, cosmeticized or leveled for mass appeal, sterilized for upper-class gentilities, or otherwise tamed and overtamed to avoid real or imagined dangers.[2]

The soteriological sentiments (yamas and niyamas) and their mercies became mere rules of the rigid-mandatory, or lip-service varieties. The grace of sequence and consequence of karma was mechanicalized into an arch law, in contrast to the dionysian teachings that the soteriological power is independent of "karmic laws." The mysterious flow of lineage stiffened into the rigidities of caste, also in contrast to the dionysian rejection of caste prejudice and the "crazy wisdoms" that ridicule it.[3]

The reverentially ecstatic "Dance of Siva, Lord of Yogis," became stylized in public rituals, "classical" music and dance, and in the yogic asanas themselves, or withered in the severe asceticisms of the fakir. By the second century A.D., Patanjali's dualistic, "classical" *Yoga-Sutra* had formalized an overseparation between Nature (*prakriti*) and Ultimate Subjectivity (*purusha*), thus "rejecting the idea that the world is an aspect of the Divine" (Feuerstein 1989, p. 412).

Thus the shamanic or dionysian yoga and its bond with mystical phenomenology maintained in the living moment through oral transmission in the hoary past (and still, with all manner of attendant difficulties), arose and then fell into evermore secularized, scriptural fundamentalisms. The sequence of its "fall" *from* dionysian-soteriological t,t,t,t, time and in-the-moment narrative utterances into the apollonian mundane time and its "formalized narratives and "histories of events" is as follows:

1. the spirit-in-time revealed as a superlative, private bodily experience (ecstasy or enstasy),
2. emergent publicly as presemantic ecstatic-catalytic utterances and dancing-swaying movements, then
3. languaged orally as sheer *descriptions* of *the experience*, then
4. memorized and scriptured into an orthodox text or externalized liturgical commemoration (yoga and meditation as teachings; the movements classicalized as ritual forms),
5. its lessons fableized for charm (the ancient myths), then
6. in search of a genteel purity, its sparkling and sensual phenomenology put into disembodied descriptions of "heaven realms" or sheer "higher states of consciousnesses," and
7. as texts and practices exported into the West, formulized for mass pedagogical ease (the contemporary yoga books and aerobicslike classes, stress-reduction courses, and other holistic applications or new-age appropriations),
8. made abstract or "symbolic" of something else, or "primitivized" by scholars for learned discouse (the transpersonalist's synthesizing schemas),[4] and, at all junctures,
9. suppressed or championed by religio-political forces; eroded by sectarian rivalries and scandals; desiccated as the legalistic, purely academic word, or scorned as mere superstition.

Thus the yogic textual metaphors that paint accurate pictures of various phases of the inner experience of certain neuroendocrinal maturations—of, for example, "fluids raining down from the heavens" and "sacrifices made into further sacrifices," referring to the transmutation of subtle melatoninlike pineal secretions as they *appear* (to the *rishika*, "the one who *sees* the described referent *actually happening*") with the eyes closed in ecstatic witness to their flickering precipitations as cast ever higher ["sacrificed and further sacrificed"] into the ever-spiraling-higher center of the cathedral-domed cranium's "*Krishna*-dark space"—were transposed to the externalized space of the firmament and, ironically, buried within the homologous *brahmanic* sacrificial rituals (or myths) which were meant to be subservient pointers to the *inner hormonal developmental experiences*. The "higher and higher heavens" became abstractions, instead of aesthetic descriptions of how *it* floatingly actually feels when the cerebral puberty unfolds meditative glimpses of the infinity of love-space-time.[5] For, what are all pubescent hormones but the "sacrificial" materializations of the infinite? And what are these sacrifices, except givings-to-physical-humans of the sensual path to their own highest joys and matured clarities?

Via further translations into the modern pragmatic-scientific vernacular, instead of an inner awe of wonder and delight, we now speak of "spiritual *practices*," "visualization *techniques*," yogic "states of consciousness" and quasi-Newtonian "spiritual *energies*." Instead of a well-mapped but dynamic, esoteric phenomenology of marvelous fluttering, whorling, meditative experiences of cerebral-hormonal flowing juices (*soma*) and brilliant sunlight (*savitri*, a Vedic term for kundalini illuminating the mind and for which Elizarenkova counts more than fifteen verbs denoting its brilliance in the *Rig Veda*) we have the dry brahmanic (Indian or Western) abstractions or translations depicting only exoteric ritual libations, transrational evolutionary schemas, tantric visualization practices, and theonyms for sun worship.[6] The Burning Bush, whether Western or Eastern, as aptly describing the overwhelming, experienced glow of kundalini in the cerebrum, is lost in its own metaphor. But sometimes not, as Allama Prabhu, the tenth-century dionysian bhakti yogi sang:

Looking for your light	[of hope],
I went out	[into meditation]:
it was like a sudden dawn	[of eternal ttt]
of a million million suns,	
a ganglion of lightnings	[the cerebral puberty]
for my wonder	[soteriological awe].
O Lord of Caves	[hearted flesh bodies],
if you are light,	
there can be no metaphor	[narrative equivalent].
(Ramanujan, 1973 p. 168)	

And why kundalini is called serpentine should not rest upon its coiled shape or as a symbol of the infinite, but to convey the *charm* of its mercurial irridescence when it is actually seen or felt: the inexplicable glimmer of human developmental detail, down to each glittering bone cell or mitochrondrial fibril thrill as the incessant t,t,t, resurgence of creation t,t,t. To hear a lifelong yogi choked up, unable to speak in daunted admiration of his predecessors while describing their inner maturations: Perhaps this memory of one of my interviewees conveys my point.

For kundalini names those degrees of our own potential that, like conception and birth, the shimmerings of the surf, or the unpredictiblity of Brownian movements, exceed the leveling grasp of too-formulaic developmental models, narratives, or measurings. Thus, the complexity of Indian classical music and the greater complexities beneath it: the *dhun* (chant) and din resolving to Aauummmm and returning to Maaaaaaa. What else could enrapture us to the point of climax for eternity but the marvel of the never-before, *forever*? What else could wean us of every selfishness, vengefulness, and even the fear of death? Such is the next puberties: the rebirth into soul Time that all religions point to.

Yes, by imitating others' endogenously originated movements, heartfelt utterances, righteous actions, or rapt concentrations, we can go through the back door (literally via a ventral [front door] or Eastern bodily channel) into the same depths of wonder, wisdom, and delight. And, by motionless meditation, too, one can enter. Thus, we have numerous helpful yogic texts, new and ancient, and a proliferation of yoga and still-meditation classes. But when kundalini is reintroduced (via the Westerly and more body-involving spinal channel) to our understanding of yoga and meditation, something deep and primordial ripples through the viscera, and yoga or meditation "practices" can no more be considered mere teachable techniques than gestation or puberty can be. For kundalini yoga surfaces from the same bodily depths as gestation, the first breath, adolescent puberty, and now, beyond.

KUNDALINI YOGA: A DEVELOPMENTAL ANATOMY OF ULTIMATE HOPE

However compelling our sufferings might be and however coherent our etiological mappings of their engendered effects, without the irony of a nearby blessedness, we will fail to grasp the spiritual poignancy of the human condition. Such is the soteriological challenge of faith and promise of eventual deliverance of any religion. Spiritual maturation is thus often defined as the ever-strengthening of faith in the availability of some nonomnipotent, but temporally inexhaustive succor amid the melee of confusions and adversities of worldly life.

Kundalini yoga not only asserts that such blessedness is our endless soul condition, it goes on to trace its exact anatomical structure and maturational epigenesis: This ultimate hope and beneficence glows radiantly from the base of the spine, the armature of all vertebrate evolution and embryological embodiment from which all bodies emerge. This root location suggests a singular developmental trajectory begun in utero with the body-shaping, early formation of the neural groove (the protospine) initiated from this inceptive point, with all major developments thereafter originating as pulses from this premonitory source. Hope and human development converge as the scent, sound, feel, or taste of future possibilities fructifying in the radiant juices and humming in the quivering tissues of the body and in the dazzling eternality of consciousness.

Thus, yoga depicts as *physiologically immanent* the impetus of all human searching for unencumbered or absolute wisdom and bliss, in their many forms. "Hope" or "searching" is literally the *feeling* of our own genetico-spiritually propelled maturation via the tricklings of this subtle force (and its derivatives) always throughout the body and, then, specifically and concentratedly, into the anatomical substrate of all spiritual paths: the tree of life and knowledge, the middle way, the core teachings, the shamanic rope climb and mountainous ascent: the spinal channel known as sushumna, "the space where the spiritus-wind flows by grace alone." Joseph Campbell's catchy "follow your bliss" vocational aphorism reveals its endogenous fundament. A particular vein of possible ecstasies proves to be the purest of guides to our own growth, if we can but find it among the myriad less profound satisfactions and follow it devotedly, that is, with unbroken, meditative allure.

At a mundane level, the scientific verification of a yogically attained, "theoretically impossible" interaction between the conscious will and the autonomic or primordial physiologies first occurred in 1926, as documented by V. G. Rele:

> In the year 1926, under the auspices of the Bombay Medical Union, Deshbandhu demonstrated certain phenomena . . . with the chestpieces of our stethoscopes on his heart, we listened to the stopping [sustained fibrillation] of his heart. (Rele 1927, pp. xxii–xxiii)

and has been followed up by numerous successive laboratory experiments and measurements. In some mysterious way, egoic intentionality and the involuntary nervous system had formed a cooperative (perhaps ecstatic) union. Here we see a mundane version of the mystical search to unify the personal will with That of God. The subsequent interest in stress reduction, visualization healing, and other psychosomatic or autogenic health practices proceeded, in part, from this modest degree of verified yogic attainment.

Yet, as profound a depth of knowledge of the life force and the body as this ability would seem to indicate, what remains to be revealed of kundalini yoga will have far more profound consequences. For where this bodily control or, rather, intelligence, comes from and where it can ultimately lead to has remained obscure, in spite of theories of hypnosis, autosuggestion, or biofeedback or even the collective unconscious or dynamic ground.[7]

For while health is a function of normalcy, both must be contexted developmentally, that is, both must be understood temporally as what quality of embodied life *next* becomes possible as a result of such "health" or "normalcy." And, then, from that basis, what quality of life next becomes possible, and so on. As Sartre mused, the meaning of things is to be derived destinally or by where, finally, they tend toward. Thus, "the normal" could be attuned to "the Absolute," if we but knew what the Absolute was, and then dedicated ourselves to it, absolutely, as the discovered, most matured possibility for homosapiens sapiens. In this case, let us consider that to be homosapiens kundaliniens.

I am aware of the rhetorical impact of making such grand word choices—"postgenital puberties," "the Absolute," "homsapiens kundaliniens"—and of embarking on significant constructive efforts after some one hundred-fifty pages of largely deconstructive labors. I know as well that I risk provoking dismissive skepticisms by hoisting a claim for ultimate truth and a teleological evolutionism. But the indeterminacy, impermanence, eros-as-mystery, and uncertainty that I tried to free from clinical misapprehensions in previous chapters via deconstruction should not be construed as a final end, as taking nonabsolutism, individual freedom, or adaptive diversity as a final truth.

The postmodern project of laying bare the hypothesis of metaphysical closure (that the constructs of reason might eventually exhaust their explanative effectiveness) and the insubstantiality of the authoritative subject does not guarantee its own finality. A consequence of noncynical, profound doubt regarding all received wisdom can be that, within it, something utterly new or "foreign" might be noticed and granted credibility by the community of experts (or by any individual). Yet not just a grasping after yogic exotica, or the utter novelty of each new moment—but the Absolute as a (lost? obscured?) vast developmental continuum underlying the moments and hopefulness of our lives.

In a state of radical doubt or openness we must no longer dare to assume that answers to the timeless questions must easily fit in with established theory, nor that they must originate within traditional Western research institutions or discursive methods. The strange discipline in Western academic philosophy and psychology of seeking answers primarily, if not exclusively, within the established Western canon can seem like working with one hand tied behind the back, or worse.

The sectarian approach to spiritual truth is another unfortunate and at times tragic limitation. That the search is best done in chairs, with the eyes fastened to books and the ears to discourse, or in a lab where the researcher does not change, or even in motionless contemplations with no attention to the glands, interior vibrations, the spine, and the rest of the body, will seem from within the yogic methodologies to be overly apollonian and distinctly restrictive.

However, only a scientifically verifiable new discovery concerning human possibility would be compelling enough to foment a "reworlding" (after Heidegger's verb *to world* a world) breakthrough beyond the postmodern shifting play of words, time, and ideologies of difference; for example, repeatedly measurable alterations of endocrine secretions resulting from the serpentine intelligence of kundalini yoga.

Yet, in a theological, political, and then in a prepotent semantic sense, Western science is prevented from exploring spiritual matters not so much by the grossness of its methods as by a lingering dualism that has long minimized the spirituality of the physical world. "If science *can* or has studied it, then it probably should not be deemed 'spiritual,'" is the syllogism preempting the intermingling of these "two" domains, finally, of spirit and body. DNA may be profound, but it cannot be "spiritual" because it is (merely) molecular. For the limitations of dualism to be obviated, we must grant spiritual import to the body. But, to avoid a too-facile nondualism, we will have to look much more profoundly into the body.

POSTGENITAL STIRRINGS: A SPIRITUAL PREPUBESCENCE

The long-developing, prepubescence ramping toward the kundalini spinal puberty is known as pranotthana ("intensified, uplifted life energy," perhaps emergent within cellular mitochondria). This is clearly the same force of quivering uprightness active in Quakerism, Shakerism, Judaic *davening* (torso-rocking prayer), charismatic Holy Ghost phenomena, the swaying *zikr* and whirling dervish of Islam, the quiverings of the Orthodox hesychast, the Goddess-worshipping circle dance, the Dionysian revel of the Greek mystery schools, the flowing movements of tai chi, the ecstatic shamanic dance, the yogically derived Andalusian flamenco, the Middle-Eastern belly dance, and the orgonic quivering-streamings of bioenergetics (which Reich deemed as beyond sexuality). Poetically, Rumi personified this way of vibrational spiritual development that calls beyond one's current level of maturation toward the more distant puberties.[8]

> Drumsound rises on the air,
> its throb, my heart.
>
> A voice inside the beat says,
> "I know you're tired,
> but come. This is the way."
> (Rumi 1996, p. 122)

The *Mahayana* and *Hinayana Buddhist* and *raja yoga* focus on the straightened spine (*uju-kaya*) is merely an intentionally taming approach to the same spinal puberties (an uprightness that, too, emerges endogenously as the serene tumescence of the awakened spine), as are other erect-back Western sects. Here the "straight and narrow paths" attempt to obviate the complexities of the bodily awakenings in pursuit of the transcendental, with more or less severity.

Pranotthana is also vividly apparent in the developmental movements and perpetual stretchings of infants and in the maturational glow of children and energetic zest of adolescence. As the thirteenth-century attainer of the final maturations, Shri Jnaneshvar stated:

> 51. That is called [yogic developmental] action of the body in which reason takes no part and which does not originate as an idea springing in the mind.
>
> 52. To speak simply, yogis perform actions with their bodies, like the movements of children. (Jnaneshvar 1987, p. 102)

The various willfully practiced asanas of hatha yoga are, more accurately, apollonian formulations of their dionysian originary emergence as sahaja yoga, or the yearning, quaking, shaking, davening, throbbing, swaying, and bodily tumescences of various other traditions. *Hatha* as meaning "forceful" grows ambiguous. Is it that a force, a divine *shakti*, compels the yogini to worshipfully stretch and develop her own body, beyond her own will's choices and dictates into further maturation? Or does hatha refer only to her own willful storming of the heavenly gates? Or is there a point of humbling recognition where even that leeway of freedom called "the will" is seen as yet another expression of the Goddess, more or less attuned to the rhythms of the postgenital pubescent stirrings?

All such movements, vocalizations, and emotionalities are yogic to the degree they foment the neuroendocrine transformations which comprise *urdhva-retas* ("refining maturation of bodily essence") grasped rudimentarily as "sublimation" by Freud, thinly as psychological "alchemy" by Jung, and externalized with uncertain results in medicinal alchemies. Urdhva-retas ripples through all religions, sexual liberations, and love relationships that sense there is "more to sex (or, rather, eros) than sex itself." Thus, the conflictual history of sex and spirituality is merely the confusion attendant to the transitions of *any* puberty.

The emotional crucibles of commitment, monogamy, open marriage, or the pursuit of honest communication in any marital or caring relationship can be considered as part of this maturational alchemy. For all the soteriological sentiments belong to its phenomenology, as does the processing of upsets via the fires of apology and forgiveness. The many erotic permutations of tantric practice, with more or less success, are also the bubblings toward urdhva-retas. Certainly the ecstatic celibacies and unconditional loves of saviors, saints, and yogis must be included here.[9]

The Postgenital Pubescent "Alchemies"

Known in Vedic times as *shamanica medhra* (releasement beyond genital puberty, and from which the term *shamanism* is likely derived), the essential alchemy of urdhva-retas is the distillation of the soteriological secretion-radiance of *ojas* (subtle glycogen or health-energy radiance) such that desire-based love (the alchemical lead or mercury) begins to mature into ever more *un*conditional love (the alchemical gold, or the nectar of endless love).

Via the dionysian actions of body, breath, sentiment, and the utterly allured concentrations known in the apollonian formulae as meditative stages, various hormonal secretions (felt as evermore poignant longings and gratitudes) undergo the alchemical maturation. These once-distilled secretions, (elixirs, soma, philosopher's gems) are then reabsorbed into the body as a kind of nourishing fuel. So uroborically nourished, the body grows in the "yogic direction" to next time issue slightly "higher octane" radiance secretions, whose hypervitalities are distilled into still higher octaned secretions, and so on. In the first line of Hymn VII.5 of the *Atharva-veda*, this quintessential distillation process is described: "By sacrifice the gods sacrificed to the sacrifice." The "gods" are, of course, the finest points of origination of the scintillations of these inwardly seen radiances, and the series of inner alchemical distillations, their "sacrifices to sacrifices."

At some point, the glowing radiances and soteriological longings resulting from a longstanding urdhva-retas foments an opening of hymenlike *granthis* (knots) along the spinal sushumna. Kundalini awakens and enters. Thus, the long, spinal prepubescence of pranotthana enters its puberty and one hears of yogic disidentifications with the body and the ego and reidentifications with the soul within its temple-body. Later there will be identifications with the Womb-Void and Eternal Body, or even the disidentification with all word forms, denoting that other puberties have begun. For "kundalini" merely names that motherly force that carries the body-soul from zygote through teenaged puberty and beyond, in what Ken Wilber has called the full-bodied opening to development and ecstasies "beyond the genitals."

The Traverse from a Genital to a Post-Genital Developmental Psychology

Wilhelm Reich came close to the yogic perception of an energetic, psychophysical developmentalism in declaring that

> the act of desiring had to be grasped in a much deeper way than analytic psychology was capable of doing. Everything pointed to a deep biological process, of which the "unconscious" desire could only be an expression. (Reich, *The Function of the Orgasm*, 1973, p. 66)

But as Foucault was the first to point out in his groundbreaking *The History of Sexuality*, Reich could not think beyond the "deployment of sexuality" of his times and equated desire with sex desire, as his title denotes. Lacking information regarding the vibrant energetics of kundalini yoga, he, as did Freud, misconstrued and pathologized yoga as a "killing of the instincts."

> One may . . . hope to be freed from a part of one's sufferings by influencing the instinctual impulses. . . . The extreme form of this is brought about by killing off the instincts, as is prescribed [sic] by the worldly wisdom of the East and practiced by Yoga. If it succeeds, then the subject has, it is true, given up all other activities as well—he has sacrificed his life; and, by another path, he has once more only achieved the happiness of quietness. (Freud 1961 [1930], p. 26)

Through its pathologizing concepts of self-stimulation, somatic cocooning, and autohypnotic states, psychoanalysis continues to obscure its view of yogic phenomena. Even Winnicott's "self-soothing" misses the spiritual depths from where this "internal mothering" emerges and what further nurturance it is fully capable of providing. As well, the more bodily oriented therapies of Reichian orgonomy and bioenergetics focused its therapies exclusively on orgasmlike emotional releases or catharses to increase energetic flow. Characterized as a mere bioelectrical energy, the motherly force lost more of her nurturing powers. As Reich's innovator, Alexander Lowen asserts with confident authority:

> When growth has reached its natural limits, some other use must be made of the excess [sic] energy that is being produced. . . . In the higher animals, the excess energy is discharged in the sexual function, as Wilhelm Reich showed.
> Maturity means that the energy that was formerly needed for the growth process is now available for discharge. (Lowen 1967, p. 57)

Repeatedly, conventional developmental theory is delimited by its unfamiliarity with any postgenital maturational stages—stages that require the very energy that is otherwise construed as having no other purpose than its availability for discharge, perhaps lovingly, perhaps not. Anyone who differs with this view was to be seen as naive, repressed, and perhaps even insane, as was Freud's pronouncement while ostracizing Jung for asserting that the life force was a "psychic" and not a sexual energy. And Western religions' garbled understanding of the postgenital puberties depicted genital puberty as a sinful, barely tolerable state. Its severe guidances on how to continue the maturational traverse has soured the whole affair for most Westerners for centuries. Thus, the church and its suffering Savior were an easy mark for the too-confident

Maturation of the Ensouled Body 157

psychoanalytically based ideologies of "sexual liberation."

Yet, in this postmodern era, Foucault grasped the historicity and narrowness of what he called the medico-psychoanalytic "deployment of sexuality." For, in this near-allegorical history, psychoanalytic sexology wrote itself in as delivering a final and complete "erotic liberation" from the age-old grip of centuries of religious/cultural "repressions" and "unnatural sublimations." Foucault noted that although many social gains have occurred, a mandated and specifically formulaic and inherently limited sexuality, a scientia sexualis, had been deployed.

One limitation was guaranteed by the rebellious thrust of this scientia sexualis, a rebellion against spirituality that defined the new "science." Thus, Foucault claims that to have this sexuality has become "more important than one's soul."

> By creating the imaginary element that is "sex," the deployment of sexuality established one of its most essential operating principles: the desire for sex—the desire to have it, to have access to it, to discover it, to liberate it, to articulate it into discourse, to formulate it into truth.... And it is this desirability of sex that attaches each one of us to the injunction to know it, to reveal its law and its power; it is this desirability that makes us think we are affirming the right of our sex against all power, when in fact we are fastened to the deployment of sexuality that has lifted up from deep within us a sort of mirage in which we think we see ouselves reflected—the dark shimmer of sex. (Foucault 1980a, pp. 156–57)

Foucault went on to distinguish this conflict-forged, biomedical scientia sexualis of Western sexological science and psychoanalyis from the radically different ars erotica developed by various Indo-Arabic cultures under very different circumstances:

> In the erotic art, truth is drawn from pleasure itself, understood as a practice and accumulated as experience; pleasure is not considered in relation to an absolute law of the permitted and the forbidden, nor by reference to a criterion of utility, but first and foremost in relation to itself, it is experienced as pleasure, evaluated in terms of its intensity, its specific quality, its duration, its reverberations in the body and the soul. Moreover, this knowledge must be deflected back into the sexual practice itself, in order to shape it as though from within and amplify its effects. In this way, there is formed a knowledge that must remain secret, not because of an element of infamy that might attach to its object, but because of the need to hold it in the greatest reserve, since according to the tradition, it would lose its effectiveness and its virtue by being divulged.... The effects of this masterful art, which are considerably more generous than the spareness of its prescriptions would lead one to imagine, are said to transfigure the one fortunate enough to receive its privileges: an absolute

mastery of the body, a singular bliss, obliviousness to time and limits, the elixir of life, the exile of death and its threats. (Foucault 1980a, pp. 57–58)

The several-thousand-year-old Eastern somatic spirituality of kundalini yoga and its expansive developmental path belong to this Foucauldian ars erotica where spirituality and philosophical pursuit—along with the body's vast capacities to move and to feel—cohere together as a unitary whole. As Marcuse noted in his critique of psychoanalysis, *Eros and Civilization*, "the instincts are to be understood spiritually." The body or incarnation becomes the essential text, and its logos: the immortal soul.

Indeed, that these ars erotica ways yielded "an absolute mastery of the body, a singular bliss, obliviousness to time and limits, the elixir of life, the exile of death and its threats" has an additional purport: We must wonder whether the extent to which eros can liberate us has been dramatically underestimated by the deployers of the scientia sexualis. As Ken Wilber quipped, "God-consciousness is not sublimated sexuality, sexuality is repressed God-consciousness," and Patanjali: Bodily asana "becomes perfect . . . when [the mind] makes the idea of its infinity its own content [*anantasamapattibhyam*]" (Eliade 1958, p. 53.)

Without making use of the entire kundalini yoga schema, we have another basis from which to develop a psychotherapy, one somewhat anticipated by contemporary psychoanalysis's exchanging its instinctive-drive theory for the more relationally oriented "self-psychology" and "object relations." In a post-Freudian economy of time and meaning, beyond preoccupations with a predetermining past and a single desire, another form of life exists.

For, in the kundalini theory of the body, our deepest sensations are understood, not so much as inklings of a buried past, but more as tremors of an emergent and hopeful present-future. In interpreting a client's body language of gestures, emotion displays, and reported sensations according to this depth, a spiritually inspiring therapy emerges. The tinglings of the future, not merely variously hidden wounds and pain, can be mapped out and guided forward.

This therapist sees and hears "glimmers of hopefulness" in perhaps fleeting eye glows or warbling speech. Indeed, she uncovers "sheer presence as hopefulness," and, even though morbidly, fathoms the perversity of "suicidality as hopefulness." While the postgenital puberties are not part of the exoteric clinical narrative, the soteriological sentiments are. An etiological past of conclusive wounding events is exchanged for a redemptive past where hope still lives. For, indeed, it does.

Certainly, the phrase *the body* has long disguised a crucial insight:

Maturation of the Ensouled Body 159

There are as many "bodies" as there are *theories* or representations of something very real *called* "the body." Such could be said of many psychotherapeutic phrases that we have examined such as *the self, the feeling,* or *the past*. But in the case of *the body*, matters are particularly acute.

For, at this time, transpersonalists, feminists, and body psychotherapists use the term literally to point to a ground of unquestionably assumable certainty, a ground that is, all the while, heavily dominated by psychoanalytic beliefs. Having exposed the limitations of the mind of traditional, patriarchical authority, they hope *the* body will be infallible. Yet, they merely take up again the old methods and beliefs and urge clients to contact, again and again, more and yet more stored pain.

Just as a preteenager can know, via her own bodily changes and the culturally pervasive messages that repeatedly inform her (enthusiastically or, as can be the case in the postmodern era, despondently) of her emergent adulthood, so should all adults understand their everyday bodily sensations as saturated with a profoundly auspicious, developmentally challenging significance. In such a body, imagine the sense of mystery and wonder about the future. Such is the substrate of the spiritual life of kundalini yoga.

In considering the "kundalini body" (and there are various subtheories describing this body too), we confront that therapists have been all along operating with a *psychoanalytic* body using the Freudian hermeneutic to decode sensations, tensions, and conversion symptoms. Thus it should not surprise us that when the Freudian drive theory dominated, we had bodies saturated with sex desire, while now in these times of ego developmental theory, we have futureless bodies saturated with an etiological childhood. Of course, in previous times when the church reigned, bodies were assumed to be saturated with original sins, temptations, and fallenness.

Arrival at the Base Camp

The obvious question would seem to be: How could maturational phenomena worthy of such a genetic characterization as I assert be so unknown and rare? Part of the answer lies in:

1. The psychoanalytic retrospective distortion depicting meditative states as autistic regressions to the womb; its pathologization or minimization of sublimative eros, what Marcuse called a "hyperrepressive desublimation" of human spiritual imports, and what Foucault noted as the "mass deployment of sexuality" that has anchored Western culture paradigmatically at the level of a conclusive and inherently gratifying genital puberty; as Foucault mused ironically,

we need to consider the possibility that one day, perhaps, in a different economy of bodies and pleasures, people will no longer quite understand how the ruses of sexuality, and the power that sustains its organization, were able to subject us to that austere monarchy of sex. (Foucault 1980a, p. 159)

2. The limited exploration of the positive role of the body in spiritual development by various world religions and their missed appreciation of any *continuity* of genital puberty with "spiritual rebirth" and their consequently short-sighted and, thereby, often repressive moralities and dry monasticisms; the inherent richness of genital puberty and sex that can obscure the existence of any further bodily awakenings and any interest in cultivating them.

3. Centuries of Western biases against "animism," "vitalisms," and "heathen religions" and, more recently, in the developing third world against its own superstitious "backwardnesses." (The cross-cultural sensitivities noted throughout the *DSM-IV* are a significant improvement, in this respect.)

4. Misinterpretations of Hindu relics and texts that result when researchers are deprived of the yogic bodily referenced hermeneutic. For example, the "Ganges River" is to be often understood homologously as the main flow channel for certain maturational radiances; references to "dancing in the sky (ethers)" or "cow worship" esoterically refer to the tongue (the "cow") giving up its articulations of words in *khecari* (*khe*: "sky," *cari*: "dance in") *mudra* to stretch upward nonverbally into a vibrationally churned, subtler, "milky buttery" (the cowherd Krishna's quintessential delight), sensational-endogenous medium of truth; natural elements (diamond body, mercury, gold, moonlight or sunlight) as the phenomenal luster of internally sensed hormonal distillates; the "heaven realms" as the eyes-closed cranial-vault space (replicated universally as cathedral domes) in which the flickering nonverbal truth nectars of infinite time-light-sound-bliss flow; while the proverbial "mountainous ascent" describes what the spinal puberty of Mt. Meru, Mt. Olympus, Mt. Moriah, Mt. Kailash, or Mt. Carmel *feels like* and its glorified bodily locus.[5]

5. The many *gurus* who came to the West and breached their spiritual vows and numerous exposed religious scandals and ensuing cultural cynicisms. War, bloody religious crusades, inquisitions, sect rivalries, and other social devastations that erode faith in the existence of any true saints or spiritual Absolutes.[10]

6. The unfortunate association of yogic Sanskrit terminology (*chakras*, kundalini, mantras, etc.) with the superficiality of new-age rhetoric; the highly circumscribed exercise yoga taught widely in the West and in India and the obvious marketing problems in promoting

sublimative yoga in the West; thus, the widespread misfitting of tantric yoga into a genital puberty context, instead of the reverse.

7. Yogic archival and cult tendencies to exaggerate, mythologize, or conceal in metaphors the spiritual practices and attainments of yogic saints; the formulization of yogic phenomena into teachable, willful practices, as Patanjali devised in his *Yoga-sutra* and by many others that marginalize or miss the endogenous quality of sahaja ("spontaneous") yoga or *kriya-vati*: "spontaneous maturation movements";

The tendency of intensive spiritual lifestyles to become remote from mainstream culture, and thus "esotericized" while secularized lifestyles that dilute the teachings proliferate as exoteric "churches" or "religions"; the arising of misleading fanaticisms in esoteric groups and in mistaking licentious debauchery for the dionysian spontaneities and ecstasies resulting from careful cultivation.

8. Centuries of yogic pedagogical secrecy and the often unassuming humility of many spiritually matured, inconspicuous yogis. The safety that reclusion promises for those with spiritual powers otherwise beseiged or even feared and not uncommonly harmed by others.

9. The slow progress in Western science to measure instrumentally subtle bodily phenomena such as "energy" and the lack of biofeedback research on the spine's role in meditation.

10. Foreclosure on the possibility of reincarnation when the matter should be left as merely, if even highly, uncertain.

11. The glib use of such phrases as "Realizing Your True Self," "In One's Beingness," or "Core of Being," in popular psychology that depict advanced stages of spiritual maturation as reachable in a few years, or during a few weekends. This includes popular and academic works in transpersonal psychology where kundalini, being the only yogic energy term known in those circles, is commonly misused in naming the vast expanse of precursor states (pranotthana), rendering the happy, democratically appealing but false sense that many people have "awakened" kundalini.[11]

Furthermore, kundalini has become a catch word at this early time in its entry in American culture (it first appears in the third edition of the *American Heritage Dictionary* in 1992: "Energy that lies dormant at the base of the spine until it is activated, as by the practice of yoga, and channeled upward through the chakras in the process of spiritual perfection") and attracts those with unspecified, chronic neurological/psychiatric complaints in search of an explanation for their symptoms; the use in the West of Gopi Krishna's problematic kundalini experiences as a standard giving the awakening a reputation as more dangerous than it is.

12. The popularization and simplicity of straight-back meditative paths, which tend to marginalize or eliminate bodily movements, emotional utterances, and the like, from the spiritual path.

162 WORDS FROM THE SOUL

13. The numerous hours per day in yogic worship that development toward this physical-spiritual Absolute comes to consuming, as the fundamental purpose of life, time, and the body seems to be to enact the yogic cultivations and then to contribute to one's community; the developmental importance of initiating yogic practices before the age of thirty-five, in keeping with its biogenetics basis; and even then, the inherent difficulties affecting appetite, sleep cycles, and the Promethean temptations of hubris that can short circuit the completion of the path and generate false accounts of its requirements.

14. The time and energy demands—a kind of repressive back pressure or cultural inertia—of contemporary world structures that exist only if these stages do not unfold except perhaps rarely. In a vicious-circle fashion, this "wheel of worldly life" includes the dramatic and real need for extensive altruistic service to address the extreme deteriorations of society and the environment ironically resulting from missing these endogenous joys and then compensating by overusing the outer world. (I am reminded that in the 1970s when Burmese farmers were taught modern ways to triple their crop yield for cash export purposes, many chose to work one-third as much and to instead increase their meditation time.)

With these conjectures noted, let us continue toward those little-known lands of the yogic postgenital puberties.

Kundalini Developmentalism

Patanjali's "eight-limbed" *ashtanga* apollonian formulization of yogic maturations can serve as our starting point:

YAMA	soteriological sentiment observations
NIYAMA	soteriological sentiment cultivations
ASANA	bodily development through postural movements (the popularly known postures of hatha yoga)
PRANAYAMA	breath or vital-energy development
PRATYHARA	perception and inward attention-span development
DHARANA	inward concentration-understanding development
DHYANA	meditative knowledge development
SAMADHI	enstatic wisdom liberation development

In keeping with our approach, which views kundalini yoga as endogenous, we must strip away this formulaic structure and look at the stages as if they could be seen as fitting in a generalized way into the following developmental schema:

BEGINNING. Sperm-ovum fertilization: zygote, blastula, and gastrula stages develop;

FIRST MONTHS. Starting at the embryonic spinal base, kundalini energy-intelligence guides the formation of the neural groove, the evolutionary fundament of all evermore complex vertebrate bodies, from amphioxus on; gill arches, tail, and other "ontogeny phylogeny recapitulation" vestigial phenomena emerge and vanish; organs form, heart beats as *ananda-maya kosha* (causal body), *vijnana-maya kosha* (reflective-mind body), *mano-maya kosha* (neuroendocrine-based mind/emotion body), *prana-maya kosha* (mitochondrial-meridian vital energy body) and *anna-maya kosha* (food-eating or ordinary fleshy body) develop;

MIDDLE MONTHS. *Jiva* ("the one who lives") enters the causal body;

LATE MONTHS. Continued gestation of the fetal body toward fragile sufficiency by the sixth or seventh month as kundalini completes its formation of the body and recedes into dormancy at the spinal base; the more generic life energy of prana of the prana-maya kosha (*udana, samana, apana, prana, vyana* circuits of head, gut, elimination, respiration, and circulation, respectively) continues as the flesh body's (anna-maya kosha's) sustaining force, as nourished with earthly foods and oxygen via the umbilical connection to mother;

BIRTH. First breath, umbilicus cut, eye contact;

FIRST HOURS. Reaching, anahata-nada (polysignificant neuroendocrinal developmental utterances that are related to the yogic developmental breathing of pranayama—a "crying" that can be overassociated with adult anguish); psychomotor developmental movements akin to sahaja ("spontaneous") yoga asanas and hand and finger mudras emerge; nursing;

FIRST DECADE. Teething, walking, play; glandular secretions underlying soteriological sentiments of yamas and niyamas begin to fructify within the child's social and family context; language appropriates mind, tongue and psychosomatic enculturation occurs; prepubescent pranotthana ("intensified life energy") sustains the child's growth, visible as "the glow of childhood";

SECOND DECADE. Childhood pranotthana intensifies, fomenting genital puberty/fertility as the embodiment of infinite future human possibilities (the basis of the "endless impermanence" or survival of the species); hormonal-temporal urgencies quicken as gender-oriented desires; intermediate puberty of yama and niyama neuroendocrine secretions emerge, with emphasis upon developmentally sublimative *brahmacarya* (first *ashrama*, or "neophyte learner" stage of "following the Telos"); basic prepubescent asana and pranayama emerge in willful and minimal sahaja or "spontaneous" forms, further maturing sapient embodiment toward kundalini embodiment;

THIRD DECADE. Karma yoga, the life of responsible action and character maturation; the mind matures beyond childhood's scattered vitality toward pratyahara, the capacity for sustained perceptions and careful attention; second ashrama of "householder" family creation of *pravritti* path or the solitary mystic *nivritti* path is entered; diverse worldly involvements are varyingly *dharmic* or aligned (a*lign*ed, as in re-*ligi*on) with the endogenous maturational process; the maturations known as the mensch, good neighbor, or well-balanced person emerge; if pranotthana continues to intensify via dharmic life, the postgenital puberties of urdhva-retas quicken.

FOURTH DECADE. Dharana begins: the dawning of awesome awareness of/as endless impermanence and soteriological radiance-secretions of *tejas* ("brilliance-radiance" of spiritual zeal) and virya ("virtue-secretion/radiance") emerge; advanced asanas, mudras, *bandhas* (inner yearning contractions) and shaking mature the body for more intensified energies; dhyana begins: devout and unwavering appreciation of the flow of endless impermanence and the poignant grace of life; the puberties of the linguistic anatomy (tongue, larynx, brain centers) underlying further meditative/mental maturations begin: *simha-asana* (tongue-extended "lion pose" seen in certain goddess images) and *nabho mudra* (inward-turned tongue, "heaven-delight gesture") precursors of khecari mudra (tongue curls back in delight above the soft palate), initiating the puberties of the hypoglossal, larnyx, hypothalamus, pituitary, and pineal; *anahata-nada*, known rudimentarily as "speaking in tongues" and resounding in the sacred chantings of numerous cultures, emerge;

FIFTH DECADE. The desire-self identity matures toward the immortal soul-self identity; soteriological radiance of auras (halo-auric glow of spiritual maturity) emerges; continuation of khecari mudra, culminating in the soteriological (subtle pineal?) secretion-radiance of *soma* or amrita ("immortal-time essence," revitalizing endorphinlike hormone), the uroboric embodiment of endless impermanence; kundalini awakens, initiating the puberties of the six chakras and the inner shamanic heat; *shambhavi mudra*, the puberty of the eyes and the pineal leading to inner vision of the soul's (melatoninlike) radiances and the matter-time-space-scent-taste-light-bliss continuum emerges as a phenomenon of embodied eternal impermanence; unmani mudra, the "delight-gesture of free consciousness" cerebral puberty emerges; internal or breathless respiration in the *akashic*-ethers emerges; grandchildren emerge for householders and then the third ashrama of retirement and the fourth ashrama of worldly renunciation; great-grandchildren emerge for householders.

Sabija-samadhi and *Nirbija-samadhi*: fully matured origin-consciousness with, and then without, future waverings emerge;

REPEAT TWENTY-FIVE TO FIFTY INCARNATIONS. *Divya sharira*: exceedingly rare full maturation of the ensouled body as "divine light body" and *moksha*: complete maturation of all soul-body potentials; ultimate liberation.

Also, consider this brief description of the successive passions involved in the unfoldment of the psychospiritual puberties as they emerge within the chakra subtle-energy system along the Jacob's Ladder of the spinal axis: *muladhara* (root): passion of survival and locus of latent kundalini; *svadhishthana* (pubic): passion of genital puberty; *manipura* (navel): passion of willfulness and of urdhva-retas heating; anahata (heart): passion of longing and love; *vishuddha* (throat): passion of expressed longing, gradually nearing union; *ajna* (midbrow, hypothalamic-pineal): unitive fulfillment and dispassion.

In sahaja yoga, specific mudras and asanas emerge in conjunction with each chakra. Yoga mudra, spinal twist, back stretching, fish pose, reverse pose, and cobra pose, respectively, is one possible correlation of chakras and asanas. Here, we also have the basis for a "chakra developmental psychology," which bears some resemblance to the psychoanalytic psychosexual oral, anal, latency, phallic, and genital stages of maturation.

Endogenous Yama-Niyama Development and the Superego

In this schema, the yama-niyama development of the soteriological sentiments comes in two directions throughout the entire lifespan: (1) pedagogically, as moral teachings passed on from one generation to the next, and (2) endogenously, as the neuroendocrinal substrate for the sentiments of forgiveness, contrition, and so forth (commensurate with that of anger, sadness, desire, etc.)

Since psychoanalysis focuses exclusively on the first direction with its purely "introjected superego" and contingent "ego," we have inherited a sense of moral sentiments as being unnatural or external to human nature, and of anger, sadness, and so forth, as the only endogenous emotions. The myth of "Ten Commandments" being handed down from a mountain top seems also to corroborate the view of morals as being external teachings, but not if we interpret yogicly these "mountainous heights" (and other scriptural mountains) as being the lofty cranial vault into which the lightning of kundalini arises to then reign down from the cerebral heavens its matured soteriological wisdom. Phenomenologically, one may *feel as if* the teachings are handed down "from above," thus the mountainous metaphor fits experientially, too.

For, while the exoteric aspect of all moral-spiritual teachings is social harmony, the esoteric aspect is an internal harmony or balance that allows the central spinal channel to open and more fully mature. One develops "moral backbone" or "rectitude." Certainly, as well, the snake-encircled, hermetic caduceus healing symbol represents the congruence of health with the balancing of *ida* and *pingala*, the spiraling channels to the left and right of sushumna.

Grounded thus in the body, vitality and morality can both enhance or distort one another. Thus, certain vitality-enhancing yogic practices still cannot be given out in some subcontinent locales under the penalty of state statutes, for they are believed capable of circumventing the otherwise requisite moral development.

In resting in the immaturities of one's desirous or aggressive feelings, too much encouraged in conventional psychology due to their exogenous understanding of the soul sentiments, the unfoldment of yama and niyama can be inhibited. Certainly when apollonian moral formulations become overly severe, due to an insensitivity to the endogenous nature of moral strivings, their emergence in childhood and thereafter can be disturbed.

Clearly, certain moral teachings regarding sexuality will only make sense when understood as fragmentary attempts to support the postgenital puberties. Lacking much understanding of these stages, Western moralities grope in the half-light with their well-intended proscriptions. The minimal understanding of the spirituality of gender—what *did* Jesus feel for Mary?, St. Theresa for St. John?—in these religions is in contrast to the Hindu pantheon, where nearly every diety is openly paired with her or his beloved. Indeed, a prominent line in tantric scriptures declares, "Where man/woman worship one another is the play of the divine."

The long-developing postgenital puberties resolve the problematic relationship between sexuality and spirituality that has plagued various religions, and some of the limitations of the so-called "sexual liberation movement" of the sixties and seventies, to the present times. The monasticisms of various religions result from their tremblings. From the yogic perspective, the "sexual liberation" of recent years refers primarily to the genital stage of development, which in itself had been subjected to a cultural repression.

Maturation of the Ensouled Body 167

The possibility of "too much sublimation" has been addressed most clearly by kundalini and tantric guidances, which emphasize that merely reading about yoga or passionlessly performing any practices will also miss the point. The sensuality, the seething, serpentine *sublimative* sensuality of yoga must be felt or a kind of spiritual repression can result.[12] As Allama chided:

> With all your manifold yogas,
> you achieve
> a body, but no spirit
> (Allama Prabhu in
> Ramanujan 1973, p. 147)

Likewise, these sublimations originate from the subtler *tanmatric* (subtle potencies of sentience) dimension of human potentials, which then effect the bodily maturations.

From Worded Truth to Wordless Gnosis:
The Puberties of Khecari, Shambhavi, and Unmani Mudras

Khecari Mudra: Linguistic Transcendence and Hypoglossal Maturation. The rediscovered meditation practices of both Eastern and Western spiritualities have bequested transpersonal psychology an appreciation for the "wisdom beyond language." Psychologies of meditation now abound. Yet, when movement is kept within apollonian forms, further maturations of the body can be inhibited. Thus, the postgenital puberty of the tongue and hypothalamus known as khecari mudra ("the skydancer delight-gesture"), so supportive of the meditative maturations, is little known. (I am not referring to the intentionally contrived practice of lengthening the tongue, but the mudra that emerges spontaneously via pranotthana.)

During this puberty, the anatomy underlying speech and linguistic knowing outgrows the grip of language and its limitations and passes through all manner of maturational longings and sacred utterance. Thus, it holds special significance for our interest in linguistic deconstruction, temporality, and spirituality for, during khecari mudra, we hear evermore clearly the words of the soul in its own time and mother tongue in which semantic purport, somatic auto-developmentalism, and ecstatic worship converge in the mercurial now-now-now.

Thus, the impact of the khecari puberty is wide ranging. It spiritualizes the voice, alchemically distills mental energies to a quivering stillness, and revitalizes the body. Subjectively, a compelling, "sensual-cognitive certainty" (seemingly more precise than those provided by linguistic-discursive means) or longing, arises throughout the yogicly maturing body and into the pharnyx. Radiating into the hypoglossal nerve, the tongue literally moves beyond its linguistic-enunciating function into an esoteric vocabulary of tumescent archings and developmental "delight gestures"—mudras—and panlinguistic utterances.

As the tongue leans fore- and backward in graceful or empassioned, ecstatic worship, it is fulfilling its linguistic recitations and the yogi knows it. Whatever theological discourse is for-the-sake-of is drawing to its completion and now finds a more effective bodily means to conduct its researches for divine truths. The articulative mechanics of utterance become the sonic and somatic props for this oral-spiritual ascent. Here, the gap between words and wordless meditation, or body and spirit, is filled in exquisite detail, like the warbling lark at dawn.

These particular swaying, arching, and yearning tongue, and other bodily movements and soundings—moreso than all those of the logico-semantic ilk—unfold now a somatic-aesthetic way to the truth. Guided inwardly by the alluring scent, glow, taste, cool then heat, and eternally beckoning yin-yang whorl of the subtle-pineal's heavenly portal, the tongue takes on this postlinguistic purpose. The central nervous system, with its elaborately beautiful structural networks and energetic subtleties, becomes its own highest thought and proprioceptive feeling, and the tongue its now-silenced and prostrate devotee.

Comparative anatomy reveals that homo sapiens has the most elaborately ennervated tongue of all lifeforms. That this anatomical fact should be interpreted by sociobiologists as an evolutionary advantage or selective adaptation whose purpose is precise verbal articulations is cast into the background of a far more profound bodily potential, in the light of khecari mudra. The unusually complex hypoglossal nerve gives the tongue the sensitivity and muscular-articulating capacity to stretch back toward an inner calling, thus stimulating the brain/mind in its maturation beyond language-knowing toward meditative gnosis.

Embryology as well suggests that khecari mudra is part of a developmental continuity from the earliest to this most advanced stage of bodily manifestation. For we find that the timely secretion of sweet-tasting mucopolysaccharides causes the prototongue to lick itself away from its embryonic contact with the hypophysis (the rudiment of the hypothalamus and pituitary) and out of the then-forming cranial cavity and into the just-developing oral cavity. It is interesting, then, to find that after years of pranotthana, other sweet-tasting brain secretions (soma, amrita) will again draw the tongue toward further bodily maturations in khecari mudra. This time, the sweetness guides the tongue back behind the soft palate proximal to the hypothalamic appetitive-drive satiety center and the pituitary developmental master gland. The breathless "hermetic" meditative alchemies that proceed during its arousal quicken the maturations of this puberty.

For, during certain breathless meditative passages, which emerge during the mudra's hypoglossal tumescence, a "psychic membrane" opens, certainly related to the hypothalamic overseeing of blood oxygenations. Through this permeable boundary between psyche and soma, an internal respiration, known as *kevala kumbhaka*, begins to gasp sustenance. The yogini becomes like the first amphibious fish who risked crawling ashore breathing no longer through gulps of water, but now of atmospheric oxygen.[13] She finds a motionless way of breathing life into her body from the "lungs" of the akasha, the glowing pranic ethers of her own endless mind. This motionless inspiration feels interminably deep, going to the source of life itself, and even without khecari, is common to many meditative paths. For here the mind-brain, which is, in part, based in pranic vibration, deepens its meditative maturation and the meditator begins to identify with such wordings as "The Self," "Atman," "Space," or with the Ineffable of "not this yet 'not-not' this." But, this is just one aspect of the mudra and its pubescence.

Anahata-Nada: From Apollonian to Dionysian Utterance. During adolescent puberty, a characteristic beat, hip, or cool jive talk emerges laden with rad, or far-out nuances and innuendos in pursuit of being with it, of being in synch with the historical moment, outside of handed-down narratives. The ever-slipping-away history of fleeting impermanence is vitally but immaturely embodied in the become-fertile teenager. His now-now-now time comes up against the apollonian, traditional discursive structures of previous generations that live in older narratives, grown distant from the dionysian time. In teen talk, the ontological-temporal tension of the generation gap becomes audible.

Puberties essentially are somato-temporal quickenings. In this postgenital puberty of khecari mudra and the vishudda, (throat) muladhara (sacral base) and ajna chakras (hypothalamic-pineal area), this heightened temporal sense enters utterance in search of "being with it," but this time from a more matured, spiritual-philosophical level. That is, the mudra's hypoglossal yearnings and utterings seek to be in synch with eternal time and the emerging identity, not of the fertile adult, but of the immortal soul.

For what unfolds in the decades-long (multi-incarnational, would be more accurate) emergence of khecari mudra and its precursors, *nabho mudra*, and the "roaring lion" (who mythically emerges from a [spinal] pillar to reward the faithful) simha-asana yogic pose, is an outpouring of vocal signs and intended significances, radiating with lilting trills, sentimental nuances, and enticing innuendoes, of anahata-nada. The flood of maturationally with-it sounds extends from mmuuh to Mmmaaa to aaahh to auummm, rrr, Alah, Yawi, to tears, laughter, melodious or gutteral ecstatic singing, or roaring.

This hypersemantic speaking in tongues skims the mad genius of James Joyce: "*au trop de livre,*" as Lyotard admired the dionysian-linguistic expanse of *Finnegan's Wake*, in contrast to those "academic forms, as rituals originating in piety (as Nietzsche said) which prevent the unrepresentable from being put forward" (Lyotard 1991, pp. 80–81). The ecstatic transcendence of word sense is echoed tragically in the word salad hyposemantic flights of glossolalia, clangings, and neologisms symptomatic of schizophrenia where, under disturbed pranic intensifications, language too breaks down. Thus, the realms of anguishing madness, creative genius, and mystical elevation commingle, as many previous researchers have noted.

The essential difference between transcending or deconstructing narratives for greater clarity, and horribly deconstructing into an agonizing confusion can waver moment to moment for anyone. One's course is often a matter of sustained faith in perhaps the subtlest of trustworthy indications. The difference is in how one feels during and after such speaking and, often, how others around the ecstatic feel, that is: one must have "a place" in this world. But regarding where there is neither sanity or insanity, what can *we* say? (Thus also the traditions of crazy wisdom, suffering gods, and courtly wise fools.)[3]

From the yogic perpective, the egoic orator (from *os*, mouth, to the Latin, *Auriga*, the charioteer, to the *Bhagavad-Gita*'s Arjuna, the yogic charioteer of the five senses and recipient of the eternal wisdom from the Dark One, Krishna), with his great plots is dispersing his overly sublimated linguistic energy back into the body and its potentials. Not genital-sexually, as in the innocent sex-liberational hopes of the sixties, but more as Norman O. Brown mused in his multilayered "erotic sense of reality." Or, as in Lyotard's postmodern call for a world "heterogeneity of language game elements" (1991, p. xxiv). The soul-narrator now utters the grand metanarrative entwined through the patchwork of the world's manifold languages: the dithyramb of a diverse oneness.

In the West, the almost unpredictable immediacy of live improvizational jazz points perhaps most clearly to the same spiritual-temporal dimension as anahata-nada. Cecil Taylor's flurry of piano and hands; Coltrane's back-arching, eye-squinting, warbling squeals, issuing their mittances at the edge of breath and creation. So too, with expressive intricacies too elaborate and mercurial to imitate, the manifold *ragas* and Sanskrit grammatical precisions merely attempt mathemathical formulizations of anahata-nada's efflux of whirring devotional sentiments, dynamic intensities, and esoteric yogic functionings. Thus, noteworthy, is the absence of any written Indian musical notation system, for ragas are to be learned interiorly by feeling, that is, they are to emerge endogenously.

Only via an apollonian classicism does this music enter from without to be learned by rote memory. In its endogenous dionysian form, the call of the maturational moment prevails: just the right innuendo at just the right developmental moment, sometimes as a correlate to the tongue "needing" to arch in just *this* way, to expand the throat in *that* way, opening the heart, offering it to the highest. Perhaps once uttered while looking to the left with arm raised, fingers spread, and head thrown back and then, never again in the same way because there is no developmental-expressive reason to do so, ever again. Thus unfolds through the vibrational medium of sound and feeling each individual's *vocatio* or unique response to the spiritual calling.

The vibrations of one's yearnings thus serve to alchemically churn and heighten the hormonal secretions: such are the endocrine maturations of bhakti yoga "practices" of devotional longing. These "heightened" secretions are depicted mythically by the Dark One, Krishna's love of butter—that is, the love of the Dark Innerspace for the fructified radiances. As they are endogenously reabsorbed into the body, these distillates, from *bindu* to *ojas* and *ambrosial amrita*, prove to be evermore nourishing, perhaps even psychedelic and rejuvenating, in the purest sense. The next round of secretions and emotive sentiments are thus, alchemically, even more ardent and matured.

Altogether, such hormonal-emotional transformations contribute to the sublimative, maturational urdhva-retas process. From the perspective of anahata-nada, conventional therapeutic emotional releases of the same few emotions—anger, sadness, fear—appear as short-circuited by the lack of a spiritual-soteriological direction, even if khecari mudra never emerges but only its distant, foreshadowing lip quiverings of hope.

Shambhavi and Unmani Mudras: The Inner-Outer Visual Puberty. The expanse between shambhavi ("delight gesture of divine knowing-seeing") and unmani mudras ("no-mind mind delight gesture") tracks visual attentiveness from the outer seeing to the inner, esoteric visions and finally, into the enstatic samadhis of the fully matured ensouled body. Here, dualism becomes vestigial, as visual depth perception expands as well into the temporal dimension.

In these puberties, the pineal's ecstatic endorphinlike, light-sensitive melatoninlike, amrita/soma reveals the visual sense of eternal-impermanence temporality. The immortal light of the soul appears at the ajna chakra in the midbrow—the Eckhartian Eye of God through which Individual and Deity simultaneouly see One Another. Endless impermanence becomes visible, the clear light which, purportedly, survives even bodily death. Mind-body, life-death, name-form—various enigmatic dualisms shimmer toward resolution.

In popular parlance, a soft focus of the eyes into the space in front of one's face is a way into shambhavi, as are the various interpersonal gazing meditations of tantra. The clinical eye movement techniques known as "EMDR" (Eye Movement Desensitization and Reprocessing) derive from the release of ocular tensions while focusing mentally on traumatic memories moreso than on the openness of perception that just then emerges as ocular tensions have been released. Thus, gazing or abreactive techniques, however helpful, can divert us from the more endogenous depths where the beauty and poignancy of seeing into sheer-space-in-time can catch our attention. Whatever chronic tensions there may be, and whatever memories one might associate with them, we can become naturally allured and spellbound by the now-emergent simplicity: the innate blossoming-open of the eye-mind-heart complex.

As tensions of all sorts are shed (that one has identified with, like an old shoe), self-identification shifts toward the immortal soul. The gender sense comes into an oscillating balance of the "inner marriage," which mirrors a matured respect and appreciation of the full range of so-called gender traits, which emerge in vivid, if not confusing, contrasts from genital puberty on.

As the rejuvenative secretion of amrita heightens, a fragrant sweetness comes into one's mouth. The spine becomes straight endogenously, as a kind of tumescence of its own long-developing puberty. Thus, the mind enters a matured stillness known as *citta nirodha*, "cessation of mind," or *laya*, "dissolution." Yet, technically, shambhavi mudra covers concentrations only so far as the eyes remain open, and somewhat downward in focus. As the eyes enter a kind of tumescence, they raise slightly. This indicates the beginning of unmani mudra, described below.

Thus, shambhavi mudra is an important phase in raja yoga, or silent, still-bodied meditations. Those paths which ignore the postgenital puberties of the spine, heart, throat, and tongue, typically aim for such concentrations. The held-in-place spine inhibits the full-bodied puberties, as does the minimal attention to the alchemies of urdhvaretas.

Unmani Mudra: Puberty of Cortical Consciousness. In the next puberty, unmani mudra, the cerebrum-mind further outgrows the grip of semantic processing. This "no-mind mind" correlates with various stages of Buddhist and other meditations, whereby the originating Source of moment-to-moment consciousness is lived into with sustained, fully consumed concentration, thus preempting any "later" generations of thoughts, recalled images, or comparative multiplicities of any sort (*smritis*). This is the mental puberty otherwise known as "enlightenment," continuous flow of *shruti* (revealed truth) develops in the silent hush of this womb of consciousness: "The uninterrupted news that grows out of silence" (Rilke 1963, p. 25); Or, as J. D. Salinger put it, "God pouring God into God."

The expanse of these maturations of consciousness begins with pratyahara, the capacity to focus attention to the degree that this focusing itself can be felt and attended to. Next emerges dharana, such focus sustained to the level of a flow of concentration hovering in sheer impermanence itself. Dhyana next emerges as impermanence is continuously dissolved into as the temporal nature of the onflowing of attention, on and on and on and on.

Thus quickens the consolidation of truths: being-in-time, quiddity, the love-bliss of pristine creation as first, sabija-samadhi, constant knowing of the Source, beyond the need for explication, yet with the seeds of thought; and then nirbija-samadhi, constant knowing of the Source so convincingly as to extinguish all seeds of hankering. Time is now let-to-be, as maturation is now complete.

After many lifetimes of yogic gestation at this advanced level of maturation, so it is said, the body enters its fully matured status of divya sharira ("divine light body"). Thus, kundalini yoga logs maturations beyond the meditative absolute of the "enlightened mind" which correlatively fructify in the body as its regenerative rebirth.

For a maternal mystery is found living in that womb space of "neither this nor that" of the meditatively perfect *almost*-void. An inexhaustive generativity arachnidlike lets spin a forever from the *almost*-void that reaches into the tissues of nerve, gland, bone, and blood with an endless love, a cradle of miracles out of which the yogi emerges, again and again. Inching forward each lifetime, she now devotes half of each day to the yogic worship. At the precipice of eternity, she hovers and then falls back into that womb at bodily death again and again. And then, eventually, growing straight through her own death while remaining alive without pause or interruption, she is born into an endless immortality.

Complete Maturation: Divya Sharira and Ultimate Possibility—The Body Becomes One with the Immortal Soul

Thus, in the spinal paths, after some twenty-five to fifty lifetimes of dedicated postgenital cultivations (Krpalvanand 1979, p. 11), the entire body more and more partakes of this fundamental deathlessness, as body, mind, and eternal soul become a fully integrated whole. The term *embodied spiritual truth* leaves the realm of metaphor or vague adjectival and becomes as concretely literal and remarkable as a newborn baby.

Although exceedingly rare and seemingly outlandish, the divine body (divya sharira) is held to be no less or more miraculous or unnatural than the matured pubescent body that supports progenitive immortality and the awe of conception, gestation, and childbirth. (Here I am offering a heightened way of looking at ordinary reproductivity.)

On the one hand, taking a stand for the legitimacy of divya sharira invites a dismissal that might totally unwind my credibility from the perspective of a wide range of thoughtful readers. From the yogic perspective it is just such disbelief in *any, ever*, supernormal spiritual attainments that must also be inspected for its limitations. Such conclusive skepticism and the range of life pursuits that can ensue form the essence of a "worldliness" warned about in many spiritual traditions. It is just such a worldly attitude that, one at a time, can preempt the concerted involvement in the yogic path for each individual.

The last recorded attainment of divya sharira in 1874 is described in *Pathway to God Trod by Saint Ramalingar* (Vanmikanathan 1976), and describes the Saivite yogi, Ramalingar of Mettukkuppam, Tamil Nadu, whose body purportedly dematerialized into a florish of light. The next previous attainment was in the thirteenth century by the South Indian Saint Jnaneshvar, author of the *Jnaneshvar-gita*, a Marathi commentary on the *Bhagavad-gita* from the perspective of kundalini yoga and of *Amrita-Anubhava*, "Experience of Immortality" and the devotional *Abhanga*. In the latter he writes, "Love throbs; I have seen the intensive form of God. He is full of sound and light" (Ranade 1994, p. 195). The most recent appearances of a saint of this maturity (at the turn of the century and in the early 1950s) I have come across were documented in the book *Hariakhan Baba: Known and Unknown* by Baba Hari Dass, a lifelong Indian yogi residing in Santa Cruz, California. Other references to this Babaji, or perhaps to his guru, appear in Govindan's *Babaji* and Satyeswarananda's *Babaji*.

Known by various names, Satyeswarananda and Baba Hari Dass maintain that Hariakhan Baba (literally, "the holy man of Hariakhan Forest") is the several-thousand-year-old "Babaji" who initiated Neem Karoli Baba, known as Richard (Ram Dass) Alpert's guru, and the lineage of Paramahansa Yogananda, one of the first yogis to come to the West at the turn of the century. Yogananda attained additional esteem after his death in 1952 when his corpse showed no signs of decomposition, even after some twenty days. According to Los Angeles Mortuary Director, H. T. Rowe's notarized statement:

> The absence of any visual signs of decay in the dead body of Paramahansa Yogananda offers the most extraordinary case in our experience. . . . No physical disintegration was visible in his body even twenty days after death. . . . No indication of mold was visible on his

skin, and no visible desiccation (drying up) took place in the bodily tissues. This state of perfect preservation of a body is, so far as we know from mortuary annals, an unparalleled one. . . . No odor of decay emanated from his body at any time. . . . There is no reason to say that his body had suffered any visible physical disintegration at all. (Yogananda 1977, p. 575).

According to the late Vinit-muni of Pransali, India, Hariakhan Baba/Babaji is also Lakulisha (150 A.D., born in Kayavarohan, India; organizer of the *Pashupata sect*) who initiated Swami Krpalvanand (whose corpse showed no signs of rigor mortis during the two days before his burial [Kripalu Ashram 1982, p. 30]) in the early 1950s (and perhaps many other unknown yogis). His image remains embossed in the Elephanta Island carvings (dated 500–600) near Bombay, which purport the "practicing [of] yoga as the origin and culmination of all life" (Collins 1988, p. 48).

To help Westerners grasp the significance of these carvings, Indologist James Forbes ranks them with the Pyramids of Egypt; I would also include the mound at Golgotha and the Darwinian Galapagos Islands research. The *Vayu Purana*, the *Kurma Purana*, and the *Linga Purana* discern Lakulisha (or "Nakulisha") as the twenty-eighth incarnation of this immortal embodiment, known first as Shiva, Lord of yoga. The upright club or staff he carries (for which he is also named) represents urdhva-retas, the full evolutionary maturation of homo erectus via his spinal flowing kundalini.

According to the *Pashupata Sutra* and the *Ganakarika Sutra* (Collins 1988, pp. 137–38), the Lakulisha sect practiced an ecstatic ritual including wild laughter, sacred singing, "dancing consisting of [all possible] motions of the hands and feet: upward, downward, inward, outward and shaking motion," a sacred "sound produced by the contact of the tongue-tip with the palate . . . after the dance when the devotee has again sat down and is still meditating on Siva," an "inner worship," and prayer.

Thus we find signs of endogenous pranotthana, sahaja yoga, khecari mudra, and anahata-nada in these dionysian yogic gatherings. We encounter the seamless unity of the emotionally, fully ecstatic with the serenely meditative: that is, sheer fun totally indiscernable from deep profundity: the wild (not misunderstood as a ferocious chaos, but as sahaja) ars erotica bloom of the postgenital puberties as a joyous singularity of mind, body, and spirit.

The *Pashupata* sect, which spread throughout Hindu, Buddhist, and Jain India for some six hundred years (and originating the yogic lineage of Gorakhanath and Matsyendranath and all modern hatha yogis), was most unique in Indian history in its scorning of the caste system and its belief in a diety capable of bestowing forgiveness and soteriological grace beyond the mechanistic dictates of karma, that is, of utter mercifulness not governed by the severe logic of retribution. They believed that, as homeless forest dwellers, they transformed the enmity of city dwellers who derided them by never striking back and instead blessed them. Given the openheartedness, the breadth of emotionality inclusive of anahata-nada outpourings and shamanic, animallike dancing within the Pashupata yoga, I conjecture that this sect functioned not only as a sainted spiritual community, but, for some few, as a psychiatric haven, drug and criminal rehabilitation center, and homeless shelter. As with the appearance of many other saints, heaven lived on earth, and those within its fold were, for a time, redeemed into real life.

As Feuerstein reasons, one of the explanations for the success of the Pashupata sect was that "it offered a sense of belonging that was not based on the prevalent caste system" and that it allowed for a wide range of "emotion-based experience of the sacred" (Feuerstein 1989, p. 203). Clearly, although austere and devoted to the soteriological sentiments and yogic worship, this was not an elite religious order. I would add that in such a community, the concepts of "sanity" and "insanity" had been blurred or transcended in the discovered all-embracing (panaceaic?) sense of belonging and forgiveness.

Yet, probably not through analytic group explorations of childhood pasts were these integrations of "persona" and "shadow" attained. In fact, these Jungian terms may be inapt. Likewise their "animallike roars" must not be termed "regressive catharses." Instead, whatever growth came to the Pashupatis (and their cross-cultural similars) was more likely through contact with the forward flow of the dionysian Mother-Father of flowing t,t,t, time. Thus, for a while for all concerned—and a most wide-ranging "all" it was—there was a place in the world, and a spiritual one, at that.

As the first Western "spiritual psychologist," Ludwig Feuerbach (from whom Buber took the phrase "I-Thou") noted in his critique of the Christian penchant to overly revere suffering, such "heathen religions" as the Pashupata sect may have something to offer a postmodern, post-Freudian world:

> To suffer is the highest command of Christianity. . . . While amongst the heathens [sic] the shout of sensual pleasure mingled itself in the worship of the gods, amongst . . . the ancient Christians, God is served with sighs and tears. But as where sounds of sensual pleasure make a part of the cultus, it is a sensual God, a God of life, who is worshipped, as indeed these shouts of joy are only a symbolical definition of the nature of the gods to whom this jubilation is acceptable; so also the sighs of the Christians are tones which proceed from the inmost [Chris-

tian] soul, the inmost nature of *their* [my emphasis] God. The God expressed by the cultus . . . not the God of sophistical theology—is the true God of man. (Feuerbach 1957 [1841], p. 61)

Suffering—"getting in touch with buried pain"—as verifying the depth of a redemptive-healing path permeates both Western Religion and psychotherapy. Indeed, the psychotherapeutic ministrations bear an unsuspected continuity with the type of sin-oriented soul searching of the former. That even the cries of anguish and longing could turn *ecstatic*: such is another path of redemption. As Feuerbach notes, it is a path of longing, penitence, and devotion, *and* joy and sensual pleasure. It is a path of life. Yet, the yogic depth in which "the sensual" and "the spiritual" merge in ecstatic physio-spiritual maturations is as undreamed-of in the West (before or since Feuerbach's "blow to Christianity," which helped inaugurate "scientific psychology") as is the notion of postgenital puberties of the spine, heart, throat, and mind of the flowing kundalini. It is a soul-bodily depth that forms the basis of another sort of psychotherapy that aims to make life as beautiful as possible, for this precious fleeting time.

Indeed, consider the existence of innate pleasures and optimisms convincingly more potent and rewarding than those surges associated with the capacities of genital puberty, with the (over)accumulations of wealth and property, with the anxious passions for "life" born of exaggerated fears of aging and dying. Consider *that* spiritual pleasure and much more than another form of psychotherapy looms before us as a redemptive-healing path.

CHAPTER 4

Spiritual Emergence: Toward a Spirituality-Inclusive Psychopathology

INTRODUCTION

In 1994, a step was taken by mainstream psychology toward admitting kundalini phenomena and spiritually oriented narratives into clinical practice. I refer to the newly devised Religious Issues Nonsyndromatic V 62.89 Code and Glossary of Culture-Bound Syndromes (Appendix I) in the *Diagnostic and Statistical Manual-IV (DSM-IV)*. These inclusions in the psychiatric lexicon could at least nuance many of the diagnostic categories by granting them an influx of spiritual import. Further, the integration of somatic and spiritual-psychological realms that kundalini yoga attempts correlates with various recent scientific findings.

BODY, SOUL, AND THE SCIENCE OF THE SPIRIT

Psychoneuroimmunological studies have verified that soteriological sentiments (love, compassion) are significant factors in ameliorating medical conditions (Boryeshenko and Boryeshenko 1994; Cantin and Genest 1986). That the healing biochemistries of compassionate feelings are found in the saliva (as "sIgA"; McClelland and Kirshnit 1987; Rein and McCraty 1994; Rein, McCraty, and Atkinson 1995)) also suggests an association with amrita precursors, which also appear in saliva. These psychosomatic findings linking admiration, compassion, and love to physical healing are thus relevant to *DSM-IV* Section 316, "Psychological Factors Affecting Medical Condition," which is "reserved for those situations in which the psychological factors have a clinically significant effect on the course or outcome of the general medical condition" (American Psychiatric Assoc. 1994, *DSM-IV*, p. 676).

Thus, in a holistic, spiritually informed *DSM-V*, *positive* psychological factors affecting medical conditions would also be included in Sec. 316. It would, therefore, seem helpful to catalogue in future *DSM*'s the *characteristically healthy* aspects or talents which coexist specifically in people suffering from each of its hundreds of more psychological disorders. Such data would help guide clinicians in seeing these relative strengths, and thus contribute to the therapeutic process. And, more complexly, as Byrd's double-blind (subjects and testers are unaware of control and experimental group assignments) study of the power of prayer in healing published in the *Southern Medical Journal* purports, the beneficient wishes of unknown and distant others can prove salutory. Should therapists cultivate the best in clients to treat their disorders, and think well of them too?

Further, the National Institute on Aging sponsored "Nun Study" on the reduced incidence of Alzheimer's and other degenerative diseases as related to a lifestyle based upon soteriological sentiments is noteworthy. Recent studies of pineal melatonin verifying its light-transducing and antiaging capacities have already corroborated some five thousand years of yogic praisings of soma-amrita, the radiant, antiaging "nectar" of the pineal (and its cognates in African, ancient Greek, and many indigenous cultures). As Klatz and Goldman note, "scientists now believe [the light-sensitive pineal] is a kind of natural clock, helping us to synchronize our activities with nature" (1996, p. 28). Yoga would add that by a soteriological lifestyle of feeling the lovable aspects of oneself (esoterically, via meditative love of the gods of the pineal locus and beyond) and others, dharmic ("synchronized with nature") development ensues engendering the tastable nectars of eternal impermanence and the amritic immortal-soul sense.

While pineal expert Pierpaoli notes that melatonin "tells the body when to enter [genital] puberty" (ibid., p. 29), I draw from kundalini yoga to also assign the triggering of the postgenital puberties to the pineal locale (and the medically unexplored spinal sacrum, and other sites). Likewise, sustained levels of melatonin are being considered by scientists as "age reversing." Yet, only endogenous melatonin has, so far, reliably shown any such effectiveness. Thus, cultivation of the soteriological sentiment secretions within their yogicly originating locations are being scientifically verified as salutory and perhaps regenerative, if not also spiritually redemptive.

The inclusion in Appendix I of the "*qi-gong* psychotic reaction," so similar to the "kundalini syndrome" or, more accurately, pranotthana manifestation, is clearly significant. For Americans involved in qi-gong, meditation, or yoga have also reported problematic experiences of nonordinary consciousness (Sannella 1977). That some problems arise as a result of the most auspicious of spiritual experiences, long documented in diverse religions, must, in such cases, also be considered.

The Appendix I conditions of *dhat, jiryan,* and *sukra prameha* of the subcontinent and *shenkui* of China are more esoteric and may seem like cultural oddities from a conventional perspective. Yet, from the yogic viewpoint, these seminal concerns (and their female correlates) reflect, albeit hypochondriacally, the importance of urdhva-retas and the hormonal maturation of endogenous soteriological sentiments (inclusive of amritalike endorphin/melatonin). As physical precipitates of temporality itself—felt as biorhythms, puberties, awe, lineage hopes, longings, and satieties—these mutable secretions are held as underlying the ever-maturing sense of eternal impermanence and soul identity. Here we must resort to Marcuse's suggestion that the instincts be understood spiritually. And, following Foucault, in order to understand these other-cultural concerns, we must free our view from the psychoanalytic mono-interpretation.

At a more detailed level of symptomatology, as we learn more about khecari mudra, the fact that those with schizophrenia often have an overly arched palate (*DSM-IV*, p. 280) becomes curious, as do their "word salad" verbalizations. Such phenomena, along with the common rocking movements, crawling sensations, and religious delusions imply some connection with pranotthana and the puberties of mind beyond language and its ego-narrator gone awry.

While the *DSM-IV* distinction between self-induced, nonpathological meditative states and pathological Dissociative/Depersonalization states is important diagnostically, the implications of their continuity is perhaps more noteworthy. For *why* it is that "voluntarily induced experiences of depersonalization or derealization [do, in fact,] form part of meditative and trance practices that are prevalent in many religions and cultures" (*DSM-IV*, p. 488) reaches into cross-cultural explorations at the very edge of the mystery of life and death, and into the possibility of a continuity of consciousness from the former, eternally into the latter. As theologian-psychologist, Ludwig Feuerbach proposed:

> [C]onsciousness is essentially infinite in its nature. The consciousness of the infinite is nothing else than the consciousness of the infinity of consciousness; or, in consciousness of the infinite, the conscious subject has for his object the infinity of his own nature. (Feuerbach 1957 [1841], pp. 2–3)

It is in such vertiginous sentient depths that one can find or lose joys and terrors, personalizations and depersonalization, realities and derealities. And it is in contrast to such depths that the language we ordinarily use to describe the external world can grow ambiguous and seem inadequate. (Perhaps we approach Wittgenstein's ineffable "silence.") Indeed, "ordinary" consciousness (consciousness unappreciative of the "essential nature" Feuerbach and others have ascribed to it) and the averaged appraisal of the soulful emotionalities can seem like shadows of their full potentials. Or one might say surreally, "everything feels up for grabs."

At such times of shaken faith in what is real—whether induced through voluntary meditations or some trauma—we might use the words *unreal, unfamiliar, strange, mechanical,* or *feel[ing] like an automaton* (as in *DSM-IV*, p. 488) to describe the ordinary world and know quite well why we are speaking thusly. Similarly, the discourses of meditative traditions commonly note that enlightenment includes a sense of not "being" the body, a body which seems to live with the simplest of needs, autonomically—that is, by the power of some mysterious grace. As Meister Eckhart told his inquisitors: "I live because I live." In this "draft of the infinite" (as Heidegger termed it), one might report understatedly a mere "disturbance in one's sense of time" (*DSM-IV*, p. 488).

And in this "other time sense," we might achieve (or be shown by a therapist) greater competencies with faith, hope, gratitude, and forgiveness than we previously believed possible, as many successful meditators claim. We might find greater despair than we thought possible too, but, then, what do we *really* believe, as the hours, months, events, and years go by? And, then, what do we want to believe at the end, and what will we *then* experience? These are questions of faith and "reality."

Thus, within conventional psychopathology, dissociative states are seen as part of a "built-in" posttraumatic survival response where consciousness goes "somewhere else" to minimize the shock of a painful experience. This "elsewhere" might be more than a numbing flight from terror, anger, or grief: In a soteriological healing narrative, it might include breakthroughs into tearful moments of "saintly understanding" and "detachment" too. (See chapter 1, note 3.)

Thus, depersonalization can be seen as degrees of awe, from the reverential to the overwhelming, which have perhaps suddenly and violently initiated the ego into a realm where spiritually oriented psychotherapies might help convert any disorientations into moments of enlightenment, a maturational challenge that is spiritually paradigmatic. For such experiences belong to the long and highly vulnerable prepubescence of those postgenital puberties which can culminate beyond the normative "ego" as a matured soul-identity within the daunting currents of eternal impermanence temporality. That the *DSM* notes that "depersonalization is a common experience" could indicate that such phenomena are just part of human development, a kind of molting of identitifications.

From the spiritual states of detachment known in yoga as *vairagya* (a hallmark sign of the spinal puberty), a grievous sense of tragic absurdity can seem to surround traumatic events. The depersonalized trauma victim is thus in the grips of a spiritual maturation, an anguishing rite of passage where his compassionate faith might grow beyond a felt emptiness and any diminished emotionalities provoked by the devastating event.

Violence and abuses can themselves come to appear as the sadly unnecessary reverberations of underutilized soteriological sentiments. Thus, what one is to "relive" as the "unrepressed truth" in abreactive posttrauma therapies becomes more complex from this perspective. From "Nothing happened" to the destination of "It really happened" can land on a more emotionally complex "It" than is conventionally maintained. And the reliving might be more effectively and less riskily done from the stance of a maturing adult rather than as a regressed child identity.

As the soul identity matures, the actual horrors can seem far less real than more ideal possibilities that lived in potentia, everso nearby. Thus, derealizations and realizations of one sort or another—"trials of faith"—are crucial shiftings in the soteriological maturation. For the so-maturing, what seems real or possible (or who or what one is) is affected by maturing moods of faith, confidence, and optimism, yet is susceptible as well to the false optimisms of fantasy, mania, and grandiosity.

Change on ever-larger scales can feel trepidly possible, whether for the addicted whose Higher Power gives him some detachment from his bodily cravings (or from his own desparate grandiosity [denial] whereby he brags of his invulnerability to drug addiction) or those saints such as Gandhi and the Dalai Lama (or people you know) who have matured to the Buberian "dreadful point" of loving all people and who pray for their own attackers (even *while* horribly outraged).

Yes, under the pressures of multiculturalism, the growing interest in spirituality, and recent laboratory findings, a door in the thick walls of conventional psychology has most certainly been cracked opened. Walls of empirical standards that kept out the dross of "evil spirit" mental illness etiologies of the past, now admit the gold of benign spiritual potencies. The light that now enters, however, could become far more than a glimmer buried in the back pages of a psychiatric text or in isolated holistic medical studies, or in transpersonal meditative experiences of endless presence. This light, already widely known as the common sentiments of gratitude, awe, apology, and forgiveness, could, for some, grow exceedingly bright as Allama sang, like "a million million suns."

AWE OF ENDLESS IMPERMANENCE: THE CRUX OF SPIRITUAL EMERGENCE-EMERGENCY

In continuing our explorations of time, psychotherapeutic narrative, and spirituality, I will suggest that in vivo even the most psychotic, psychopathic, suicidal, or organic conditions are riddled with spiritual poignancy and even the most profound enlightenment confronts its attainer with new problems and challenges. For the essence of "crisis" is a *temporal* urgency which can hover ambiguously between "danger" and "maturational opportunity."

Some have said this is the import of The Cross (or Crux-crisis): the vertical breakthrough of the Eternal into horizontal, mundane time. Thus, the inherent ambiguity in the terms *spiritual emergency* and *spiritual emergence*. For, glimmers of eternality inherent to all moments shine moreso within such hormonally heated pressures, whatever the inciting fires. And such crisis-born epiphanies of the *eternal* can easily be misconstrued as the *interminability of* some specific difficulty now at hand.

Thus, conventional therapists with their past-oriented hermeneutic can overinterpret a client's reported fears of "endless" rage or his tears as signs of "vast pockets of long-repressed affect." So assured, they proceed with years of cathartic work seeking discharges from the past exclusively. Any awe of the eternal that broke into ordinary time via the crisis and was also part of the grievous moment is missed. Bereavements, momentous beginnings, and crises of all sorts commonly stir the impermanence-awe into mundane time.

Even the child's terrible disillusionment of his parental safety net becoming a web of horrific abuse partakes of this posttraumatic awe where a vast, sheer space ruptures into his life via security-ripping events. Sheer and (nonomnipotently) benign? Perhaps so. Thus, child protection agencies and other responsible adults try to deal with those aspects of abuse beyond the nonomnipotence of spiritual succor, yet, hopefully, guided by its inexhaustive wisdom.

Far less horrifically, attachment to a moment of bliss that then passes results characteristically in a disorienting anguish. Thus, the fleetings of a too-prized ecstasy can be nostalgically gripped by the dubious inquiry of "When is that good time going to return?" instead of being appreciated as a fleeting grace of endless impermanence, or as poignant longing. The condescending impatience of "spiritual materialism," can skip one over much of life, waiting only to meditate, assume an air of superiority, or become drug dependent, seeking only repeat peak experiences.

The so-called transcendence or psychosis? overly binary diagnostic debate initiated by my predecessor at the Kundalini Clinic, Lee Sannella, often revolves around this phenomenon of some inner soteriological struggle being suddenly and oscillatingly blown up to staggering proportions by the energetic stirrings. That the first chakra, where kundalini resides, is associated with the adrenals is an anatomical way of saying that spiritual awe and fear (not necessarily danger-evoked fearsomeness, for there may be little to fear, except awe misconstrued as fear, followed by fear-inducing, imagined dangers) are close cousins.

Here we encounter the Kiekegaardian "sickness unto death": a circularity of skepticism/cynicism regarding anything benignly awesome in someone who now encounters "awe of the eternal," yet unnamed as such. Both struggling *to* believe in this eternality and unable to fully enough believe, he longs for an ending to the discomfort of this no-man's-land that does not come. For his situation is unlike longing for an ordinary discomfort to end. Indeed, *how difficult to sense an end to even a slight hint of the Infinite!* And worse when It cannot be named credibly as such. Thus, this verbal misconstrual helps accelerate fear into panic: the harrowing thought of "what *next?*" mushrooms upon itself and all around, horribly.

For, what characterizes this awe most is how completely beyond egoic intentions it stretches, even if we do name it properly. Only the soul identity can measure up, a matter that for the afflicted is incredulous. (Yet, such anxieties are exactly the prepubescent struggles of the postgenital puberties into the endless soul identity.) The alternating despair that there might be *no* ending, even in death, and then that death might be an obliterating end—whichever stand one takes, both are dreadful. To call such problems and their trials of faith a matter of "premature transcendence" underestimates the potency of the Divine Revelation which, according to their own reports, has jolted even the most matured of saints and saviors for thousands of years.

As well, any specific feeling or worry experienced within this Kierkegaardian "category of the Infinite" thus portends obsessively *to* last for an eternity. Sick with a cold, one thinks, "It's okay, in two days, it'll be over"; sick with treatable cancer, one thinks (hopes), "After the treatment, I'll be okay." But touching a moment of endlessness throws any worry onto this vast temporal context with its unique hormonal substrate, thus the inherent soteriological sentiments shudder. And, as I assert, unnamed as such, we touch it in many moments: rushing in traffic or to meet deadlines, at funerals or weddings, having colds or AIDS, or feeling the mind bloom into unmani mudra. Its extreme tumults, however, can lead to (what we call) psychotic terrors, manic flights or depressive spiralings.

Thus, unless we can make subtle temporal distinctions that include possible "Awesome Eternality Experiences," these glimmerings of the endlessness of time can result in us believing that it is our mundane *worry* that could last forever. Or, in the soteriological shudder—if deprived of a sense of the merciful and the full potencies of gratitude, apology, and forgiveness—we can become entangled in the overly deterministic purgatorial narratives of Jonathan Edwardsian moralities or of deterministic adult-child syndromatic etiologies and terminal survivorhood identities.

One feels doomed, hears inner voices of damnation, or obsessively believes herself (vengefully, then sorrowfully) to be a determined product of past events. Deprived of a yogic hermeneutic and praxes, some will fear the "strange" bodily sensations that are auspicious quickenings of the postgenital maturations. In any case, in this far more vast time sense, our problems (and the possible iatrogenics of their too severely worded narratives) mingle with the Eternal and now we begin to say we feel "doomed with no sense of an ending."

And, ironically, the greater the sense of eternal time—the eerie deathless grandeur of heaven—the greater the potential terror (or derealizing lull) of this seeming endless hell. And learning to accept or "witness" one's dread is only relatively helpful, for this guidance might never plumb the temporal depths that flow beneath it all: accepting the eternality sense itself and partaking of its mercies in which all things keep *passing* and, most particularly, perpetual "presence" itself: *This* is the uroboric "deep present," which would seem to be a far more awesome matter than many present-oriented therapies allow for.

PSYCHOPATHOLOGY AND SOTERIOLOGICAL UNDEREXPRESSIONS

Various of the *DSM-IV* disorders can be viewed, in part, as deficiencies in specific soteriological skills. Unable to recover from the incompetency in any other way and thus mature soulfully, the so-diagnosed adapt in characteristically problematic ways. Incompetent in voicing appreciative thank you's (fearing obligation or worthlessness or in the shyness of receiving), one backs away from the nourishments of receiving into the Avoidant or even Schizoid Disorder or, strives only to give and then reports feeling "unappreciated" as in Dependent or Histrionic Disorders. Incompetent in apologizing and receiving forgiveness, one obsessively seeks an impossible perfection to avoid ever needing to feel them or develops a Narcissistic, hostile fear of criticism, or plunges into "unforgiveable" guilt or Psychopathic remorselessness. Incompetent at giving forgiveness, one goes on blaming others and develops a Passive-Aggressive, or even Borderline victimistic stance.

Yet, underlying such deficiencies will be the auspicious, fearsome/awesome awakening into the flow of eternal impermanence that becoming competent in some soteriological skill foments. And, ironically, it will often be, in part, the loss of a sadomasochistic vengeful raison d'etre, an "unbearable" shyness, or "it can't last" trepidations concurrent with entering real, impermanent time that can send the soterio-neophyte back to his disorder or addictive substance. In all cases, one lives at a colder distance from the graceful flow, repelled by the first shudders of an otherwise redemptive awe, misconstrued as fear. As one matures, he, skeptically, fears being unequal to himself.

THE SPIRITUAL CRISES OF MINOR ENLIGHTENMENTS

The *DSM-IV* V 62.89 description of "conversion to a new faith" is clear enough in purport:

> Examples include distressing experiences that involve loss or questioning of faith, problems associated with *conversion to a new faith* [my emphasis], or questioning of spiritual values that may not necessarily be related to an organized church or religion or religious institution. (*DSM-IV*, p. 685)

But what if it were to cover not only sectarian, chosen conversions from one faith-tradition to another, but those "conversions" to *greater awe and faith* (not just "losses" of faith) resulting from transformative spiritual experience? "New" faith here would not mean just switching to a different sectarian denomination or questioning universal spiritual values, but a *new degree* of sensed endlessness to one's faith or a disturbing/daunting increased sense of hopefulness, forgiveness, compassion, or appreciativeness altogether. And let us assume that such revelations can occur to people with borderline, paranoid, developmentally disabled, substance-addiction, manic, depressive, or psychotic conditions. Indeed, such conditions may be concurrent with confused graspings of newly emergent soteriological sentiments in fluttering, dionysian ways "not necessarily . . . related to an organized [apollonian] church or religion."

Thus, the distressing experiences I allude to come not from questioning, changing, or losing faith, but from going forward trepidly into greater degrees of faith that emerge from our just-now, newly emergent confidence, surmounting waveringly lurking doubts or losses. Recall, this difficulty is what Kierkegaard used the term *angst* to refer to originally: what happens just before and *forever after* we begin to try, or have finally chosen, *to* believe. This is the yogic ground of sequential postgenital puberties: lifelong spirit-body maturation, and the wavering "ground" that is the essence of what the term *Religious Issues* has, for centuries, uniquely referred to in all organized or nonorganized "religion": re-alignment with the more eternal Truths.

Although V 62.89 is a welcome addition to the *DSM* for anyone interested in more spirituality-friendly psychologies, its approach to

188 WORDS FROM THE SOUL

matters of faith misses the uniqueness of this domain of human experience. Furthermore, as might be expected, there are untold ramifications to this new code for therapists to consider.

Yes, "religious concern" does not need to take the form of beliefs, or value systems found within organized church institutions, as the code clearly grants. But more fundamentally (or phenomenologically), what characterizes "religions" from psychologies, political ideologies, health philosophies, or most any other hermeneutic endeavor or life praxis is that they deal with daunting awesomeness, with wincing poignancies, with surges of hopes and longings to forgive or apologize or be forgiven, with mysteries beyond certainty, with attainments beyond the mundane.

If a church or organized faith need not be part of the client's reported situation for the presenting problem to be considered spiritual, then if some of this spiritual phenomenology is convincingly present in a client's report—even if the term *spiritual* is not uttered—a therapist might consider whether a particular client might benefit from considering his problem in nonsectarian, philosophical, or even "spiritual" terms.

Thus, far short of the postgenital puberties, however, and to avoid the problems of sectarianisms, proselytism, or dogmatism, I make one simple translation across the span of formalized religions to serve as a discrete spiritual hermeneutic principle, the grace of: Jesus, Mother, Kali, Shiva, Great Spirit, Yahweh, Allah, Buddha, Lutheranism, Calvinism, and the like, is to be understood as the inexplicable flow of precious time.

Our psychological problems, now approached as "temporo-spiritual problems," are with this very preciousness. Hot tempers, depression, substance abuse, narcissistic avoidance, and psychosis are some of their forms. And, it is within this same flow of time—no longer to be considered mere, quantifiable duration—that I locate the universal soteriological sentiments: the waverings of feeling that, we are told, can true the course of human life.

Thus, a *DSM-"V"* might augment the adjective *distressing* with terms like *confusing, unfamiliar,* or *unusually profound* or even *nondual experiences* to qualify certain Religious Issues. For, beyond too-apollonian, binary contrasts (good and bad, or *holos* and *pathos*) lives the moment-to-moment dionysian Time and the daunt of its ever-returning, ever-hopeful t,t,t,t,t mercurial nature.

Any such spiritually attuned psychopathology must reflect this auspicious and dynamically transformative, temporal side of difficult experiences, from infancy onward. Thus, the long arc of the eternal sense can underlie suicidal depression (the desperations of which the more romantic seeker names as rapturous, yet painful longings), as I described in chapter 2. The immobilities of catatonia (immobilities which the still-sitting meditator turns to her spiritual advantage) can be seen as the endless time sense turned terrifyingly morbid, if not also vengefully stationary. The bipolar swings from hopeless "overness" to a hyperhopeful limitlessness, too, pivot exaggeratedly upon the shifting sands of the temporal-hormonal moment (temporo-hormonal shifts of "cooling night-moon" and "heating day-sun," which the hatha yogi cultivates and balances with his psychophysical practices).

Let us consider briefly three *DSM-IV* Personality Disorders from our perspective of daunting eternal impermanence instead of as mere products of an all-determining developmental past and the clinical narratives that ignore or miss the constant and momentous phenomenology of sheer time passage itself. And let us note that these diagnoses range from mild neurotic styles to the more severe and intractible conditions.

BORDERLINE PERSONALITY DISORDER (BPD)

The conventional focus on inadequate "ego structure" and "superego development" in the Borderline Personality is another way of saying that this diagnosis refers to extreme difficulties with mercurial impermanence and the grace-truing powers of the soteriological sentiments. The awe and preciousness of time has become a near-constant sense of threatening urgency where eternal impermanence is felt as too fleeting and too relentless, and vengefully so.

Typically in the BPD, others are blamed for the difficult and, now, exaggerated poignancy of time passage. Merely saying goodbye or ending sessions swells into: "You don't really care about me! What good are you!" Then, again, other moments will be clinged to in desperate hopefulness, but only to the point where the nostalgia of time passing makes the clinging seem unbearable. Then the characteristic distancing behaviors emerge, in thermostatic fashion, trying to keep the sense of time passage within an exceedingly narrow range of tolerance. Or is it "the mercurial" which shifts "the so-disordered?" For, in this metapsychology, ego and time passage subjectivity are one and, as "soul," endlessly so.

What double binds such a patient is that getting better also brings him into the precious, mercurial flow where time with others becomes more valued. If the patient is not to devalue others—to avoid missing the valued others more than is so far comfortable (missing them "too much"), or getting his hopes up more than is pessimistically usual (getting "too hopeful")—based upon his current set points, a felt-as-dangerous recalibration of the previous intimacy thermostat must take place.

As skillfulness with the soteriological sentiments is gained, confidence waveringly accrues. The walking-on-eggshells sense grows into a firmer ground, dignified now as "constant impermanence." As competence with apology and forgiveness grows, reconciliations within the characteristic stormy relationships associated with this pathology become easier to accomplish. As the skills of missing and longing mature, the patient becomes more able to sustain valuing others, and her intimacy set points give berth to a wider range of the temporal phenomenology. Of course, bringing significant others into sessions with the patient can facilitate progress, to everyone's satisfaction.

Flighty vengefulness (against the "unbearable" poignancies of time passage) gives this disorder its characteristic impulsive aggressiveness and paranoid readiness for "splitting": assessing the same person in the shifting moods within just a few moments as friend, then as foe. Here, vengefulness is taken as the rebellion against time, as noted by Nietzsche, against the "It was." Thus "uncovering" therapies have proven unwieldy: they heap up the sense of difficulties with the past as their explanations can just become more of the problem.

His rages appear as sadomasochistic enjoyments of vengefulness that dissipate in the more tremulous pleasures of forgiveness, and in the greater competency with the impermanent time sense that can thereby ensue. Every gain, for months or years, is both calming in fostering a sense of how solid time passage is and immediately disconcerting as this constancy is felt to be one of relentless impermanence. Thus, therapeutic progress is extremely difficult, the very success of which is threatening because its price is the eventual termination of the so-helpful relationship. As improvements emerge, time passage is felt as fragile, boring, and then as kind of peaceful. As soteriological competences mature, a warmth comes from the soul and any berating, inner voices (the soteriological superego grown alienated and severe) undergo the transformation described under Paranoid Personality Disorder.

ANTISOCIAL PERSONALITY DISORDER

The Antisocial Disordered person has found in the fleeting impermanence and its flow of merciful forgiveness a kind of intoxication in the relentless stream of next moments. Within its glandular alchemies he brews a high of constant, illicit self-forgiveness or unforgiving vengefulness gone awry into a cold, exploitative remorselessness. The relapses of the substance abuser, "just this once," too take advantage of this mercy. In the criminal extremes and if caught, incarceration merely demarcates an amount of time-to-be-done. Thus, the criminal is thought of as particularly lacking in character, for it is only the actual soteriological sentiments that can engender it (thus his tenaciously held nonsnitching code and other gang loyalties gives him a vestige of honor).

Perhaps his redemption, should it be attained, is so inspiring because he then comes to feeling simultaneously terribly guilty and spiritually innocent and compassionately understanding of others who suffer and make mistakes. Yet, he dwells upon the need for forgiveness (but not to the exclusion of his spiritual innocence: for redemption is *of* the innocent soul and it is in knowing this that he feels hopeful and worth seeking or bestowing forgiveness) since it, moreso, can bring him character. Such gains, however, place him in the flow of impermanence, exposing him to its tempting mercies, awe, and a heightened sense of visibility, perhaps so shyly or shamefully, that recidivism seems to offer shelter.

The juvenile delinquent version of this diagnosis (Conduct Disorder) is complicated by the heightened sense of a fleeting impermanence concurrent with adolescent puberty. The immortal sense, engendered by the emergent procreative powers add a taunting, felt invulnerabilty to those youths so troubled (in "need of limits," as it is said). "You can't make me do anything. I don't care what you (authority) do to me." It is as if spiritual awe has become an intoxicating fearlessness and feigned omnipotence. That a sobering, inspiring adult, who is lovable, loving, and (somehow) *inherently* commanding of respect (a mensch) is the best therapy I have seen, further substantiates soteriological approaches, moreso than analytic ones, which the youth tries to manipulate, or purely punitive approaches, which heighten his rebelliousness and cynicism.

The psychopathological lying associated with these disorders can be seen as exploitative plays with the inherent uncertainty and referentially insecure basis of all language games. The con artist's expert way with words emerges from this sophisticated sense of the limitations of language, as does his characteristic sensitivity to psychobabble or to those whom he perceives as somehow spiritually weaker than himself. That is, as someone whose embodied walk does not measure up to his talk.

We must also consider that cultural authority can become psychopathic or insensitive and exploitative of sectors of a populace. Rebellion, from madly violent to Gandhian passive resistance, are responses to such institutionalized madness.

PARANOID PERSONALITY DISORDER

The Paranoid Personality Disordered person's "pervasive distrust and suspiciousness of others" (*DSM-IV*, p. 934) appears as a difficulty with the existential uncertainty and indeterminacy of the relentless flow of moments whose wavering subtleties are perpetually overinterpreted as "dangers." At least danger is a kind of certainty, even if there is little ostensible threat: the certainty that vigilance is necessary, for certainly, we need to be safe.

Linguistically, the uncertain "is" of narrative selfhood feels it must bear the impossible burden of constantly being safe by construing narrative certainties, no matter how outlandish. The first linguistic certainty construes the standing condition of IS as "categorically dangerous." Thus, in this logic and axiomatically so, the first-person singular of all autobiographic narratives stands as the Vigilant Endangered One. Such singlemindedness fosters the characteristic thematic obsessions which convert the maturing concentrations of pratyhara into an eye-narrowing vigilance. The inward-turning wordless gaze often proves "too dangerous" and all mental powers are devoted to excessively clever decodings of "the underlying plot" hidden in (inherent) linguistic ambiguities and mercurial body language innuendos. And, hermeneutically, the more insidious the plot, the better, for it can be used to explain more and more of the dangers that are everywhere.

When sustained glimmers of the vastness of eternal time emerge—yet unnamed as such—all previous suspiciousness is thrown onto this larger-than-life canvas and the psychotic state can arise. This "bad trip" foments, ironically, from overheated soteriological chemistries of wonder and awe of the infinite into dread and terror and the life-or-death urgencies that now seem to justify and require hostile behaviors.

The terror escalates beyond bearability as estimations of its duration merge confusedly with the (unnamed-as-such) glimmers of eternal time. Oh no! This might never end! Oh no, oh nooohaaahaaaa!! Followed by hyperventilated, morbidly triggered sahaja pranayama that, under ideal conditions, would reflect a sudden passionate love of the infinite spiritus-breath and anahata-nada postlinguistic awesome utterances. For what Grof called "the sea that the mystic swims in and the psychotic person drowns in" is the bottomless sea of nearly ineffable, infinite time.

The Wittgensteinian language game sense of all communication is greeted, not with philosophical perspicuity, but with suspicion: "You're trying to play with my head, I know it!" The innocent imprecisions of language inherent to its play has, pathologically, become a serious matter. The "play" of the play is gone. The wisdom that always prefers a good-natured game becomes a dire competitiveness. Persecution, an extreme mode of endangered otherness, is conjured and other players become frightened too. Thus the miscuings spiral and the dangers intuited in one's paranoia prove to be true. No wonder psychoanalysis, with its own suspicion that special words are hiding *something*, found paranoid schizophrenia untreatable by its classical methods.

If paranoia subsides, shyness must then be mastered so that compliments can be more fully (blushingly) received, instead of with a suspicious "*Why* (a "why" emergent from the discomfort with the soft charm of his own glowing shyness) are you giving this to me." Yet, a simple "Thank you" works unbelievably well (thus, the disbelief in its powers). The client then receives the nourishment and feels both momentarily lovable and resourceful *to* his therapist-benefactor who, too, glows with being nourished by the appreciation she has just received *from* her benefactor-client. Equality and benign sharing have been attained. But only for a while: for such is impermanence.

As in many severe "temporal disorders" such as paranoia or borderline conditions, the revealing-concealing quality of time passage and the bodily blushes or sensational surges of its rhythms can be experienced as very disturbing and very alluring. Thus, it is especially important to discuss the limitations of the therapeutic relationship as excluding nonsession friendship or romance of any sort, but instead as existing for the sake of the client's greater life outside of the session.

The discussion, clearly, must be respectful of the high hopefulness that might be invested in such imagined possibilities. For, in a soteriological therapy, a great degree of appreciation will be given to the client, who must then create such friendships or romances with others drawing from the learning laboratory of the more limited clinical setting. This "for the sake of . . ." purpose to the therapeutic relationship and its trying limitations must be embraced by both parties. The therapist disclosure: "I believe in this therapeutic structure, but I feel the loss too" can be a very helpful admission. The limitations (overdefined as "boundaries") can motivate the client to enhance her external life. Again, bringing in significant others facilitates achieving these goals.

Regarding paranoia, auditory hallucinations emerge from the same tiered sense of "higher intelligences in the head" that meditative paths call "the heaven realms of wrathful/beneficient dieties." The following therapeutic metaphor is a means of transforming such wrathful dieties into a beneficient one.

> Consider that voice in your head [soul qua supergeo] that yells and screams at you as a crusty, old drill seargent whose barkings are born of a love for you, grown harsh. Believing the stakes to be life-or-death, he is willing to be hated as he calls you an idiot, if by such harshness he can keep you from sticking your head up in the heat of battle and getting shot. Look him in the eye and you will see beneath his harshness a heart of gold that he long ago gave up believing anyone would ever see. Keep looking until you see a tear glisten as his loneliness

erodes. For he never thought anyone would actually see his heart of gold beneath his bark. But now it is happening and he feels a disarming gratitude. Feel a responding tear in your own heart. And let the two of you join together. He won't need to bark, because you are assuring him that you can hear just fine. He can see your wisdom and you can let in his pride in you, and he can rest easier and thus you can feel needed by him too.

Here, so-called ego and superego merge more and more as the maturing character and wisdom of soul. As the sadistic tones of this life-or-death inner voice receive the soteriological transfusion, the temporal urgency is refreshed with a preciousness that nourishes, yet always hints at the fragile mortal sense. The diagnostic matter of whether a "voice" *is* "hallucinatory" or *is* "spiritual" seems best deferred to considering the quality of information the voice gives, and the kindliness of its tone.

EGO DEVELOPMENT AS CHARACTER MATURATION

In this consolidation of psychic "constructs" of ego/superego/id, I suggest that the cumbersome pre/trans/non/egoic developmental language that transpersonal psychology has construed from its psychoanalytic precursor be abandoned. In its place I choose a clinical vocabulary of "character maturation" in the real-passing time of the impermanent now and in the ever-developing soteriological powers.

Here, "character" combines ego and superego into a single, resonant entity, while their division derives from the psychoanalytic assumption that moral sentiments are introjects and not at all endogenous (or from those religious narratives that depict people as precarious souls before a moralistically severe and panoptic god.) The amoral-nature-energy of the id can be traced to the Motherly Kundalini-shakti, thus locating human nature in the ultimately beneficent, yet exceedingly vast range of postgenital maturational potentials of the ensouled body. Thus, we can dispense with such vague or disturbing terms as *nonegoic core*, or *Terrible Mother* and instead draw from the anatomical clarities of yogic subtle physiology and ultimately benign, if also daunting, endogenous potentials.

And, since we find that expressions of fairness and of sharing begin, as Papineau notes, even "before [children] can speak" (1997, p. 13), let us assume that we are born as souled beings with merely immature soteriological powers. Thus, let us infer that psychoanalysis, in seeking an amoral fundament to homo sapiens as part of its scientific despiritualization of reality, became unable to see such early soteriological expressions. Indeed, from the infant's first wailings to the outcries of "Sh'ma!"

"Shiva!" "Allah!" "Hast Thou forsaken me?" and anahata-nada, one can hear an ever-maturing continuity of awe, hope, and character. This truncation has given us a sense of the psyche as far more weak, woundable, and at odds with its own biopsychic energies (as "id," "nonegoic potentials," "Terrible Mother," etc.) than I and my references maintain. For ego merely refers to the ability to function in ordinary apollonian time, while all these other terms refer to the dionysian time, once freed of hysteric hyperbole: the sheer awe of t,t,t,t . . . , not some selfishly aggressive and predatorily sexual, untamed instinctive core.

Thus, from a soteriological perspective, the psychopathologies as noted in the eight hundred pages of the *DSM-IV* appear as, simply, variated *maturational struggles with arising, dashed, and rearising hopefulness*. The struggles occur as opportunities missed or somewhat taken to: give and receive thanks or appreciation; to err, apologize, forgive and try anew, and to age evermore into the daunting impermanence. A spiritually oriented diagnostician/therapist is merely someone who can see hopefulness—that is, the human soul—in its myriad and even torturous forms, and helps it impermanently along.

Assessing psychological disorders or complaints in this way guides the therapist's specific admirations, appreciations, and inspirations of the client to also admire, appreciate, forgive, and apologize in her life. Thus, the undertapped soteriological powers of the soul are brought into fuller functioning as forces capable of transcending for a time the repetitive or unyielding tendencies ("tendencies" are always toward some fixed symptomatic [x] that is tended toward; but if [-x] is quite possible, can we really call something a "tendency," rather than merely "what can happen"), which "sustain" disorders.

For as soon as some degree of increased hopefulness, however small, emerges (and at least small degrees of progress are visible in any brief time span for anyone who might see and then cultivate them), the universal Problematic of Trepid Hopefulness and Uncertainty replaces that of Psychopathology. In that quavering moment where the paranoid has lowered his guard, or the addict has been clean for one shakey week, the substance of the previous diagnosis becomes moot, and treatment becomes a matter of these new problematics: How to deal with the auspiciously disconcerting "too good to be true" cognitive/affective awakening into greater hope.

Here, the psychiatrically disabled who approaches self-sufficiency might fearfully "turn back toward/become" symptomatic, frightened by the shift from staid chronicity to indeterminant impermanence. Here, the personality disordered's moment of trust leads him to valuing the very person his negative splitting, conartistry, or paranoia had just warned him against—a valuing that engenders new uncertainties previously covered over by his pathological pseudocertainties. Likewise, the pranotthana-aroused experiences spinal sensations that dishevel her contemporary involvements with a sense of "greater purpose": but can she live up to it in community with others?

Assessment becomes the ongoing esteeming of how the soteriological interventions are working—for example, the type of shy half smile or flashed blush and the degree of verbal acceptance upon being admired for: the courage it has taken to come to therapy; the quavering trust involved in coming to a hospital; or the insistently passionate pride in not wanting to admit to needing any help, while in the office or hospital.

For progress is a rope of hopefulness woven ever longer into the thin air of the present. And the insecurity of it all is what makes humans so great with each step they take into this fleeting impermanence.

CONCLUSION

Consider the core or ground of human experience to be the stream of eternal impermanence. See the soteriological sentiments of awe, gratitude, admiration, and praise as surrounding this core of the "deep present" and fanning out in the nourishing blush of shared appreciations and hopes.

See the rectifying or truing sentiments of apology and forgiveness as forming the next outer circumference. See these sentiments engaged with a more peripheral layer of turbulent emotions and thoughts, stirred by various problematic, yet characterologically maturing or "redemptive" life experiences. See even heinous events as rectifiable by the ever-strengthening soteriological powers, creating a culture of sharing, mercy, and spiritual growth.

Consider the body—its nerves, glands, and secretions—as a precipitate of soteriological time potencies that matures (becomes ever more embodying of the soteriological potencies, over time) via ecstatic movements, beatitudes, and utterances. Call these maturational activities "worship" or "religion" or "spirituality," for they help one to be more forgiving, grateful and hopeful.

See the psychoanalytic view of human nature as appearing at a time in Western history when the soteriological powers had grown weak, culminating in Nietzsche's outcry that pity, vengeance, and cynical materialism had "killed" God. See this weakness resulting from (1) the Judeo-Christian soteriological skew toward sorrowful and contrite passions and away from joyous passions (somewhat corrected for by the liberality of humanism) and (2) a limited understanding of the vast developmental expanse of the body's soteriological/ecstatic potentials (explored in great detail in yoga over the past five thousand years and just now becoming known in the West). See the innovative edge of psychoanalytic therapies in the seventies, eighties, and nineties as just discovering the healing power of compassion. See a soteriological psychotherapy as drawing from the full range of sentiments and, someday, facilitating the deepest of incarnate potentials revealed in the bloom of endless dionysian time ttttttt

NOTES

CHAPTER ONE

1. What difference can a choice in metaphors of causality make? Consider the causality metaphor known as the "domino effect" as used in the 1960s. Although inaccurate to the historical conditions of Vietnam's supposed "domino" neighbors, this metaphoric depiction sounded so threatening to the U.S. military that the image of unstoppable topplings became a rallying point and battle cry, mobilizing the United States into massive warfare and disillusionment. History is often metaphor's child and the various metaphors of causality its phantasmagoric seeds, each spawning a different potential future or recorded past. See also, Lakoff and Johnson, *Metaphors We Live By* (Chicago: University of Chicago Press, 1981).

2. See Marija Gimbutas, *The Civilization of the Goddess* (San Francisco: Harper Collins, 1991) for a feminist discussion of neolithic cultural worship of a regenerative Mother-Diety based in a temporality of eternally recurrent impermanence.

3. See R. Anderson, "Nine Psychospiritual Characteristics of Spontaneous Weeping" in *J. Trans. Psychology* 28(2), 1996: 167–73, for a review of "weeping in profound grief which reaches into the very core of Self, weeping at the sight of astonishing beauty, at the apprenhension of one's essential nature and that of others, and as a gift, i.e., receiving spontaneous acts of grace." Anderson quotes Catherine of Siena (*The Dialogue*, trans. S. Noffke [New York: Paulist Press, 1980, p. 163]): "When she feels the presence of my eternal Godhead, she begins to shed sweet tears that are truly a milk that nourishes the soul in true presence. These tears are a fragrant ointment that send forth a most delicious perfume." Quoting Doherty (*Poustina: Christian Spirituality of the East for Westerners* [Notre Dame, Ind.: Ave Maria Press, 1975, p. 118]): "[Spiritual] sorrow is a state of union with God in the pain of men. It is a state of deep and profound understanding. It is as if God put his hand out and the panorama of the whole world and its pain is opened before you." And drawing from metaphors suggesting the puberty of the heart: "Once you have reached the place of tears . . . it begins to shed tears. For now the birth pangs of the spiritual infant grow strong, since grace, the common mother of all, makes hast to give birth mystically to the soul, the image of God, into the light of the world to come" (Isaac the Syrian, quoted in M. Ross, "Tears and Fire: Recovering a Neglected Tradition," in *Sobornost* 9(1): 14–23).

For a discussion of the profundity of tears, ala Heidegger, Kant, and Merleau-Ponty, see Levin 1988, p. 130:

> Why do I say that crying is the *root* of seeing? . . . The connection between sight and crying, is not an a priori principle of [Kantian] pure understanding, but rather, in words that Merleau-Ponty might have used, an "organismic a priori" of the human body as we live and feel it. . . . The spontaneous, involuntary crying of the eyes . . . attests a *pre-personal, pre-objective bond of communication, a sort of primordial communion*, which always already exists between the world and the gaze.

Lacking spiritual tears and their poignant complexity and maturational necessity, does psychotherapy overuse grievous tearful catharsis to approach these "other" tears?

4. Mandatory reporting laws relate to suspected possibilities of child, sexual, spousal or elder abuse and Tarasoff dangers that a therapist believes deserve to be investigated by those empowered to do so for possible verification. He only needs to believe that such situations *deserve such attention*.

5. Washburn's (*Transpersonal Psychology in Psychoanalytic Perspective* 1994) view of midlife as a challenge to the ego to outgrow dualistic thinking: "The mental ego in late dualism is prone to undergo a deep shift in its sense of how it stands in existence" (p. 183). "[M]idlife . . . designates the transitional period between egoic maturity and transegoic awakening. The ego, having completed its development in early adulthood, begins to sense that something is amiss at the very (dualistic) bases of its being" (p. 185). In my interpretation of kundalini developmental theory, Washburn is pointing to the postgenital puberties wherein the body-psychological-identity complex can undergo a vast range of maturations.

6. See chapter 3, note 4 for comments on Wilber's similar critique on the academic contrivance of "symbolic interpretations."

CHAPTER TWO

1. In *What Is Called Thinking?* Heidegger (1968) traces Nietzsche's metaphysic to its "heart and core," where man can be "delivered from revenge: that is the bridge to the highest hope for me, and a rainbow after long storms" (p. 85). In this heart, *thought itself* would no longer arise in the rancor of the spirit of revenge, as it so often does in postmodern culture.

The gender, race, and abortion debates, the litigation explosion, and the many tabloid TV talk shows are some obvious examples of our culture's heated fascination with vengefulness, perhaps a kind of voyeuristic vengeance itself. Even the cover of *Time* (8/21/91) asked, "Have we become a nation of crybabies?"

Thus televised courtroom trials and TV tabloid audience-guest-host pseudotrials have become spectacles in the medieval sense of a jeering crowd lost in their clappings and derisions to the immediate sorrows of the human tragedies before them, and where there are no winners or real satisfactions. As Foucault notes regarding the history of public punishments in *Discipline and Punish* (1979):

[I]n punishment-as-spectacle a confused horror spread from the scaffold; it enveloped both executioner and condemned; and, although it was always ready to invert the shame inflicted on the victim into pity or glory, it often turned the legal violence of the executioner into shame. Now the scandal and the light are to be distributed differently; it is the conviction itself that marks the offender with the unequivocally negative sign: the publicity has shifted to the trial, and to the sentence; the execution itself is like an additional shame that justice is ashamed to impose on the condemned man. . . . This sense of shame is constantly growing: the psychologists and the minor civil servants of moral orthopaedics proliferate on the wound it leaves. (Foucault 1979, pp. 9–10)

And what is revenge? Heidegger quotes Nietzsche, "This alone is revenge itself: the will's revulsion against time and its 'It was'" (Heidegger 1968, p. 93). Again, Heidegger states, "Revenge is the will's revulsion against time, and that means, against the passing away and its past" (ibid. p. 96). Attaining this highest hope of freeing the will from the-past-as-revenge is to "presence" presence itself.

2. See *The New York Review of Books* (4/24/97, vol. 44(7): 60–64), "Sybil—The Making of a Disease: An Interview with Dr. Herbert Spiegel," by Mikkel Borch-Jacobsen, in which the consulting psychiatrist in the famous multiple personality case of Sybil states that he all along assessed Sybil as not suffering from M.P.D.: "I saw her (Sybil's) 'personalities' rather as a game-playing. . . . I thought this was an ingenious way of identifying different episodes and events in Sybil's life. . . . But I thought this was all emerging simply (because of) [Sybil's therapist's] wanting to make sense out of the disparate life experience that Sybil had. . . . I told (Sybil's therapist, Cornelia Wilbur and Flora Rheta Schreiber, the author of the book *Sybil*) that it would not be accurate to call Sybil a multiple personality. . . . Schreiber . . . said, 'But if we don't call it a multiple personality, we don't have a book . . . it won't sell!'" (p. 63). Thus, we find an additional narrative structure in the particular psychotherapeutic narrative of the precedent-setting "case of Sybil": the making of not only a coherent-enough etiological history, but a hoped-for, sensationalist bestseller.

3. By contrast, we might imagine a psychotherapy whose hermeneutic includes the oracular—that is, a reading from the present of inklings of what is yet to come. We might expect such therapies to engender another set of sentiments—those of yearning, dread, uncertainty, wonder, hope, suspense, excited and even manic anticipations.

4. In *The Sickness unto Death*, Kierkegaard explored the dread in which one wishes oneself to be over and finds oneself, relentlessly, to yet exist. "When death is the greatest danger, one hopes for life; but when one becomes acquainted with an even more dreadful danger, one hopes for death. So when the danger is so great that death has become one's hope, despair is the disconsolateness of not being able to die" (1946 [1849], p. 342).

5. Quotation marks remind us that such yardstick language depicting a "trajectory of time" is merely metaphoric. "Nearness" and "distance" refer more to "senses of urgency" than to "time." Here "time" might be better named "modulations of urgency."

6. As Heidegger stated, being and time are together. And when language is in the ("errant") grip of principial thought, mankind is capable of an unwieldy, technological self-destruction. Or, in our study, the individual is capable of suicide (or murder) via "technologies" of vengeance. For vengeance is the supreme antitemporal principle, which can come to dominating the aesthetic of presence. Thus, the historical, ethical, and metaphysical potency of Christ's exchange of vengeance for love and forgiveness, and of Gandhi's passive resistance.

7. The irony we are considering is that of wanting an ending to come, soon, to that which we most want to continue. Compare the mounting ambivalent pressures of those last few seconds before the termination of a successful therapy with Dostoyevsky's novelization of his own near execution (as I quoted at length, p. 25), which ends with the about-to-be-executed's redemptive vow, and its inverting irony: "'I would miss nothing [of life if suddenly pardoned, now that I am awake to its preciousness]!' He said that this thought finally filled him with such rage that he wanted to be shot *as soon as possible* [my emphasis]" (Dostoyevsky 1969, p. 81).

8. See Cashdan (pp. 139–42, 1988), who quotes Johnson (p. 298, 1985): "The final necessary step [in therapy] is *forgiveness*: forgiveness of what happened, forgiveness for what is happening, forgiveness of what may still happen."

9. Survivors of violence find their bitterness and horror with nothing to bite into as time passes, except this "what" and its phantasmic "is." Their non-omnipotence feigns the opposite in the "never" of "Never Again!"

Their "never" inverts to an "always"—a vigilant and unforgetting *is*—against the wind of impermanence and mortal limitations. (Could soteriological impermanence thoroughly and widely known engender a world within which no new horror might arise? But to let our *shared sense* of mortal impermanence reign as the lord of "is" seems an insipid affront to the horrors that can happen—although exactly this perception initiated the Buddha's enlightenment as he saw an aged, and then a crippled person, hobbling down a narrow Indian street—and then a funeral procession.) Instead of the heartful poignancy of impermanence as our truing force, we have the cycles of retaliation and ever-ready defensiveness, whether at the international level or the neighborhood gang level: "I carry my piece to school 'cause everybody does, and 'cause, well, you know (shoulders shrugged, eyes looking off to one side): stuff happens" (quoted from a Los Angeles County Prosecutor's Office juvenile interview).

10. Thus, while walking to his own execution, Robert Alton Harris comforted the inarticulate sorrow of a prison guard who had befriended him, instead of lashing out at him, murmured, "It's okay"—echoing in mundane understatement that soteriological ideal of forgiveness that has inspired hope for some two thousand years; echoing those Tibetan monks who pray for the Chinese.

11. I have admired the mother of a teenaged murderer as she stood ashamed next to her son on the day of his arraignment in the Atlantic County, New Jersey, Juvenile Courthouse (a converted youth's rollerskating rink) in 1974. Standing there in something greater than his horrible guilt, she and he came forth and stood together before the Court, bowed.

CHAPTER THREE

1. I am aware that the concept of "postgenital puberties" is a radical innovation in transpersonal psychology, and moreso in the study of comparative religions and developmental neuroendocrinology. And, as discussed on page 172, there are many spiritual paths or religions which only minimally mature the full potential of "the body" en route to meditative gnosis or enlightenment, compared to what we find in kundalini yoga. These paths do not force the radical revisions I am discussing, but they most certainly press in this direction.

Lacking information and many exemplars of the full-bodied path of kundalini, various transpersonal theorists depict kundalini as relating primarily to gross reality (Wilber 1995, pp. 608–609, via the limited information of his mentor, Avabhasa Franklin Jones), or, in the work of Michael Washburn, as a hairsplitting, ambiguous half-differentiation of sexuality and spirituality whereby the latter is a repressed version of the former.

While such a phrasing is en route to the terminology of "postgenital puberties," its convolutedness is exactly what suggests that the phenomena it tries to describe exceed its grasp, in Kuhnian fashion. Kundalini phenomena in particular constitute exactly the *type of* "anomalous data" Kuhn made famous as "*paradigm shifting* data," in this case shifting of our conventional paradigm of psychosexual development. For Kuhn, the *awkwardness* of the pre-Copernican geocentric astronomical map, forever trying to accommodate anomalous observations with its strange, epicyclical planetary orbits helped betray that "geocentricity" was an inaccurate description of the earth's *solar*-centered system. Similarly, kundalini, Wilber's, and Washburn's transpersonal developmental theories all press to decenter genital sexuality from our psychosexual map and recenter it with *something* "more spiritual."

See the definitional contortions of Washburn, (1994, pp. 310–11), who, lacking the concept of postgenital puberties, tries valiantly to distinguish "sexuality" from "spirituality" in his transpersonalization of psychosexual development—while, weaving back and forth, also depicts them as none other than each other, yet crucially different, yet none other than the one being a repressed version of the other, or the numinous power of the other, or the "spirit of the spirituality" of the ecstasy of the other, until eros is *once* awakened, yet long after its awakening in genital puberty:

> In the Tantric view, sexual ecstasy and spiritual ecstasy are *more than analogous* [my emphasis]; they are *consanguineous* [?]: the eros of sexual ecstasy *is none other than* [my emphasis, and what, exactly, is the qualifying "eros of" distinguishing?] the numinous power or spirit of spiritual ecstasy. In crediting Tantrism with this insight, *I do not [however] mean to suggest that spirituality can be reduced* [my emphasis] to sexuality. Sexuality and spirituality are not identical. Sexuality is based in a specific psychophysiological center and is a distinct experiential modality. Spirituality on the other hand belongs to embodied life generally and is expressed through all experiential modalities. This *difference is crucial. Notwithstanding this difference* [my emphasis], how-

ever, sexuality and spirituality are intimately related, I suggest, in that the *very energy* [my emphasis] that under dualistic conditions expresses itself primarily *as sexual energy* [my emphasis] is *none other than* [my emphasis] repressed [the term *repression* keeps this convolution in tune with the "validating power" of psychoanalysis, however misleading] spiritual power. . . . [E]rotogenic and spiritual experiences are expressions of the same sacred power, a power that, when awakened, is a palpable presence within the body . . . eros, *once* [only once? my emphasis] awakened, is *none other* [my emphasis] than spirit. (pp. 310–11)

Washburn's efforts to reconcile kundalini developmentalism with psychoanalysis force him into using the pathologizing concept of "repression" to describe the dormancy of kundalini and the hymenlike granthis (subtle body "knots") as the "infrastructure of primal repression" and as "layers of ossified countercathexis that block the flow of energy." Infancy is not best termed "repressed adolescence" nor is dormant kundalini best termed "primally repressed psychic energy," except if one is hoping to preserve the psychoanalytic vocabulary and map as one's ultimate concordance, at strange conceptual costs.

See also my *Passions of Innocence* (1994, pp. 172–78) on the social cost of our current, inaccurate psychosexual map.

Perhaps transpersonal psychology must speak in this slippery way, in order to both preserve the gains of sexual liberation psychology, while struggling to make room for a "new" spirituality that is both pleasurable, but not merely hedonistic, nor too sexual, yet not repressive either. Again, seeing these theoretical struggles (and their correlate existential struggles with the endogenous forces themselves) as indications of the emergence of unaccounted-for postgenital ("more spiritual," yet fleshy and pleasurable) *puberties* would seem to be helpful and warranted.

And, as an even cursory study of kundalini yoga and all of Hinduism reveals, the basis of these spiritualities is erotic transformation—the worship of the postgenital puberties—of one sort or another.

2. As Euripedes lyricized in *The Bacchae*, where Pentheus represents the apollonian powers of the state and mundane time:

PENTHEUS. Seize him! This man is taunting Thebes!

DIONYSIUS. Don't bind me I tell you. You need control, not I. . . . He was binding me—he thought—yet he neither grasped me nor touched me. Hope was all he fed upon.

Here, Dionysius is the voice of ever-fleeting eternal impermanence Time. He taunts the apollonian world with a vitality-into-the-future that lures mundane-time-Pentheus with the mere "hope" that he might ever touch the awe of the living god in his revels.

3. See Feuerstein (1989, pp. 31–37), on "crazy wisdom."

Crazy wisdom methods are designed to shock, but their purpose is always benign: to reflect to the ordinary worldling the "madness" of his or her existence, which from the enlightened point of view, is an existence rooted in profound illusion.

Thus, we find as well in the bluntness of schizophrenic accusations, and in its word-salad glossolalias, characteristic gems of insight or bitingly humorous sarcasms. Standing in line at the Safeway Market a man so afflicted repeats under his breath "Lips and hair, lips and hair, all she is is lips and hair" while waiting behind an elderly woman who is trying to deter time passage and preserve her youthful image with a silver boufant hair-do and a broad flourish of red lipstick.

4. See Wilber 1995, pp. 236–42, for a critique on the academic contrivance of the religious symbol, particularly of the work of Joseph Campbell.

> It is people such as Campbell and Jung and Eliade, *operating from a widespread access to rationality—something the originators of myth did not have* [?]—who *then* read deeply symbolic "as ifs" into them, and who like to play with myths and use them as analogies and have great good fun with them, whereas the actual mythic-believers do not play with myths at all, but take them deadly seriously and refuse in the least to open them to reasonable discourse or any sort of "as if" at all. (p. 238)

5. See J. Sansonese (1994), *The Body of Myth*. Also, see D. G. White (1996), *The Alchemical Body*, for detailed, critical study of the homologizations of body, cosmos, ritual, and myth in yoga, and of the alchemical body, which is none other than the hormonal-developmental traverse from genital puberty to the postgenital puberties: "Ashes of prior sacrifices are the seeds of future sacrifices, and so it is that the erotic ascetic Siva can call the ashes that he smears upon his body his 'seed' (p. 216). Ash, or *vibhuti*, holds the esoteric significance of transmuted or transmutable seed essence, thus within my terms, the genital puberty sacrifices itself to (is outgrown into) the postgenital puberties, wherein the secretions of the latter give rise to the soteriological elixirs of the former. Also, let us consider that "sacrifice" refers to *a making evermore sacred* via an offering up, that is spiritual growth as the outgrowing of one puberty-identity-body-emotionality into another and another, ad infinitum.

6. See also Elizarenkova (1995, p. 125) for references to the brilliance of the sun and other radiances in the *Rig Veda*. See p. 20 for her numerous located cross-references in the *Rig Veda* of "singing praises" with swallowing sacrificial libations. Here, the internal secretion of postgenital hormones (soma) becomes entangled with the ritualistic imbibing of sanctified psychoactive libations. Consider the "looking upward" quoted from verse 7.33.5 as the eyes-closed look into the meditative space:

> Finding themselves in trouble, surrounded in the Ten-kings-battle, they were *looking* upwards, as (those who are) tormented by thirst (look up) at the sky (hoping for rain [the secretion of subtle radiances in the cerebral-pineal locus]). (10.32.4)

> I was *gazing* at that pleasant place [in the pineal-cranial space] toward which milch [*sic*] cows [esoterically: the tongue in its puberty of khecari mudra] should direct (their journey) like a wedding procession. (p. 15)

The degree to which the *Rig Veda*'s syntax, phonetics, vocabulary, metaphors, metrics, and morphology all resonate with yogic catalytic significance is brought out in exquisite detail in this work, and testify to the spiritual (if also apollonian to the extreme) maturity of the *Rig Veda*.

7. In Washburn (1988, 1994), we encounter the overly abstract verbiage that comes into play when spiritual development is not fully grasped as endogenously arising postgenital puberties, and spiritual stages of maturation are yet pressed into compliance with psychoanalytic concepts. In this case, the term *the Dynamic Ground* is introduced "to designate the source of spiritual power" (1994, p. 314), which is "repressed" into "latency," leading to a "separation of the ego from the power of the Dynamic Ground [which] is a separation of the ego from spiritual power." See note 1 for comments on these convolutions.

8. As D. M. Levin (1985, pp. 293–349) notes from a Heideggerian perspective in *The Poetizing Dance, Gathering Round Dance*, "When mortals dance in a spirit of joyful piety, the Being of all beings itself is presencing, and not only as ground, but as Earth, as elemental . . . free of metaphysical encumbrances."

9. According to *ayurvedic* physiology, (in Dass and Aparna 1978, p. 66):

> The food we eat is transformed into the seven body constituents (dhatus) by an involved step-by-step transformation process. The digested food is successively converted into lymph, blood, tissue, fat, bone, marrow, sexual secretions, and an eighth constitutent called ojas—subtle light energy. The ojas, the most refined essence of the sexual secretions, in turn permeates and nourishes every cell of the body. With an increase in ojas there is a marked increase in well-being at all levels. With a loss of ojas everything deteriorates. The development of every body constituent is directly influenced by the one preceding it. Therefore, if an excessive amount of sexual energy is lost (loss of sexual energy happens mainly through sexual activity [and excessive anger]) the production of ojas suffers. . . . There is an excess of sexual secretions produced each month to allow for one monthly intercourse without detriment to physical, mental, emotional and spiritual well-being.

10. Lest we believe that yogic sectarianism has been immune to the intrigues and corruptions that permeate the history of Western religions, particularly in modern times, see D. G. White (1996), pp. 342–49.

11. In his mini-bestseller, *Emotional Resilience*, psychiatrist David Viscott teaches that meditation is a not all-together "natural process," whose "nonsense . . . Hindu mantras" like "*om nemah shevaya*" ("I bow to Siva" [God of ascetic yogis]) work to "numb your mind" and after a few sentences on "advanced technique" (visualize a "blue spot, discern a rotating star and try to stop it from rotating") declares, "That's all there is to meditation. . . . Meditate daily or once a week" (Viscott 1996, pp. 49–50).

12. See my *Passions of Innocence* for a popularized guide to the postgenital traverse.

13. D. G. White (1996) notes, regarding Matsyendranath [whose name means "Lord of the Lord of Fishes"], the original guru of the Nath yogic sect:

"What I wish to argue here is that Matsyendra's doctrine of the fish belly—a revolutionary doctrine indeed, given the perennial importance that has been attached to it in Hindu tantricism over the past one thousand years—is about diaphragmatic retention [of the breath] and its effects on the body and consciousness of the yogic practitioner" (p. 225). I would add that the yogic importance of this breathless state is the capacity to breath from the etheric akhasic dimension directly, via the puberty of the hypothalamus, which monitors blood oxygen levels (see also ibid., pp. 222–29).

CHAPTER FOUR

1. Within the yogic chakra system (*muladhara, svadhisthana, manipura, anahata, vishuddha,* and *ajna*), we can locate six dimensions of the ensouled body's participation in Feuerbach's infinity of consciousness: (1) existence (endless surviving energy-matter; terror to thrill); (2) lineage and sexual attraction (endless desire and bodily procreativity; desperate gender craving to play delights); (3) will (endless assimilative acquisitiveness, selfish competition to affiliative community); (4) love (endless circulatory giving-receiving, romantic yearning to unstoppable love); (5) linguistic and artistic expression (endless aeolic praise, confusion to unitive complexity); and (6) the nondual infinity Feuerbach describes so well (endless temporo-spatial awe: from endless numbing dread to ecstatic heavenlike wonder).

GLOSSARY OF YOGIC TERMS

Ajna chakra (cakra): midbrow nondual-knowing subtle energy center
Akasha: etheric dimension, more subtle than the gaseous
Amrita: nectar of immortality, originating in the pineal area
Anahata chakra (cakra): heart subtle energy center
Anahata-nada: spontaneous, endogenously emergent utterances
Ananda-maya kosha: subtle, causal body
Anatta (Pali term): no-constant-self
Anicca (Pali term): impermanence
Anna-maya kosha: fleshy, food-eating body
Apana prana: eliminative energetic flow
Ars erotica: approach to eros, which attuned to its profundity
Asana: bodily pose conducive to physical-spiritual maturation
Ashrama: stage of life or of existential maturation
Ashtanga yoga: eight-limbed "classicalized" yoga
Auras: subtle bodily radiance emergent in urdhva-retas process
Bandhas: muscular contractions emergent in postgenital maturation
Bhakti yoga: ardent devotional yoga
Bindu: procreative seed essence
Brahmacarya (brahmacharya): life of following the Absolute
Brahmarandhra: mind-heart subjectivity or space of the Divine
Buddhi: intellect, knowing aspect of mind
Chakras (cakras): psychoenergetic centers along spinal axis
Citta prana: energy of consciousness
Daven (Hebrew term): swaying prayer, akin to pranotthana
Daya: generosity
Dharana: intermediate maturation of sustained attentional focus
Dharma: religion, alignment with endogenous growth factors
Dhyana: advanced maturation of sustained attentional focus
Divya sharira: fully matured "divine body"; Christian "body of glory"
Hatha yoga: actions that mature the body and breath spark
Hri: modesty, humility
Iccha shakti: energy of will
Ida: feminine or "lunar" spinal energy channel
Kaivalya: unencumbered fully matured soul sense
Karma: the sequential flow of consequences
Khecari mudra: yogic puberty of tongue
Koshas: "sheaths" that make up the human organism

Kshama: forebearance or equanimity
Kundalini: mother energy or intelligence of complete maturation
Laya: absorption or matured unification of mind-as-consciousness
Manipura chakra (cakra): navel center, primary site of urdhva-retas
Mano-maya kosha: "emotional body"
Mudra: matured asanas or movements with pubertylike importance
Muladhara chakra (cakra): root, sacral center; locus of kundalini
Nabho mudra: precursor to khecari mudra
Nadis: subtle energetic flow channels, comparable to acupuncture meridians
Nirbija-samadhi: unwavering, fully matured Origin Consciousness
Nivritti marga: renunciate path; no-worldly-desires path
Niyama: soteriological sentiment cultivations
Ojas: a postgenital puberty radiance-substance
Pingala: solar, masculine spinal channel
Prana: fundamental life energy
Prana-maya kosha: vital energy bodily sheath
Pranayama: vital-spark cultivations
Pranotthana: intensified life force underlying all maturation
Pratyahara: matured attention beyond scattered distraction
Pravritti marga: with-worldly-desires path
Qi gong (Chinese term): Chinese yoga, cultivation of qi, or prana
Raga: archetypal musical theme
Rasa: essence or juice of life, or of blissful experience
Retas: procreative essence, precursor to amrita.
Sabija-samadhi: unwavering, nearly matured Origin Consciousness
Sadhana: all willful or spontaneous yogic actions
Sahaja yoga: endogenously arising yogic maturations
Sahasrara chakra (cakra): crown psychoenergetic locus
Samadhi: awareness unwaveringly and completely gathered unto its source
Scientia sexualis: Foucault's term for rule-oriented erotic models
Shakti: spiritual or charismatic force, feminine in essence
Shambhavi mudra: meditative gazing puberty of eyes
Shraddha: spiritual passion or faith
Shruti: sound as truth, in-the-moment revelation
Siddhi: highly matured spiritual capacities or powers
Smritis: recalled or remembered truth or recollections
Soma: ritual libation or inner postgenital secretion: amrita
Sushumna (susumna): spinal channel of kundalini arousal
Svadhisthana chakra (svadhishthana cakra): genital pubic center
Taluka: soft-palate energy site involved in khecari mudra
Tantra: school of Shiva-Shakti yogas inclusive of kundalini yoga
Tejas: glowing spiritual zeal
Unmani mudra: no-mind-mind puberty of stable consciousness
Urdhva-retas: postgenital hormonal maturation
Vairagya: spiritual detachment
Vijnana-maya kosha: discriminative wisdom sheath
Virya (vira): spiritual virtue derived from procreative essence

Vishuddha chakra (cakra): throat psychoenergetic center
Viyoga: mystical union during felt-sense of separation
Yama: soteriological observances
Yoga: ways of complete maturation toward the Omega-Source
Zikr (Persian term): torso-throbbing pranic prayer in Sufism

BIBLIOGRAPHY

Albee, E. *Who's afraid of Virginia Woolf?* New York: Atheneum, 1962.

Almaas, A. *Essence: The diamond approach to inner realization.* 3d printing. York Beach, Me.: Samuel Weiser, 1991.

Altizer, T. *History as apocalypse.* Albany: State University of New York Press, 1985.

American Heritage Dictionary. 3d ed. New York: Houghton Mifflin, 1992.

American Psychiatric Association, Commission on Psychotherapies. *Psychotherapy research: Methodological and efficacy issues.* Washington, D.C.: 1982.

———. *Diagnostic and statistical manual of mental disorders (DSM-IV).* 4th ed. Washington, D.C.: 1994.

Ananda, D. (Bubba Free John). *Love of the two-armed form.* Middletown, Calif.: Dawn Horse, 1978.

Anderson, R. "Nine psycho-spiritual characteristics of spontaneous and involuntary weeping." *Journal of Transpersonal Psychology* 28(2) 1996: 167–73.

Aranya, S. *Yoga philosophy of Patanjali.* Trans. P. Mukerji. Albany: State University of New York Press, 1983.

Arendt, H. *The human condition.* Chicago: University of Chicago Press, 1970.

———. *The origins of totalitarianism.* New York: Harcourt Brace, 1973.

Aries, P. *Western attitudes toward death from the middle ages to the present.* Trans. R. Ranum. Baltimore, Md.: Johns Hopkins University, 1974.

Arieti, S. *Interpretation of Schizophrenia.* 2d ed. New York: Basic Books, 1974.

Arnold, E. *Light of Asia.* London, 1879.

Aurobindo, G. *The brain of India.* Pondicherry, India: Sri Aurobindo Ashram. 1960 [1920].

Aurobindo G., and The Mother. *On love.* Pondicherry, India: Sri Aurobindo Ashram, 1973.

Avalon, A. (J. Woodroffe). *The serpent power.* New York: Dover, 1974.

Avraham of Gerona, Rabbeinu Yonah ben. *The gates of repentence.* Trans. S. Silverstein. Jerusalem: Feldheim, 1976.

Ayyangar, T. R. S. *The Yoga Upanishad.* Adyar: Adyar Library, 1952.

Bahri, H. *Learners' Hindi-English dictionary.* Delhi: Rajpal, 1993.

Baker, E. *Man in the trap.* New York: Avon, 1967.

Banerjea, A. K. *Philosophy of Gorakhnath.* Delhi: Motilal Banarsidass, 1983.

Barankin, E. *Probability and the East.* Reprint from *Annals of the Institute of Statistical Mathemathics* (16), 1964: 185–230.

Barth, J. *Lost in the funhouse.* New York: Bantam, 1966.

Bartley, W. *Wittgenstein.* La Salle, Ill.: Open Court, 1985.

Bass, E., and L. Davis. *The courage to heal: A guide for women survivors of child sexual abuse.* 3d ed. New York: Harper Perennial, 1994.

Beattie, M. *Codependent no more: How to stop controlling others and start caring for yourself.* San Francisco: Harper & Row, 1987.
Beneke, T. "Triumph of Heart." Interview of Lillian Rubin, Senior Research Fellow, Institute for the Study of Social Change, University of California, Berkeley. In *Express* 19(22) (3/7/97): 14.
Benson, H., and M. Klipper. *The relaxation response.* New York: Avon, 1976.
Bentov, I. *Stalking the wild pendulum.* New York: Dutton, 1977.
——. "Micromotion of the body as a factor in the development of the nervous system." In L. Sannella, *Kundalini: Transcendence or psychosis?* San Francisco: Dakin, 1978.
Bergson, H. *A study in metaphysics: The creative mind.* Trans. Mabelle Andison. Totowa, N.J.: Littlefield & Adams, 1965.
Bhagavad-Gita. Trans. S. Prabhavananda and C. Isherwood. New York: Mentor, 1951.
Bharati, A. *The tantric tradition.* London: Rider, 1965.
Bion, W. R. *Transformations: Change from learning to growth.* New York: Basic Books, 1965.
Boorstein, S. *Transpersonal psychotherapies.* Palo Alto, Calif.: Science & Behavior Books, 1980.
Borysenko, J., and M. Borysenko. *The power of the mind to heal.* Carson, Calif.: Hay House, 1994.
Boss, M. *Psychoanalysis and daseinanalysis.* Trans. L. Lefebre. New York: Basic Books, 1963.
Bouveresse, J. *Wittgenstein reads Freud.* Trans. C. Cosman. Princeton, N.J.: Princeton University Press, 1995.
Bowlby, J. *Maternal care and mental health.* New York: J. Aronson, 1995.
Bradley, S., R. Beatty, and E. H. Long. *The American tradition in literature.* 3d ed. New York: Grosset & Dunlap, 1967.
Bradshaw, J. *Healing the shame that binds you.* Deerfield Beach, Fl.: Health Communications, 1988a.
——. *Bradshaw on: The family.* Deerfield Beach, Fl.: Health Communications, 1988b.
Briggs. G. *Gorakhnath and the Kanphata yogis.* Delhi: Motilal Banarsidass, 1982.
Brodsky, J. "The writer in prison." In *This prison where I live.* Ed. Siobhan Dowd. New York: Cassell, 1996.
Brown, N. O. *Life against death.* Middletown, Conn.: Wesleyan University Press, 1959.
——. *Love's body.* New York: Vintage, 1966.
Buber, M. *I and thou.* Trans. R. Smith. New York: Scribner's, 1958.
Buddhananda, C., with S. Satyananda. *Moola bandha, the master key.* Monghr, India: Goenka Bihar School of Yoga, 1978.
Bugental, J. *Psychotherapy and process.* New York: Random, 1978.
Calvin, J. *Institutes of the Christian religion.* Trans. H. Beveridge. Grand Rapids, Mich.: Eerdmans, 1989.
Cantin, M., and J. Genest. *The heart as an endocrine gland.* Clinical and investigative medicine, 1986. 9(4): 319–27.

Carson, R., J. Butcher, and J. Coleman. *Abnormal psychology and modern life*. Glenview, Ill.: Scott, Foresman, 1988.

Carter S., and J. Sokol. *Men who can't love*. New York: Berkeley, 1988.

Cashdan, S. *Object relations therapy*. New York: Norton, 1988.

Chamberlain, D. *Consciousness at birth: A review of the empirical evidence*. San Diego, Calif.: Chamberlain, 1983.

Chessick, R., *The technique and practice of intensive psychotherapy*. New York: Jason Aronson, 1974.

Cole, F. *Early theories of sexual generation*. Oxford, 1930.

Collins, C. D. *The iconography and ritual of Siva at Elephanta*. Albany: State University of New York Press, 1988.

Copernicus, N. "Dedication of the Revolution of the Heavenly Bodies," in *Famous prefaces*. Ed. C. Eliot. Harvard Classics. New York: Collier, 1969.

Cortright, B. *Psychotherapy and spirit: Theory and practice in transpersonal psychotherapy*. Albany: State University of New York Press, 1997.

Coulson, M. *Sanskrit*. Chicago: NTC Group, 1992.

Courtois, C. *Healing the incest wound*. New York: Norton, 1988.

Crews, F. "The unknown Freud," *The NY Rev. of Books* (11/18/93).

———. "The unknown Freud: An exchange," *The NY Rev. of Books* (1/3/94).

———."The myth of repressed memory," *The NY Rev. of Books* (11/17/94), continued in 12/1/94, "Victims of repressed memory" and in letters to editor, 1/12/95, 2/16/95, 4/20/95).

Danielou, A. *The Ragas of northern Indian music*. New Delhi: Munshiram Manoharial, 1981.

———. *The influence of tuning and interval on consciousness*. Rochester, Vt.: Inner Traditions, 1995.

Darwin, C. *The origin of species*. Reprint. New York: Mentor, 1958 [1859].

———. *The descent of man and selection in relation to sex*. New York: A. L. Burt, 1874.

Dass, A. and Aparna. *The marriage and family book*. New York: Schocken, 1978.

Dass, B. H. *Hariakhan Baba, known, unknown*. Davis, Calif.: Sri Rama, 1975.

———. *Silence speaks*. Santa Cruz, Calif.: Sri Rama, 1977.

———. *Ashtanga yoga primer*. Santa Cruz, Calif.: Sri Rama, 1981.

DeMaria, R. *Communal love at Oneida*. New York: E. Mellen, 1978.

de Nicolas, A. *St. John of the Cross: Alchemist of the soul*. New York: Paragon, 1989.

de Rougemont, D. *Love in the Western world*, Trans. M. Belgion. New York: Schocken, 1983.

de Saint Exupery. *The little prince*. Orlando, Fl.: Hartcourt Brace Jovanovich, 1971.

Dimock, E. *The place of the hidden moon*. Chicago: University of Chicago Press, 1966.

Dossey, L. *Healing words: The power of prayer and the practice of medicine*. New York: Harper-Collins, 1993.

Dostoyevsky, F. *Notes from underground, The grand inquisitor*. Trans. R. Matlaw. New York: Dutton, 1960.

———. *The idiot*. Trans. H. Carlisle and O. Carlisle. New York: Signet, 1969 [1868–69].

Dreyfus, H. *Being-in-the-world: A commentary on Heidegger's "Being and Time."* 4th printing. Cambridge, Mass.: MIT Press, 1993.

Dworkin, R. *Law's empire*. Cambridge, Mass.: Belknap Press, Harvard University Press, 1986.

Dyczkowski, M. *The doctrine of vibration*. Albany: State University of New York Press, 1987.

———. *The stanzas on vibration*. Albany: State University of New York Press, 1992.

Eckhart, M. *A modern translation*. Trans. R. Blakney. New York: Harper & Row, 1941.

Edinger, E. *Ego and archetype*. Boston: Shambhala, 1992.

Eliach, Y. *Hasidic tales of the holocaust*. New York: Avon, 1983.

Eliade, M. *Yoga, immortality and freedom*. Trans. W. Trask. New York: Pantheon, 1953.

———. *The myth of the eternal return*. Trans. W. Trask. New York: Pantheon, 1954 [1949].

———. *Patanjali and yoga*. New York: Schocken, 1976.

Elizarenkova, T. *Language and style of the Vedic rsis*. Albany: State University of New York Press, 1995.

Epstein, M. *Thoughts without a thinker: Psychotherapy from a Buddhist perspective*. Basic Books, 1995.

Erenwald, J. *Psychotherapy: Myth and methods, an integrative approach*. New York: Greene & Stratton, 1996.

Erikson, E. *Identity and the life cycle*. New York: Norton, 1980.

Evans-Wentz, W. Y. *The Tibetan book of the dead*. London: Oxford University Press, 1978 [1927].

Evola, J. *The metaphysics of sex*. Rochester, Vt.: Inner Traditions, 1983.

Farber, M. L. *Theory of suicide*. New York: Funk & Wagnalls, 1968.

Fenichel, O. *The psychoanalytic theory of neurosis*. New York: Norton, 1945.

Feuerbach, L. *The essence of Christianity*. Trans. G. Eliot. New York: Harper, 1957 [1841].

Feuerstein, G. *Yoga, the technology of ecstasy*. Los Angeles: Tarcher, 1989.

———. *Encyclopedic dictionary of yoga*. New York: Paragon, 1990a.

———. *The yoga-sutra of Patanjali*. Rochester, Vt.: Inner Traditions, 1990b.

———. "A new view of ancient India," *Yoga Journal* 105 (July/August 1992): pp. 64–69, 100–102.

Firman, J. and A. Gila. *The primal wound*. Albany: State University of New York Press, 1997.

Foss, M. *Symbol and metaphor in human experience*. Lincoln: University of Nebraska Press, 1966.

Foucault, M. *Madness and civilization*. Trans. R. Howard. New York: Vintage, 1965.

———. *Discipline and punish*. Trans. A. Sheridan. New York: Vintage, 1979.

———. *An introduction*, vol. 1 of *The history of sexuality*. Trans. R. Hurley. New York: Vintage, 1980a.

———. *Herculine Barbin*. Trans. R. McDougall. New York: Pantheon, 1980b.
Frank, J. D., and J. B. Frank. *Persuasion and healing: A comparative study of psychotherapy*. 3d ed. Baltimore: Johns Hopkins University Press, 1991.
Frankel, V. *Man's search for meaning*. New York: Pocket Books, 1959.
Freil, J. *The grown-up man*. Deerfield Beach, Fl.: Health Communications, 1991.
Freud, S. *Civilization and its discontents*. Trans. J. Strachey. Reprint. New York: Norton, 1930.
———. *An outline of psychoanalysis*. New York: Norton, 1949 [1938].
———. *Beyond the pleasure principle*. In *The standard edition*. v. 18. Trans. J. Strachey. London: Horgarth, 1955.
———. *The future of an illusion*. Trans. W. Robson-Scott. Reprint. Garden City, N.Y.: Doubleday, 1961.
———. *Moses and monotheism*. Trans. K. Jones. New York: Vintage, 1967 [1939].
———. *Writings of Sigmund Freud*. Ed. A. Brill. New York: Modern Library, 1977.
Freud, S. and J. Breuer. *Studies on hysteria*. In *The standard edition*. v. 2 (1893–1895). Trans. J. Strachey. London: Horgarth, 1955.
Gebser, J. *The ever-present origin*. Athens: Ohio University Press, 1985.
Genova, J. *Wittgenstein: A way of seeing*. New York: Routledge, 1995.
Gimbutas, M. *The civilization of the Goddess*. San Francisco: Harper Collins, 1991.
Giovacchini, P. L. *The urge to die*. New York: Penguin, 1983.
———. *Countertransference triumphs and catastrophes*. Northvale, N.J.: Jason Aronson, 1993.
Glasser, W. *Reality therapy: A new approach to psychiatry*. New York: Harper & Row, 1965.
Govindan, M. *Babaji and the 18 siddha kriya yoga tradition*. 3d ed. Montreal: Kriya Yoga Publications, 1993.
Greenberg, G. *The self on the shelf*. Albany: State University of New York Press, 1994.
Greenwell, B. *Energies of transformation: A guide to the kundalini process*. Cupertino, Calif.: Shakti River Press, 1990.
Greer, G. *Sex and destiny*. New York: Harper & Row, 1984.
Greyson, B. "The physio-kundalini syndrome and mental illness." *Journal of Transpersonal Psychology* 25(1), 1993: 43–58.
Grimes, J. *A concise dictionary of Indian philosophy*. Albany: State Univerity of New York Press, 1996.
Grof, S. *Beyond the brain: Birth, death and transcendence in psychotherapy*. Albany: State University of New York Press, 1985.
Grof, S., and C. Grof, eds. *Spiritual emergency*. Los Angeles: Tarcher, 1989.
Grunbaum, A. *The foundations of psychoanalysis*. Berkeley: University of California Press, 1984.
Haber, R. *Dimensions of psychotherapy supervision, maps and means*. New York: Norton, 1996.
Haich, E. *Sexual energy and yoga*. Trans. D. Stephenson. New York: ASI Pub., 1978.

Haines, R. *Handbook of human embryology*. Edinburgh: Churchill Livingston, 1972.
Hamilton, G. *Self and others: Object relations theory in practice*. Northvale, N.J.: Jason Aronson, 1990.
Hanh, T. N. *Living Buddha, living Christ*. New York: Riverhead, 1995.
Heidegger, M. *An introduction to metaphysics*. Trans. R. Manheim. Garden City, N.Y.: Anchor, 1961.
———. *Being and time*. Trans. J. Macquarrie and E. Robinson. New York: Harper & Row, 1962 [1927].
———. *What is called thinking?* Trans. F. Weik and J. Gray. New York: Harper & Row, 1968.
———. *Poetry, language, thought*. Trans. A. Hofstater. New York: Harper Colophon, 1975.
Hildegard of Bingen. *Book of divine works*. Ed. M. Fox. Santa Fe, N.M.: Bear & Co., 1987 [1170–73].
Hillman, J., and M. Ventura. *One hundred years of psychotherapy and the world's getting worse*. New York: Harper Collins, 1993.
Iyengar, B. K. S. *Light on yoga*. New York: Schocken, 1976.
———. *Light on pranayama*. New York: Crossroads, 1981.
Jacobson, E. *The self and the object world*. New York: International University Press, 1971.
Janov, A. *The primal scream: Primal therapy, the cure for neurosis*. New York: G. P. Putnam's Sons, 1970.
Jnaneshvar, S. *Jnaneshvari*. Trans. V. Pradhan. Albany: State University of New York Press, 1987.
Joyce, J. *Ulysses*. New York: Vintage, 1961 [1914].
———. *Finnegan's wake*. New York: Viking, 1968 [1939].
Jung, C. *Collected works of C. G. Jung*. Vol. 12 *Psychology and alchemy*. Princeton, N.J.: Princeton University Press, 1970 [1944].
———. *The basic writings of C. G. Jung*. Ed. V. DeLaszlo. New York: Modern Library, 1959.
———. *Memories, dreams, reflections*. Ed. A. Jaffe. Trans. R. Winston and C. Winston. New York: Pantheon, 1973.
Kafka, F. *The trial*. Trans. W. Muir and E. Muir. New York: Schocken, 1970.
Kahn, M. *Between therapist and client: The new relationship*. New York: Freeman, 1991.
Kaminer, W. *I'm dysfunctional, you're dysfunctional*. Reading, Mass: Addison, Wesley, 1992.
Karasu, T. B., *Deconstruction of therapy*. Northvale, N.J.: Jason Aronson, 1996.
Katz, S., and A. Liv. *The codependency conspiracy*. New York: Warner, 1991.
Kaufmann, W. *Existentialism from Dostoyevsky to Sartre*. New York: New American Library, 1975.
———. *Religions in four dimensions*. New York: Reader's Digest Press, 1976.
Kernberg, O. *Borderline conditions and pathological narcissism*. New York: Aronson. 1976.
Kerr, M., and M. Bowen. *Family evaluation*. New York: Norton, 1988.

Kierkegaard, S. *The knight of faith and the knight of infinite resignation* [1849]; *The sickness unto death* [1849]; *Concluding unscientific postscript* [1849]. In *A Kierkegaard anthology*. Ed. R. Bretall. New York: Modern Library, 1946.
———. *The present age*. New York: Harper Torchbook, 1962a [1846].
———. *Works on love*. Trans. H. Hong and E. Hong. New York: Harper Torchbook, 1962b [1847].
———. *Philosophical fragments*. Trans. and rev. H. Hong. Princeton, N.J.: Princeton University, 1969 [1844].
———. *The concept of dread*. Trans. W. Lowrie. Princeton, N.J.: Princeton University Press, 1973 [1844].
———. *Fear and trembling*. Trans. H. Hong and E. Hong. Princeton, N.J.: Princeton University Press, 1983 [1843].
Klatz, R., and R. Goldman. *Stopping the clock*. New Caanan, Conn.: Keats, 1996.
Klotz, J. *Love and transference*. Unpublished lecture given at the San Francisco Society for Lacanian Studies, 4/17/91.
Kockelmans, J. "Daseinanalysis and Freud's unconscious," pp. 21–42 in *Heidegger and psychology*. Ed. K. Hoeller. Seattle, Wash.: Review of Existential Psychology and Psychiatry, 1988.
Kohut, H. *The restoration of the self*. New York: International University Press, 1977.
———. *How does analysis cure?* Chicago: University of Chicago Press, 1984.
Kramrisch, S. *The presence of Siva*. Princeton, N.J.: Princeton University Press, 1983.
Kripalu Ashram. *Guru prasad*. Summit Station, PA: Kripalu Ashram, 1982.
Krishna, G. *Kundalini: The evolutionary energy in man*. Berkeley, Calif.: Shambhala, 1970.
———. *The biological basis of religion and genius*. New York: Harper & Row, 1971.
———. *Kundalini for a new age*. Ed. G. Kieffer. New York: Bantam, 1988.
Krpalvanand, S. *Science of meditation*. Kayavarohan, India: D. H. Patel, 1977.
———. *Krpalupanisad*. St. Helena, Calif.: Sanatana Pub. Society, 1979.
———. *Realization of the mystery: Commentary on hatha yoga pradipika*. Unpublished ms., 1989.
Kuhn, T. *The structure of scientific revolutions*. Chicago: University of Chicago Press, 1970 [1962].
Lacan, J. *Ecrits*. Trans. A. Sheridan. New York: Norton, 1977.
Lad. V. *Secrets of the pulse: The ancient art of ayurvedic pulse diagnosis*. Albuquerque, N.M.: Ayurveda Press, 1996.
Laing, R. D. *The divided self*. London: Pelican, 1965.
———. *Knots*. New York: Pantheon, 1970.
———. *The facts of life*. New York: Pantheon, 1976.
———. *The voice of experience*. New York: Pantheon, 1982.
Laing, R. D., and A. Esterson. *Sanity, madness and the family*. Middlesex: Penguin, 1973.
Lakoff, G., and M. Johnson. *Metaphors we live by*. Chicago: University of Chicago Press, 1981.

Lao Tzu, *The Tao Te Ching: The texts of Taoism.* Trans. J. Legge. New York: Dover, 1962 [1891].
Lasch, C. *The culture of narcissism: American life in an age of diminishing expectations.* New York: Norton, 1978.
Laskow, L. *Healing with love.* San Francisco: Harper, 1992.
Lati, R., and J. Hopkins. *Death, intermediate state and rebirth in Tibetan Buddhism.* Reprint. Valois, N.Y.: Gabriel/Snow Lion, 1985.
Leary, T. *Timothy Leary: High priest.* Berkeley, Calif.: Ronin, 1995.
Lee, J. *The flying boy.* Deerfield Beach, Fl.: Health Communications, 1987.
Levin, D. M. *The body's recollection of being: Phenomenological psychology and the deconstruction of nihilism.* London: Routledge, Kegan & Paul, 1985.
———, ed. *Pathologies of the modern self: Postmodern studies on narcissism, schizophrenia, and depression.* New York: New York University Press, 1987a.
———. "Mudra as thinking: Developing our wisdom-of-being in gesture and movement." In *Heidegger and Asian thought.* Ed. G. Parks. Honolulu: University of Hawaii Press, 1987b.
———. "The opening of vision: Seeing through the veil of tears." In *Heidegger and psychology.* Ed. K. Hoeller. Seattle, Wash.: Review of Existential Psychology and Psychiatry, 1988, pp. 113–46.
Lomas, P. *The limits of interpretation.* New York: Aronson, 1990.
Love, P. *The emotional incest syndrome.* New York: Bantam, 1990.
Lowen, A. *Love and orgasm.* New York: New American Library, 1967.
Loy, D. "Avoiding the void: The lack of self in psychotherapy and Buddhism." *Journal of Transpersonal Psychology* 24(2), 1992: 151–79.
Lukoff, D. "Diagnosis of mystical experiences with psychotic features," *Journal of Transpersonal Psychology* 17, 1985: 155–81.
Lukoff, D., F. Lu, and R. Turner. "Toward a more culturally sensitive *DSM-IV*: Psychoreligious and psychospiritual problems," *J. of Nervous and Mental Disease* 180(11), 1992: 673–82.
Lukoff, D., R. Turner, and F. Lu. "Transpersonal psychology research review of psychospiritual dimensions of healing," *J. Trans. Psychology* 25(1), 1993: 11–28.
Lyotard, J-F. *Heidegger and the Nazis.* Minneapolis: University of Minnesota Press, 1990.
———. *The postmodern condition: A report on knowledge.* Trans. G. Bennington and B. Massumi. Minneapolis: University of Minnesota Press, 1991.
Macdonell, A. *A Sanskrit grammer for students.* Cambridge: Oxford University Press, 1927.
Machiavelli, N. *The prince.* Trans. G. Bull. London: Penguin, 1981 [1514].
MacMillan, M. *Freud evaluated: The completed arc.* New York: North Hollan, 1991.
Mahler, M., F. Pine, and A. Bergman. *The psychological birth of the human infant.* New York: Basic Books, 1975.
Malmkjaer, K., ed. *The linguistic encyclopedia.* New York: Routledge, 1995.
Marcus, S. *Freud and the culture of psychoanalysis.* Winchester, Mass.: Allen & Unwin, 1984.

Marcuse, H. *Eros and civilization.* New York: Vintage, 1955.
Maslow, A. *Toward a psychology of being.* Princeton, N.J.: Van Nostrand, 1968 [1962].
———. "Neurosis as a failure of personal growth." In *Psychopathology today: Experimentation, theory, and research.* Ed. W. S. Sahakian. Itasca, Ill.: Peacock, 1970.
Masson, J. *The assault on truth: Freud's suppression of the seduction theory.* New York: Penguin, 1984.
McClelland, D., and C. Kirshnit. "The effect of motivational arousal through films on salivary immunoglobin A." *Psychology and Health* (2), 1987: 31–52.
McKenna, T. *Food of the gods.* New York: Bantam, 1993.
Melville, H. *Billy Budd, sailor, and other stories.* New York: Penguin, 1986.
Menon, R. *The Penguin dictionary of Indian classical music.* New York: Penguin, 1995.
Merleau-Ponty, M. *The essential writings of Merleau-Ponty.* Ed. A. Fisher. New York: Hartcourt, Brace, World, 1969.
Metzner, R. "The Buddhist six-world model of consciousness and reality." *Journal of Transpersonal Psychology* 28(2), 1996: 155–66.
Miller, A. *Pictures of childhood.* New York: Farrar, Strauss, Giroux, 1986.
Miller, J. "The unveiling of traumatic memories and emotions through mindfulness and concentration meditation: Clinical implications and three case histories." *Journal of Transpersonal Psychology* 25(2), 1993: 169–80.
Mindell, A. *Working with the dreaming body.* London: Arkana, 1985.
Minuchin, S. *Families and family therapy.* Cambridge, Mass.: Harvard University Press, 1974.
Monier-Williams, M. *A Sanskrit dictionary.* Oxford: Oxford University Press, 1990.
Monk, R. *Ludwig Wittgenstein: The duty of genius.* New York: Penguin, 1990.
Mookerjie, A. *The tantric way.* Boston: Little & Brown, 1977.
———. *Kundalini: The arousal of the inner energy.* New York: Destiny, 1982.
Moore, T. *Care of the soul.* New York: Harper, 1992.
Morris, D. *The naked ape.* New York: Dell, 1967.
Moses, P. J. *The voice of neurosis.* New York: Grune & Stratton, 1954.
Motoyama, H. *The theory of the chakras.* Wheaton, Ill.: Quest, 1981.
Muktananda, S. *The play of consciousness.* Campbell, Calif.: Shree Gurudev Ashram, 1974.
Neumann, E. *The origins and history of consciousness.* Princeton, N.J.: Princeton University Press, 1954.
Nietzsche, F. *On the genealogy of morals* Trans. W. Kaufmann. New York: Vintage, 1969 [1887].
———. *Thus spake Zarathustra.* Trans. W. Kaufmann. In *The portable Nietzsche.* New York: Viking, 1970 [1883–85].
———. *The birth of tragedy.* Trans. S. Whiteside. New York: Penguin, 1993 [1872].
Nisargadatta, M. *I am that.* Trans. M. Frydman. Bombay: Chetana, 1979.
Norwood, R. *Women who love too much.* Los Angeles: Tarcher, 1985.

Osoff, J. "Reflections of *Shaktipat*: Psychosis or the rise of *kundalini*? A case study," *Journal of Transpersonal Psychology* 25(1), 1993: 29–42.
Otto, R. *Mysticism, East and West*. Wheaton, Ill.: Quest, 1987 [1932].
Oxford compact English Dictionary. Oxford: Oxford University Press, 1994.
Papineau, D. *The philosophy of science*. Oxford: Oxford University Press, 1996.
———. Review of *The origins of virture* and *Bonobo* in *New York Times Book Review* (5/11/97): 13–14.
Parnell, L. "Eye movement desensitization and reprocessing (EMDR) and spiritual unfolding." In *Journal of Transpersonal Psychology* 28(2), 1996: 129–53.
Perls, F. *Gestalt therapy verbatim*. New York: Bantam, 1976.
Perry, J. *The far side of madness*. Englewood Cliffs, N.J.: Prentice Hall, 1974.
Peterman, J. *Philosophy as therapy: An interpretation and defense of Wittgenstein's later philosophical project*. Albany: State University of New York Press, 1992.
Quine, W. *Ontological relativism and other essays*. New York: Columbia University Press, 1967.
Rajarsri, M. *Yogic experiences*. Kayavarohan, India: D. H. Patel, 1977.
Rama, S., S. Ajaya, and R. Ballantine. *Yoga and psychotherapy*. Honesdale, Pa.: Himalayan Institute, 1976.
Ramanujan, A., ed. & trans. *Speaking of Siva*. Baltimore: Penguin, 1973.
Ranade, R. *Jnaneshvar, the gurus's guru*. Albany: State University of New York Press, 1994.
Raphael, S. J. *Finding love*. New York: Jove, 1984.
Reich, W. *The function of the orgasm*. Trans. V. Carfagano. New York: Simon & Schuster, 1973.
———. *The sexual revolution*. Trans. T. Wolfe. New York: Farrar, Strauss, & Giroux, 1974 [1945].
Rein, G., and R. M. McCraty. "Long-term effects of compassion on salivary IgA," *Psychosomatic Medicine* 56(2), 1994: 171–72.
Rein, G., R. M. McCraty, and M. Atkinson. "Effects of positive and negative emotions on salivary IgA," *Journal for the Advancement of Medicine* 8(2), 1995: 87–105.
Rele, V. *The mysterious kundalini: The physical basis of the kundalini, (hatha) yoga in terms of Western anatomy and physiology*. 10th ed. Bombay: Taraporevala, 1960 [1927].
Richardson, W. "The mirror inside: The problem of the self," pp. 95–112 and "The place of the unconscious in Heidegger," pp. 176–98, in *Heidegger and psychology*. Ed. K. Hoeller. Seattle, Wash.: Review of Existential Psychology and Psychiatry, 1988.
Rilke, M. *Letters to a young poet*. Trans. M. Herter. New York: Norton, 1934.
———. *Duinos elegies*. Trans. J. B. Leishman and S. Spender. New York: Norton, 1939.
Robinson, R. *Survivors of suicide*. Santa Monica, Calif.: IBS, 1989.
Rogers, C. *On becoming a person*. New York: Houghton Mifflin, 1961.
Rolt, C. E. *Dionysius the areopagite on the divine names and the mystical theology*. New York: Macmillan, 1966.

Rorty, R. *Objectivity, relativism, and truth.* Cambridge, England: Cambridge University Press, 1996 [1991].
Roszak, T. *The making of a counter culture.* Garden City, N.Y.: Anchor, 1969.
Rothberg, J. *Technicians of the sacred.* Garden City, N.Y.: Anchor, 1969.
Rubin, L. *The transcendent child.* New York: Harper, 1996.
Rumi, J. *The essential Rumi.* Trans. C. Barks with J. Moyne. San Francisco: Harper, 1996.
Russell, D. *The secret trauma.* New York: Basic, 1986.
Russell, E. "Eastern meditative and Western psychotherapeutic approaches," *Journal of Transpersonal Psychology* 18(1), 1986: 51–72.
Sahakian, W. *Psychotherapy and counseling: Techniques of intervention.* 2d ed. Chicago: Rand McNally, 1976.
St. Clair, M. *Object relations and self-psychology.* Monterey, Calif.: Brooks/Cole, 1986.
St. John of the Cross. *The dark night of the soul.* Trans. K. Reinhardt. New York: Ungar, 1957.
Salinger, J. D. *Nine stories.* New York: Little, 1953.
Sannella, L. *The kundalini experience.* Lower Lake, Calif.: Integral Press, 1987 [1977]. Original title: *Kundalini: Transcendence or psychosis?*
Sansonese, J. *The body of myth.* Rochester, Vt.: Inner Traditions, 1994.
Sartre, J-P. *Being and nothingness: An essay on phenomenological ontology.* Trans. H. Barnes. New York: Philosophical Library, 1956.
———. *The transcendence of the ego.* Trans. F. Williams and R. Kirkpatrick. New York: Noonday, 1970 [1957].
Satir, V. *Conjoint family therapy: Your many faces.* Palo Alto, Calif.: Science & Behavior Press, 1974.
Satyeswarananda, G. B. S. *Babaji.* Vol. 1. San Diego: Sanskrit Classics, 1992.
Schaef, A. *Co-dependence: Misunderstood-mistreated.* San Francisco: Harper & Row, 1986.
———. *When society becomes the addict.* NY: Harper & Row, 1987.
Schleiermacher, F. *On religion: Speeches to its cultured despisers.* New York: Harper Torchbook, 1958 [1799].
Schopenhauer, A. *The world as will and representation.* New York: Dover, 1969.
Schurmann, R. *Heidegger on being and acting: From principles to anarchy.* Trans. C-M. Gros. Bloomington: Indiana University Press, 1987.
Schwarz, J. *The path of action.* New York: Dutton, 1977.
Searles, H. *Collected papers on schizophrenia and related issues.* New York: International University Press, 1965.
———. *Countertransference and related subjects.* New York: International University Press, 1979.
Shabad, P. "Resentment, indignation, entitlement: The transformation of unconscious wish into need," *Psychoanalytic Dialogues* 3(4), 1993: 481–94.
Shakespeare, W. *Hamlet.* Baltimore: Signet, 1967.
Shapiro, F. *Eye movement desensitization and reprocessing.* New York: Guilford Press, 1995.
Shengold, L. *Soul murder.* New York: Fawcett, 1991.

Shneidman, E., and N. Faberow, eds. *Clues to suicide*. New York: McGraw-Hill, 1957.
Silburn, L. *Kundalini: Energy of the depths*. Albany: State University of New York Press, 1988.
Sivananada, S. *Kundalini yoga*. India: Divine Light, 1971.
Sivaramamurti, C. *Indian sculpture*. New Delhi: Allied, 1963.
Smith, M., G. Glass, and T. Miller. *The benefits of psychotherapy*. Baltimore: Johns Hopkins University Press, 1980.
Sontag, F. *Wittgenstein and the mystical: Philosophy as an ascetic practice*. Atlanta, Ga.: American Academy of Religion, 1995.
Sophrony, A. *Wisdom from Mount Athos*. Trans. R. Edmonds. Crestwood, N.Y.: St. Vladimir's Seminary Press, 1974.
Sovatsky, S. "Eros as mystery: Toward a transpersonal sexology and procreativity," *Journal of Transpersonal Psychology* (Summer 1985): 1–32.
———. "Eros as mystery: The shared-gender mystery," *Journal of Humanistic Psychology* 33(2), Spring 1993: 72–90.
———. "Clinical contemplations on impermanence: Temporal and linguistic factors in client hopelessness," *Review of Existential Psychiatry and Psychology* 21–23, 1993: 153–79.
———. *Passions of innocence*. Rochester, Vt.: Inner Traditions, 1994.
Spence, D. *Narrative truth and historical truth: Meaning and interpretation in psychoanalysis*. New York: Norton, 1992.
Spinelli, E. *The interpreted world*. London: Sage, 1992.
Spinoza, B. *Works of Spinoza*. Trans. R. Elwes. New York: Dover, 1951.
Stern, D. *The interpersonal world of the infant*. New York: Basic Books, 1985.
Stolorow, R., B. Brandchaft, and G. Atwood. *Psychoanalytic treatment: an intersubjective approach*. Hillsdale, N.J.: Analytic Press, 1987.
Stolorow, R., and G. Atwood. *Contexts of being*. Hillsdale, N.J.: Analytic Press, 1992.
Strasser, S. *The soul in metaphysical and empirical psychology*. 2d impression. Pittsburg, Pa.: Duquesne University Press, 1962.
Sullivan, H. S., *The interpersonal theory of psychiatry*. New York: Norton, 1953.
Symons, D. *The evolution of human sexuality*. Santa Barbara: University of California Press, 1979.
Taimini, I. *The science of yoga*. Wheaton, Ill.: Quest, 1967.
Tart, C., ed. *Transpersonal psychologies*. New York: Harper, 1975.
Teilhard de Chardin, P. *The phenomenon of man*. New York: Harper, 1961.
Thirumoolar, S. *Thirumandiram, A classic of yoga and tantra*. Vol. 1–3. Trans. D. Nataranjan. Montreal: Babaji Kriya Yoga, 1993.
Time Magazine. New York: Time-Warner, August 21, 1992.
Tipler, F. *The physics of immortality*. New York: Anchor, 1995.
Tirtha, S. S. *A guide to shaktipat*. Paige, Tex.: Devatma Shakti, 1985.
Tirtha, S. V. *Devatma shakti*. Delhi: S. Shivom Tirtha, 1948.
Tola, F., and C. Dragonetti. *The Yogasutras of Patanjali*. Trans. K. Prithipaul. Delhi: Motilal Banarsidass, 1987.
Turner, R., D. Lukoff, R. T. Barnhouse, and F. Lu. "Religious or spiritual problem: A culturally sensitive diagnostic category in the *DSM-IV*," *Journal of Nervous and Mental Disease* 183(7), 1995: 435–44.

Tyberg, J. *The language of the gods: Sanskrit's key to India's wisdom*. Los Angeles: East-West Cultural Center, 1970.
Urbanowski, F., and J. Miller. "Trauma, psychotherapy, and meditation," *Journal of Transpersonal Psychology* 28(1), 1996: 31–48.
Vanmikanathan, T. *Pathway to God trod by Saint Ramalingar*. Bombay: Bharatiya Vidya Bhavan, 1976.
Vasu, R., trans. *The Siva Samhita*. New Delhi: Oriental Book Reprint Co. (no date).
Venkatesananda, S. *The concise Yoga Vasistha*. Albany: State University of New York Press, 1984.
Viscott, D. *Emotional resilience: Simple truths for dealing with the unfinished business of your past*. New York: Harmony, 1996.
Vishnudevananda, S. *The complete illustrated book of yoga*. New York: Julian Press, 1960.
Vyas, D. *Science of soul*. Rishikesh, India: Yoga Nitekan, 1972.
Waldman, M. "The therapeutic alliance, kundalini, and spiritual/religious issues in counseling: The case of Julia." *Journal of Transpersonal Psychology* 24(2), 1992: 115–49.
Walsh, R. "What is a shaman? Definition, origin and distribution." *Journal of Transpersonal Psychology* 21(1), 1989: 1–11.
Walsh, R., and F. Vaughn. "On transpersonal definitions." *Journal of Transpersonal Psychology* 25(2), 1993: 199–207.
Washburn, M. *Transpersonal psychology in psychoanalytic perspective*. Albany: State University of New York Press, 1994.
———. *The ego and the dynamic ground*. Albany: State University of New York Press, 1988.
Watts, A. *Wisdom of insecurity*. New York: Random, 1968.
Webster, R., *Why Freud was wrong*. New York: Basic Books, 1995.
Weil, A. *The meaning of the sun and moon: A quest for unity in consciousness*. Boston: Houghton Mifflin, 1980.
Weschler, L. *Seeing is forgetting the name of the thing one sees: A life of contemporary artist Robert Irwin*. Berkeley: University of California Press, 1982.
White, D. G. *The alchemical body*. Chicago: University of Chicago Press, 1996.
Whitfield, C. *Codependence: Healing the human condition*. Deerfield Beach, Fl.: Health Communications, 1991.
Whitman, W. *Leaves of grass*. New York: Signet, 1958.
Wilber, K. *The spectrum of consciousness*. Wheaton, Ill.: Quest, 1977.
———. *No boundary*. Boulder: Shambhala, 1979a.
———. "Are the chakras real?" In *Kundalini, evolution and enlightenment*. Ed. J. White. Garden City, N.Y.: Anchor, 1979b.
———. *The atman project: A transpersonal view of human development*. Wheaton, Ill.: Theosophical Publishing House, 1980.
———. "The pre/trans fallacy," *Re-Vision* (3), 1980: 51–72.
———. *Sex, ecology and spirituality*. Boston: Shambhala, 1995.
———. "Transpersonal art and literary theory," *Journal of Transpersonal Psychology* (28)1, 1996: 63–91.
Wilhelm, R., Trans. *The secret of the golden flower*. Commentary by C. G. Jung. New York: Harcourt, Brace, 1935.

Winnicott, C., R. Shepherd, and M. Davis, eds. *D. W. Winnicott, psychoanalytic explorations.* Cambridge, Mass.: Harvard University Press, 1989.

Winnicott, D. W. *Collected papers.* London: Tavistock, 1958.

———. *The maturational process and the facilitating environment.* New York: International University Press, 1965.

———. *Playing and reality.* New York: Basic Books, 1971.

Wittgenstein, L. *The blue and brown books.* Ed. R. Rhees. New York: Harper Tourchbook, 1965.

———. *Lectures and conversations on aesthetics, psychology and religious belief.* From notes of Y. Smythies, R. Rhees, and J. Taylor. Ed. C. Barrett. Berkeley: University of California Press, 1967.

———. *Philosophical investigations: The English text of the third edition.* Trans. G. E. M. Anscombe. New York: Macmillan, 1968.

———. *On Certainty.* Ed. G. E. M. Anscombe and G. H. Wright. New York: Harper, 1969.

———. *Remarks on the philosophy of psychology II.* Ed. G. H. von Wright and H. Nyman. London: Blackwell, 1980.

———. *Culture and value.* Ed. G. H. von Wright and H. Nyman. London: Blackwell, 1980.

———. *Tractatus logico-philosophicus.* Trans. C. K. Ogden. New York: Routledge, 1992.

Wolpe, J. *The practice of behavior therapy.* New York: Pergamon, 1969.

Wolstein, B. *Countertransference.* Northvale, N.J.: Jason Aronson, 1995.

Wood, D. *The deconstruction of time.* Reprint. Atlantic Highlands, N.J.: Humanities Press International, 1991.

Yogananda, P. *Autobiography of a yogi.* Los Angeles: Self Realization Fellowship, 1977.

Yu, L. *Taoist yoga, alchemy and immortality.* New York: Samuel Weiser, 1973.

Zimmer, H. R. *Artistic form and yoga in the sacred images of India.* Trans. G. Chapple and J. Lawson. Princeton, N.J.: Princeton University Press, 1984.

INDEX

abandonment, 23; and death, 128; fear of, 34–36, 85–86; and missing, 96–98
Abhanga (Jnaneshvar), 174
Absolute, 152; disbelief in, 160; time-consuming pursuit of, 162
abused adult-children, 64–65; Menendez case, 48
abused children, 35, 184; and reporting laws, 200n.4
addiction, 99, 183, 190; and impermanent progress, 187, 195
admiration, in therapy, 37–38, 53, 60–62, 92–93
adolescent speech, 145; and anahata-nada, 169; and apollonian narratives, 169; and Conduct Disorder, 191, 202n.9; and dionysian time, 169
ageing, 26, 107; parental, 128; in therapy, 115–16; and victimhood, 111–12. *See* cynicism
ajna chakra, 165; and khecari mudra, 169
alchemy, of bhakti yoga, 171; emotional, 21, 33, 154–55; and forgiveness, 88–89, 190; hermetic/breathless, 26, 168–69; as hormonal sacrifices, 155; and Krishna, 160, 171; yogic, 148–49, 205n.5, 206n.9
Allah, 188
allegorical reductions, 115
Alpert, R., (Ram Dass), 174
alternative dispute resolution (A.D.R.), 67, 75–76
ambiguities, lost, 115; and paranoia, 192

American Heritage Dictionary (1992), 161
amrita, 73–74, 164, 168, 171; and melatonin, 180. *See also* soma
Amrita-Anubhava (Jnaneshvar), 174
anahata chakra, 165
anahata-nada, 145, 164, 169–71; and infantile crying, 36, 163, 194–95; and paranoia, 192; and Pashupata ritual, 175
analogy making, and conscious mind, 103; and insight, 79; and masochism 85–87; and newness, 107–108
ananda-maya kosha, 78; and embryological development, 163
anatta, 80, 137
anger, 68–78; as bad, 72; and frustration, 70, 77; and hypopotency, 72; inducing, 71; misnamed, 68, 77; and motivation, 71; overusing, 69; perseverated, 64; releasing, 70–74; repressing, 70–73; and spiritual principles, 69–70; as weapon, 68, 76
anicca 16, 21, 80
anna-maya kosha, and embryological development, 163
Antisocial Disorder, 190–91. *See also* psychopathic disorder
anxiety, 23, 24, 34–36; archaic, 114; Kierkegaard on, 187; and uncertainty, 86
apana prana, and embryological development, 163
apollonian, moral severity, 166; religion, 147–48, 152, 187; time, 148, 195; yoga, 154, 155, 162

227

apology, 19, 22, 37–38, 87–89; and admiration, 87–88; as inconsistent, 67; repeated, 62
Arendt, H., 2
Arjuna, etymology of, 170
ars erotica, 137, 157–58; kundalini yoga as, 158
asana, 142, 147, 154, 164; in ashtanga schema, 162; becoming perfect, 158; in infancy, 163; specific to chakras, 165
ashramas, 164, 165
ashtanga yoga, 162
Atharva-veda, 155
aural fading, 111; and melancholy, 124–25
auras, 74, 164
Aurobindo, S., 60, 144, 146, 147
author-reader oneness, 102–103
Avoidant Disorder, 186
awakening to impermanence, 22, 30, 31, 79–80; and the infinite, 51, 182–86
awe, 5, 21, 24, 29, 94; and boundaries, 50; consciousness as, 80, 94; and fear, 82, 94, 182–86; of soul, 137; and suicidality, 134
ayurvedic physiology, 206n.9

Babaji (Govindan), 174
Babaji (Satyeswarananda), 174
bandhas, 164
basics of conventional therapy, 11, 20
belly dance, 153
Bergson, H., 108
Beyond the Pleasure Principle (Freud), 138
Bhagavad-Gita, 170; kundalini interpretation of, 174
bhakti, 142
bipolar disorder, and sun/moon yoga, 189
blushing, 79, 90, 91, 95, 136, 137–39; and paranoia, 193
bodhisattva, 146
body, as basis of religion, 143, 196; despiritualized, 160; as path, 2, 7, 33, 41, 47, 150–51, 163–65; as infallible, 82–83, 159; and kundalini 42, 104, 141–42, 150–51; and moral backbone, 142; purpose of, 162; as theoretical construct, 159. *See also* kundalini yoga
body psychotherapy, 82–83, 158–59
Borderline Disorder, 186, 189–90; and ego structure, 189; and missing, 98, 189–90
Boss, M., psychoanalytis, 17
boundaries, 18, 33, 43, 79, 138; and I/Thou, 50: as politico- military metaphor, 50; and respect, 50; in soteriological therapy, 193
Bouveresse, J., 11–12, 101, 102
Bradshaw, J., 13
brahmacarya, 164. *See also* postgenital puberty
Breuer, J., 15, 136
Brodsky, J., 60
Brown, N. O., 170
Buber, M., on enemy love, 53, 146; *I/it* and *I/Thou*, 50
Buddha, 144, 188; enlightenment of, 202n.9
Buddhism, Hinayana, 153; and impermanence, 16, 84; Mahayana, 153; and no self, 79; and unmani mudra, 172. *See also* anatta; anicca

Campbell, J., 151
catatonia, and meditative stillness, 189
cathartic discharge, 121, 127, 133; limits of, 145, 171, 184, 200n.3; as orgasmlike, 156; and spiritual yearnings, 171, 176; and tears, 38; and vindication, 133
Catherine of Siena, on spiritual tears, 199n.3
certainty, and familiarity, 117; and temporal conclusivity, 118, 135; and vengefulness, 112

chakras, and ensoulment of body, 207n.1; and psychoanalytic stages, 165
character, 79, 194, 196; and Antisocial Disorder, 190–91 and dispute resolution, 75–76;
Christ, 144; as Eternal Time, 39, 188; and forgiveness, 71, 202n.6 and Mary, 166; as pure love, 116–17
citta nirodha, 172
clanging, 170
client-centered inquiry, 12
clinical efficiency, 56
codependence, 93
coherency, 32; and being convincing, 67; and lifestories, 65–67; and new events, 65
Coltrane, J., 170
complaints, as longings, 56
Conduct Disorder, 191
confidence, 49, 50, 78; and deeper knowing, 84
conflict resolution, 68–69, 74–76; and character maturation, 75
Confucian formalism, 97
consciousness, and depersonalization, 181–83; as infinite, 26, 181, 185–86; and methods of mind, 103
contractions, 125–26; and suicidality, 118, 121. *See also* grammatic contraints; it's
contradiction, limitations of, 66
contrition, 67. *See also* apology
coparenting, 20, 61
countertransference, 13, 37, 124; and vengefulness, 68
crazy wisdom, 147, 170, 204–05n.3
Crews, F., 13, 20
crisis, as breakthrough, 23, 183–84
The Culture of Narcissism (Lasch), 48
cynicism, 4, 22, 23, 30, 62, 76; and ageing, 52; as certainty, 128; end of, 53; and the inquisitional attitude, 116–17; and soteriology, 76; touched by love, 122–23

Dalai Lama, 144, 183
Darwin, C., 146
dasein, 39, 50; and family therapy, 60
Dass, B. H., 174
davening, 153, 154
death, 25, 39, 46, 91, 100; by one's own hand, 118, 132; as an elsewhere, 118–20; as an end, 118; as final pardoning, 27–28, 132; as hope, 119–20, 133–34; and immortality, 173; and oblivion, 108; as a revulsion, 128; as "soon", 119; as "then", 119
The Deconstruction of Time (Wood), 16
Deleuze, G., 16
demands, as frustrated invitations, 99
denial, 183; as hope-against-hope, 43; as resistance, 116
Dependent Disorder, 186
depression, and little faith, 124; personification of, 129; and time-passage, 113, 117
dervish, 153
desire, and mystery, 80. *See also* sex desire
despair, as distant hope, 21. *See also* dread
destiny, 39, 118, 132; and the Absolute, 152
development, 30, 32, 46–47; via articulation, 104; infantile, 114; as lifelong, 144–45. *See also* anahata-nada; kundalini yoga; puberty
dharana, 142, 164, 173; in ashtanga yoga, 162. *See also* meditation
dharma, 164
dhyana, 142, 164, 173; in ashtanga yoga, 162. *See also* meditation
Diagnostic and Statistical Manual of Mental Disorders (DSM-IV), 55; cross-cultural sensitivity of, 160; and Dissociation/Depersonalization, 181–83; Religious Issues V Code, 179, 187–89; Section 316, 179–80; and urdhva-retas, 180–81

dialog, and otherness, 125
dionysian, misunderstood as debauchery, 161; religion, 147–48, 204n.2; revel, 137, 153; time, 147–48, 176, 188, 195, 196; yoga, 154, 155
Dionysius the Areopagite, 19
disappointment, 68–69, 71, 72–73; and masochism, 127–28
dissociative/depersonalization states, 181–83; and awe, 182–86; and spiritual detachment, 182–83
divya sharira, 165, 173–75; and supernormality, 174
doing time, 130, 190
doom, 117, 130
Dostoyevsky, F., execution scenario, 25; Grand Inquisitor, 116–17, 122–23; Prince Mishkin, 73
doubt, and wonder, 29
dread, 23, 25; Kierkegaardian, 51, 185–86; as projected fears, 117; and psychosis, 192. *See also* anxiety
dream interpretation, 31, 101
dualism, 147, 153; resolution of, 171, 200n.4
dynamic ground, 151; 206n.7

Eckhart, M., 144, 182; and Eye of God, 171
economy of meanings, 70, 74, 77, 144; post-Freudian, 158
economy of time, 18, 81–82; post-Freudian, 158
ecstatic, celibacies, 154; Pashupata ritual, 175; utterance, 148, 175. *See also* anahata-nada
Edwards, J., and inquisitional narratives, 114, 185–86
ego, as character, 194; precarious, 113–14. *See also* self-sense
ekstasis, 29, 39, 84
Elephanta Island, 175
Elizarenkova, T., 149, 205–06n.6
embodying soul, 71–72
embodying vocabularies, 71, 77, 159; in childhood, 163

EMDR (Eye Movement Desensitization and Reprocessing), 172
emotional transmutation, 74. *See also* alchemy
empathy, 11, 37–38; limits of, 49, 66, 124
endings, 26; and getting better, 128; as relief, 126–27; of sessions, 32–33, 115, 125; and suicidality, 120
endorphin, 164, 171
enlightenment, 27, 28, 36, 84, 172–73
entrustment, 92–93
Epstein, M., and Buddhist psychoanalysis, 66
eros, 91; as scent of impermanence, 120; and suicidality, 120, 133
Eros and Civilization (Marcuse), 158, 159
eternal recurrence, 39
eternality, 26–28
etiological past, 5, 11, 13, 14, 18, 36, 44, 107, 121; as all-consuming, 113–15, 131, 186; and bad blood, 113, 132; and the body, 159; and contradiction, 67; and demonizing parents, 54; and genetic explanations, 132; and melancholy, 116; and multiple personality, 116; and pop psychology, 115; and redemptive past, 158; and vengefulness, 59
evanescence, and mercy, 121–22
exacting standards, 58–59, 114; and Christ's love, 117; narratives of, 51, 185–86; and temporal poignancy, 113–14, 127; and The Fall, 113
execution, 25, 202n.10; and soul, 52
existentialism, 16; emotionality of, 99; and mortal ground, 97–98; issues of, 99
extrasensory perception, 101
eye contact, 62–63

failure, clinical, 48; of social programs, 47–48
faith, 35, 39, 49–50; distressful increases in, 187–88; during breakdown, 170, 182, 187–88; and humility, 53
false memories, 13
familiarity, as certainty, 117
family history, 20, 84, 115, 121; as temporal occlusion, 28. *See also* etiological past
family therapy, 39, 53–54, 60–62; and sharing missing, 96–97
family values, 7, 39; and parenthood, 40–41
fee, hourly, 60, 115; and resentment, 125, 126, 133
Feuerbach, L., on consciousness, 26; and depersonalization states, 181; on ecstatic spirituality, 176–77; on suffering in Christianity, 176–77
Feuerstein, G., on crazy wisdom, 204–05n.3; on Pashupata sect, 176; on Patanjali, 147
Finnegan's Wake (Joyce), 170
flamenco, 153
for, 43, 46, 48, 62, 78, 79, 95, 145
Forbes, J., 175
forebearance, 21; and anger, 72–74; and repression, 38, 74; as yogic tapas, 74
forgiveness, 19, 22, 38, 87–88, 202n.8; difficulty of, 122; healing power of, 68; as optional, 63, 129; as premature, 64, 129; repeated, 62–63; as spontaneous, 124, 135–36. *See also* apology; Schwarz, J
Foucault, M., on ars erotica, 157; on deployment of sexuality, 156–57, 159–60, 181; on gender, 80–81; on punitivity and vengeance, 200–01n.1; on scientia sexualis, 157. *See also Herculine Barbin*
Frankel, V., and spiritual resilience, 51

freedom, 6, 27, 74, 116–17; and evanescence, 121–22, 124; misunderstood as licentiousness, 161; from suicidal narrative, 132; and the will, 154
Freud, S., 7, 13, 14; as archeologist, 18, 82; on blushing, 91, 138; dream interpretation, 101, 105; "future of an illusion," 15, 39; genital primacy, 143; good little boy, 138; on Jung as insane, 156; pathologizes yoga, 156; and scientia sexualis, 137; and sublimation, 154. *See also* psychoanalysis
fullness of time, 27
future, 25; as bodily depth, 158–59; as doubt, 29; as expectant fantasy, 108; hermeneutics of, 201n.3; as next, 66–67, 80, 185, 106–107; and psychotherapy, 81–82, 158–59. *See also* kundalini yoga

Ganakarika Sutra, 175
Gandhi, M., 183, 191; passive resistance, 202n.6
Gebser, J., 146
gender, 80–81
genital puberty, and Conduct Disorder, 191; and infinite future, 163
Genova, J., 15
Gimbutas, M., 199n.2
giving and receiving, 89–95; challenges of, 90; clinical skills of, 90–95; phenomenology of, 90; and tearfulness, 94–95
glossolalia, 170
God, as idols, 106; as inner radiance, 155; as IS, 108; love of, 28
Goddess-worship, 153, 199n.2
Goldman, R., 180
Gorakhanath, 175
grammatic constraints, 28, 74. *See also* contraction
grandiosity, 183
granthis, 155, 204n.1

granting credibility, 92
gratitude, 21, 90; in psychotherapy, 12, 42–43; 93–95
Great Spirit, 188
grief, as missing, 45–46
Grof, S., 192
Grunbaum, A., 20

haiku, 15, 18 108, 138
Hanh, T. N., and interbeing, 79
happiness, 77, 78, 91
Hariakhan Baba: Known and Unknown (Dass), 174
Harris, R. A., it's okay, 202n.10
hatha yoga, 142, 154; as exercise, 161. *See also* sahaja yoga
heaven, 27; as cranial homologue, 148, 160, 166, 205–06n.6
Heidegger, M., on horizon of being, 65; on infinity, 182; on Nietzschean revenge, 200–01n.1; on overpowering power (deinotaton), 103; on presencing presence, 136; on principial thought, 202n.6; on reworlding, 152–53; on thinking temporally, 123–24, 136; on thinking/thanking, 13
hell, 27, 32; as indeterminable suffering, 119; psychosis as, 131
Herculine Barbin (Foucault), 80–81
heterosexuality, 80–81
Higher Power, 183
Hildegarde Bingham, 144, 146
Hillman, J., 7
The History of Sexuality (Foucault), 156, 157–58 159–60
Histrionic Disorder, 186
Holy Ghost, 153
homosexuality, 80–81
honesty, as accurate naming, 69; as negative statements, 87
honoring parental origins, 28
hope, 17, 18, 19, 23, 36, 81; alluring, 24; and cynicism, 41; as future, 25, 151; problematic of, 195; and procreation, 39–40; and relationship, 92–93; and selfhood, 92; and soteriology, 42, 88; and suicidality, 119, 121, 133, 158; tears of, 46
hopelessness, 23, 25, 76, 88; circularity of, 129–30; progress during, 55–56
hormones, as temporal precipitates, 131, 181, 147, 189, 196. *See also* alchemy; amrita; endorphin; melatonin; Nun's Study
how to, 43–44
hypergeneralizations, 13
hyperindividualism, 7
hypothalamus, 36, 146; and khecari mudra, 168, 169;

iatrogenia, 4–6, 12, 13–15, 17, 43, 95; and feigned certainty, 83–84; and needs, 59; of word *pain*, 45–46; and retrospection, 83–84; and self-help lists, 121
id, 194, 195
ideal, in glow of shyness, 138; as hoped for, 38; as real, 31, 76, 109, 183; as therapeutic goal, 95–97
immortality, 27, 107, 173; and clear light, 171
impermanence, disguised by narratives, 119; eroticism of, 136; as forgotten history, 84, 104; as given condition, 2, 16; as happiness, 29; as heartless, 127; phenomenology of, 16, 83–84; poignancy of, 27, 46; of progress, 31, 42, 195–96; slipperiness of, 29; and trying, 129–30; as visible, 171; withering effects of, 47, 56. *See also* time; time passage
independence, 93
indeterminacy, 25, 26. *See also* uncertainty
Indian music, complexity of, 150; lack of notation in, 170–71. *See also* anahata-nada
individuation, 12, 50; and shyness, 137–38

infinity, 23; as dread, 32, 184–86; wisdom of, 35
inner child, 15–16; as misnamed innocence, 137; therapeutic ruse, 112, 115, 128
innocence, 13; as endless understanding, 73; fall from, 112; and forgiveness, 124; glow of, 70; as redemptive, 64, 132, 135
inquisitional narratives, 113–14, 128. *See also* exacting standards
Institute of Holocaust Reconciliation and Remembrance, 63
intellectualization, 13
interminability, 184–86; and spiritual emergence
interrogatives, 28, 30
intersubjective field, 7
ironic emotionalities, 3, 19, 25, 29; and hidden goals, 97; and spiritual blessedness, 150
is, 124–26; as endless condition, 131, 202n.9; impotence of, 131; as missed complexity, 130–32; and paranoia, 192; as perpetual was, 131; and suicidal conclusivity, 118; to be/not to be, 130; as vengeful izzz, 133
Isaac the Syrian, on spiritual tears, 199n.3
Islam, call to prayer in, 145; whirling dervish in, 153; zikr in, 153
it/it's, 36, 118, 121, 202n.10; as effigy, 125; as hip Absolute 145, 169; as implacable, 125–26, 129; as the ineffable, 42; as unrepressed trauma, 183

jazz, 18, 122, 170
jiva, 137; and embryological development, 163
Jnaneshvar, S., and diva sharira, 174; on spontaneous yoga, 154
Jnaneshvar-gita (Jnaneshvar), 154, 174
Joyce, J., 115, 145, 170
Judaism, davening in, 153; nigune in, 145

Jungian, alchemy, 143, 154; dream interpretation, 101; and psychic energy, 156
justice, and vengeance, 132–33
justifiable homocide, 73

Kafka, F., and postmortem shame, 128
Kali, 188
Kaminer, W., 7, 20
karma, 147, 176; yoga, 164
khecari mudra, 42, 144, 164, 167–71; as bodily substrate of meditation, 167; and comparative anatomy, 168; and embryology, 168; misinterpretations of, 160; as outgrowing of linguistic articulation, 167–68; and Pashupata ritual, 175; and revitalization, 167; and schizophrenia, 181
Kierkegaard, S., on angst, 187; on category of the Infinite, 185; on dread, 51; on faith, 187; on "sickness unto death," 185, 201n.4
Klatz, R., 180
koan, 5, 77
Krishna, 148; alchemical significance of, 160, 171
Krishna, G., 146, 161, 170
kriya-vati, 161. *See also* sahaja yoga
Krpalvanand, 173; and incorruptibility, 175
kundalini awakening, 141, 155, 161, 164; and *American Heritage Dictionary*, 161; as body intelligence, 151; as charm of impermanence, 149; as dangerous, 161; defined, 141; and embryological development, 163; as mountainous ascent, 160; as rare, 161. *See also* pranotthana
kundalini yoga, and adult development 6, 8, 21, 39, 42, 82, 141, 159; and emotional sublimation, 73–74; as endogenous, 142, 146–52; and id,

234 INDEX

kundalini yoga *(continued)*
194; as motherly, 155; and nonegoic core, 194; and oversublimation, 167; as secret discourse, 157–58, 161; and spiritual body, 36, 81, 159; and Terrible Mother, 194; and unspecified complaints, 161. *See also* kundalini awakening, postgenital puberty
Kurma Purana, 175

Lacan, J., and jouissance, 138–39
Laing, R. D., 24, 31–32, 34; and mask of insanity, 55
Lakulisha, 175–76
language, as developmental phenomenon, 104, 145. *See also* anahata-nada
language games, 137; death in, 119; and lying, 191; and paranoia, 192–93; rules governing anger in, 73; and sadomasochism, 73; and vengeance, 73. *See also* Wittgenstein, L
Lao Tzu, 31, 144
Lasch, C., 7, 48
laya, 172
Leary, T., 144
Lennon, J., 13
Levin, D. M., on spiritual dance, 206n.8; on spiritual tears, 199–200n.3
liberal agenda, 6, 47–49
lifetime, as spiritual path, 21
linga, 105–106
Linga Purana, 175
logic, and conscious mind, 103; and suicidality, 118, 120, 121; and war, 118. *See also* exacting standards
longings, as distant love, 21; as fulfilling, 60; hidden in anger, 3, 56
Lowen, A., on sexuality, 156
love, 21; covered by hatefulness, 54–55, 89, 193–94; and disappointment, 78; dread in awakening to, 51; enemies, 53, 88; as high optimism, 49; and humility, 53; as merciful, 117; as nonomnipotent, 100; receiving, 89–90; as spiritual purpose, 64; unconditional, 154, 183
Lutheranism, 188
Lyotard, J-F., on academic restraint, 170; on limitations of memory, 16–17

MacMillan, M., 20
Maharsi, R., 144
mandalas, as developmental stimuli, 103–104
mania, 183
manipura chakra, 165
mano-maya kosha, and embryological development, 163
mantras, 104. *See also* anahata-nada
Marcuse, H., on hyperreppressive desublimation, 159; on spiritualized instincts, 158, 181
masochism, 38, 46, 85–87, 127–28; and missing, 96; and pop psychology, 121
Matsyendranath, 175; on breathless yoga, 206–07n.13
McKenna, T., 144
McLuhan, M., on self as verb, 78
medication, 8, 33; as temporal pharmacology, 130
meditation, 33, 39, 104–105; Burmese appreciation of, 162; and mind breathing, 168–69, 206–07n.13; stages of, 142, 144; and subtle observation, 124; and unmani mudra, 172–73
melatonin, 36, 148, 164, 171, 180
Melville, H., and Billy Budd, 73
memory, false, 13; as memorial, 108; as precarious, 17; as venegeance, 108
mensch, 5, 164, 191. *See also* character
mercy, 73, 122, 124, 135

metaphors, of causality, 199n.1, deceptiveness of, 14–16, 106; of depth, 14–16, 106; and literary analysis, 104; of mountainous heights, 166; and suicidality, 119; of time, 201n.5. *See also* symbol
metaphysical closure, 152
midlife crisis, 143
Mirabai, 144
missing, 21; affection, 96–98; and impermanence, 98; as pain, 45. *See also* Borderline Disorder
moksha, 165
Moore, T., 51
mortality, 32, 39, 97–98
Mother (The), 144, 146, 188
mudra, 142, 164; in infancy, 163
muladhara chakra, 165; and adrenalized states, 184–85; and khecari mudra, 169
multiple personality disorder, 16; and Sybil, 201n.2
mystery, 15, 18, 30, 34; as alluring, 108, 120, 121, 136, 139; of continuation, 39; of endless time, 101, 113; of God's ways, 65; maternal, 173; and morbidity, 120, 134; and *mu*, 39; as now, 41, 102–103, 124; and sadomasochism, 73; and sexuality, 80, 136, 137; and shadow, 99; and uncertainty, 80, 83, 112; and the unconscious, 100–106. *See also* next

nabho mudra, 164, 169. *See also* khecari mudra
Narcissistic Disorder, 186
narrator, as precarious, 28
needs, 57–60; developmental, 57–58, 113–14; getting met, 3, 5; hysteria, 59; infantile, 34–36; and longings, 57; recipient complicity, 58, 59; severity of, 57, 59, 114; and uncertainty, 59. *See also* exacting standards
Neem Karoli Baba, 174

neologisms, 170
new age, superficiality of discourse, 160–61
newness, as awe, grace, hope, insecurity, panic, anxiety, dread, 23; as freeing, 122; and the future, 107; and greetings, 125
Neumann, E., 146
next, 25, 30, 31, 66–67, 80, 106–07, 185. *See also* future
Nietzsche, F., 8, 36; on academic piety, 170; and death of God, 64, 196; and eternal recurrence, 16, 84, 117; and higher man, 146; on last men, 112–13; on play of impermanence, 136; and revulsion against 'It was,' 132, 190, 201n.1; and self-overcoming, 64
nigune, 145
nirbija-samadhi, 165, 173
nivritti, 164
niyamas, 21, 142, 147; in ashtanga schema, 162; in childhood, 163; as endogenous, 165–66
no-harm contract, 134
nondualism, 147, 153
nonomnipotence, and anger, 64, 72–73; and inexhaustibility, 51–52
nonself-disclosure, 11
nostalgia, and depression, 83; and dusk, 115; and session endings, 115
note-taking, as singular retrospective, 115
now, 18; living in, 145–46; as mystery, 41, 102–03, 124; as too late, 27, 125
novelty, 18, 24. *See also* newness
Nun's Study, 180

object relations, 11, 158; and self-structures, 79
obligation, fears of, 18, 40–41
oblivion, 18; and clinging, 108; and letting pass, 108
oedipal complex, 28, 81, 136
of, 44, 46, 138

ojas, 155, 171
omnipotence, feigned, 64
ontogeny phylogeny recapitulation, 163
optimism, 18, 39, 41–42, 49–51, 78
oral transmission, 147–48
Otto, R., on F. Schleiermacher, 27
Oxford English Dictionary, 72

pain, 45–46, 84; and grateful tears, 94; uncovering, 125
panic, 23, 36, 185
Papineau, D., on moral development, 194
Paranoid Disorder, 191–94; and anahata-nada, 192; and auditory hallucination, 193–94; and pratyahara, 192; and shyness, 193
Parker, C., 122
Pashupata sect, 175–76
Pashupata Sutra, 175
passions, and chakras, 165; of sublimation, 167
passive-aggression, 73, 127; disorder, 186; and lateness, 98
past, as over, 125
pastoral counseling, 52
Patanjali, 144; and ashtanga yoga, 162; and dualism, 147; formulized yoga, 147, 161, 162; on infinity, 158
Pater, W., on artist's resilience, 60
Pathway to God Trod by Saint Ramalingar (Vanmikanathan), 174
patterns, 13, 18, 24; and coherent etiologies, 67; as verb, 107
personality disorder, 136, 186, 189–94
perspicuity, 12, 43–44
pessimism, 23, 41
pineal, 36, 180; and khecari mudra, 168, 169; and shambhavi mudra, 171
pituitary, 36
Platonic cave, 104
pop psychology, 3, 4, 43, 93, 115, 121, 161; and meditation, 206n.11

postgenital puberty, 8, 164; as basis of religions, 143–44, 166; of chakras, 164; kundalini awakening as, 142; misunderstood in West, 156–57, 166, 186, 203–04n.1; rarity of, 159–62; spinal puberty 6, 104, 105, 150, 155, 160;*See also* puberties; sexuality and spirituality
posttraumatic stress, 136, 182–85; in childhood, 184; and soteriology, 88
Prabhu, A., 149, 167, 183
prakriti, 147
prana-maya kosha, and embryological development, 163
pranayama, 142; in ashtanga yoga, 162; and infantile crying, 163
pranotthana, and adult development, 123; in childhood, 34, 154, 163; and emotional expression, 77; and Pashupata ritual, 175; unknown to transpersonal psychology, 161; in world religions, 153. *See also* kundalini awakening
pratyahara, 142, 173; in ashtanga yoga, 162; in mental maturation, 164; and paranoia, 192
pravritti, 164
presence, 3, 5, 7, 18–19; as accentuating losses, 127; deep, 186, 196; as fleeting, 17; as lost, 113; in psychotherapy, 124
psychoanalytic, depth, 14–15; pathologization of meditation, 156, 159; "spell" 4, 14, 37–38, 54, 60, 86, 93; stages and chakras, 165; sublimation, 142, 143, 159; terms, 3–4, 11; unconscious intentionality, 100. *See also* Freud, S.
psychobabble, 5, 191
psychoneuroimmunology, and amrita, 179; and soteriological sentiments, 179
psychopathic disorder, 186; and lying, 191. *See also* Antisocial Disorder

psychopathology, 1, 3, 4, 186–87, 189–94; as soteriological struggles, 195; and spiritual emergence, 144; and word-choices, 24, 36, 44; and vengeance, 85
psychosis, 131; and lonely hope, 55, 99; and paranoia, 192; or transcendence, 184–86
psychotherapeutic progress, 18, 19, 30, 31, 41–43, 90–92; problematic of, 19–20, 41–43, 90; sustaining, 91–92
psychotherapist, defined, 30; as guide, 54–55, 93, 195; as idealist, 97; specialists, 64
psychotherapy, as hope, 92–93; and present-future, 81–82; as too late, 125
puberties, of eyes, 104, 164, 171–72; and identity-change, 145–46, 155, 164, 169, 172; of larynx, 145, 164; of mind, 145, 147–48, 164–65; as somato-temporal quickenings, 169; of spine, 82, 153–54, 172. *See also* khecari mudra, unmani mudra, sambhavi mudra
punctuation constraints, 28. *See also* grammatic constraints
purusha, 147

qi-gong psychotic reaction, 180
Quakerism, 153
Quine, W., and referential indeterminacy, 124
quivering, and forgiveness, 123; and khecari mudra, 171; and psychotherapy, 123; spiritual, 122–23, 153

ragas, 170
raja yoga, 153, 172. *See also* meditation
Ramakrishna, 144
Ramalingar, 174
rasa, 73
receiving, 92–95; compliments, 94; gratitude, 12, 94; love, 89–90

redemptive healing, and impermanence, 21 1, 18; and the past, 17, 36
reframing, 42
Reich, W., on desire, 155–56; and orgone, 138, 153, 156; on sublimation, 91
reincarnation, 13, 161, 173
Rele, V. G., 151
religious conversion, and *DSM-IV* V Code, 187
respect, 18
Rig Veda, 149, 205–06n.6
Rilke, R., on silence, 103, 172–73; on sublime terror, 34, 36; on unshieldedness, 50, 122
Rossi, P., on social programs, 47
Rowe, H. T., on incorruptibility, 174–75
Rubin, L., 20; on resiliency, 36–37
Rumi, 144; on inner vibration, 153
run-on sentences, as state alterers, 148, 149; and time, 5–6
Russell, B., on L. Wittgenstein, 5

sabija-samadhi, 165, 173
sadomasochistic emotions, 3, 5, 24, 76, 127–28, 132–33; and Borderline Disorder, 190
safety, limits of, 26, 33
sahaja yoga, 147, 154; and infancy, 163; marginalized, 161; and Pashupata ritual, 175
St. John of the Cross, 60, 144; and St. Theresa, 166
Salinger, J. D., 173
samadhi, 142, 171; in ashtanga yoga, 162;
samana prana, and embryological development, 163
Sannella, L., 180, 184
Sartre, J. P., 152
savitri, 149
Schaef, A. W., 14
Scheman, N., 15
Schizoid Disorder, 186
schizophrenia, 64, 205n.3; as pranic disturbance, 170, 181

Schleiermacher, F., on absolute dependence, 95; on immortality, 27
Schurmann, R., on impermanence of ultimates, 108–109
Schwarz, J., and forgiveness, 68
scientia sexualis, 136, 137, 157, 158
self psychology, 11, 50, 158
self-sense, 49–51, 78–79; in dreams, 101; as fragile, 114; as locus of hope, 92–93; as narrator, 28
separation anxiety, 34–36
serotonin, 36
sex desire, 80, 156; as derivative of impermanence, 136
sexual liberation, 157, 170; limits of, 158, 166
sexuality and spirituality, 143, 146, 154, 177, 203–04n.1; history of, 154; misunderstood, 156–57, 160, 166. *See also* postgenital puberties
shadow, as constrained emotions, 99; fascination with, 100; and light, 99; as temporal finitude, 99–100; as transmutable, 99
Shakerism, 153
shakti, 154
shamanic heat, 164
shamanica medhra, 155
shamanism, and kundalini, 141, 153; and original yoga, 147
shambhavi mudra, 164, 171–72; and EMDR, 172; and gender sense, 172; and inner marriage, 172
sharing, admiration, 40; fear, 22–23; fertility, 40; gratitude, 21; hope, 53–54; impermanence, 22, 32–33, 137, 202n.9; innocence, 136; missing, 96; in Platonic cave, 104; pride, 97; striving, 56
Shengold, L., and soul murder, 51–52
Shiva, as eternal time, 188: Dance of, 137, 147; as Lakulisha, 175
shruti, 172–73
shyness, in awakening, 21; as crux of transformation, 129, 136–39; in feeling *seen*, 87, 95; and paranoia, 193; in receiving, 12, 18; unbearable, 186–87
simha-asana, 164, 169
sinner, and the body, 159; doomed, 131; hopeless, 129; precarious, 114; worthless, 53
skepticism, 2, 3, 152
smritis, 172
Socrates, 144
soma, 149, 155, 164; and khecari mudra, 168; and melatonin, 180; and shambhavi mudra, 171. *See also* amrita
Sontag, F., on L. Wittgenstein, 5
soon, and suicidality, 119
soteriological sentiments, 1, 20–21; and *DSM-IV*, 179–83; distortions of, 3, 114, 127, 206n.10; as efflux of soul 20–21, 90–91; as endogenous, 7, 165–66; and internal harmony, 166; as introjects, 7; Judeo-Christian skew, 7, 196; lack of, 2, 66, 132; and maturation, 2, 21, 79, 88, 196; as moral teachings, 165–66; and psychopathology, 186–87, 195; and social harmony, 166, 196; as superego, 165–66; and vitality, 166; as weak, 124; working-through, 67
soteriology, 68; etymology of, 88
soul, as atman, 119; and character, 194; as diagnosable, 15, 51; divine spark, 52; as ego/superego/id merger, 194; as inexhaustible/nonomnipotent, 51–52; as infinite, 84, 185; as lost, 52; murder, 51–52, 117
speech actions, 85
Spence, D., 20
spirit of revenge, 8, 117, 200–01n.1
spiritual emergence (emergency), 4, 27, 141, 179–86; as endogenous, 143–46; as evolutionary, 146; and interminability, 184–86; and medication, 8; and soul identity, 182

spiritual jurisprudence, 75
spiritual materialism, 184
spiritual power, 4, 161
splitting, and Borderline Disorder, 190; as circular, 126–27; and impermanence, 126
Stolorow, R., and parental ineptitude, 89; and validation, 37–38; and vengeful exaggeration, 85
straight-back paths, and postgenital puberties, 153–54, 172; as repressive, 161
subtle emotions, 77, 89–90; and abused adult-children, 64–65; and newness, 108; and therapeutic possibilities, 123, 135–38
suicidality, as conclusive narrative, 117–18; and deficient vocabularies, 80–81; intimacy of, 134; and moral ought, 127; and no-harm contract, 134; and the past, 111; and repeated phrasings, 120; and romantic longing, 188; teenaged, 112; as a way out, 119, 132
superego, as inquisitor, 113–14; as soul, 3, 5, 7
sushumna, 2, 155; and moral rectitude, 166
suspense, 65
suspiciousness, 13, 15, 16, 17, 38; and inquiry, 87; in receiving, 94, 96; and wonder, 22, 94
svadhishthana chakra, 165
symbol, 103–106; as academic contrivance, 106, 148, 205n.4
Symons, D., on evolution of sexuality, 146

tai chi, 144, 153
tantra, and brain evolution, 146; defined, 142; dieties, 166; and gazing, 172; misunderstood, 160–61
Taoist, metaphysics, 16; yoga, 142
Tarasoff law, 200n.4
Taylor, C., 170

tears, of gratitude, 94–95; spiritual, 38, 199–200n.3
Teilhard de Chardin, 146
tejas, 164
temporal balance, 8, 81–82
temporal poignancy, in "life is too short, " 99; misinterpreted, 113–14; and suicidality, 118, 127; and war declarations, 118
termination, 128, 190
then, and suicidality, 119. *See also* next
Theresa of Avila, 144; and St. John of the Cross, 166
Thomas, D., on language and behavior, 48–49
time, distortions of, 16, 182; Grace, 2; as incessant flux, 5, 16; metaphors of, 201n.5; as past-present-future, 108; preciousness of, 46, 134; problematics of, 2, 5, 112, 184–86. *See also* impermanence; time passage
time passage, 41, 186; and fifty-minute hour, 25, 115, 126; as malevolent, 112; as slipping away, 111–12, 117, 129; as too late, 113; as weakness, 125. *See also* impermanence
to, 43–44, 62, 77, 104, 193
too good to be true, 23, 61, 89, 90; mercy as, 124; progress as, 127–28, 195; reconciliations as, 63
Tractatus Logico-philosophicus (Wittgenstein), 42
transference, 20, 124; as nuances of hope, 136; and vengefulness, 127
transmute, 74
transpersonal psychology, 143–44; and the body, 158; and kundalini, 161; terminology of, 79, 194, 203–04n.1
triangulation, 29, 62
Truffault, F., *The 400 Blows*, 132
Tweedie, I., 144

udana prana, and embryological development, 163

uju-kaya, 153
uncertainty, 22, 25, 33, 36; as danger, 191–92; and fear, 80, 82; and progress, 30
unconscious, 15, 100–106; known via awe, 101–106; as puzzle, 101. *See also* mystery
unmani mudra, 164–65, 171, 172; and Buddhist meditation, 172
urdhva-retas, and alchemy, 154, 171; chakra location, 165; defined, 154; and still meditations, 172; and sublimation, 154–55; and upright spine, 175
urgency, 35, 36; crises as, 184; as erotic, 136; as too late, 27, 113
uroboric play, 44, 52; and yogic alchemy, 155

vague feelings, 26, 73
vairagya, 182–83
Vayu Purana, 175
vengeance, 8, 18, 24; against It Was, 125, 133; circularity of, 132–33; collapse of, 75, 129, 135, 150, 202n.9; cultural, 200–01n.1; and eternal recurrence, 117; and justice, 132–33; as narrative theme, 119; as pleasurable, 127; as preferred, 88–89; as raison d'etre, 132, 186–87; as soteriological resistance, 124
Ventura, M. 7
vijnana-maya kosha, and embryological development, 163
Vinit-muni, 175
vipassana, 80
virya, 74
vishuddha chakra, 165; and khecari mudra, 169
viyoga, 60, 96
vocatio, 171
vulnerability, 85, 124, 137
vyana prana, and embryological development, 163

Washburn, M., on spiritual development, 143–44, 200n.5, 206n.7; on spirituality and sexuality, 203–04n.1
Watts, A., 36
Webster, R., 20
Weschler, L., on *seeing*, 103
We've Had One Hundred Years of Psychotherapy . . . (Hillman and Ventura), 13
wheel of worldly life, irony of, 162: time demands of, 162
while, 30
Whitman, W., 97, 100; on author-reader union; 102–103 on goodness, 99
Who's Afraid of Virginia Woolf (Albee), 73
Wilber, K., 16; and postgenital development, 155, 158; and spiritual evolution, 146; on symbolic interpretation, 205n.4
Winnicott, D. W., and good enough mother, 34; on holding environment, 123; on infantile psychopathology, 114; on parental destructiveness, 54; and self-soothing, 156; on separation anxiety, 34–36; and therapeutic austerity, 66; on therapeutic rocking, 123
wistfulness, 117, 134
with, 44; it, 145, 169
Wittgenstein, L., 11, 12, 15; dream meanings, 31, 102; forms of life, 6, 21, 41, 45, 56, 57, 75; language games, 137; metaphors, 106; newness, 23; perspicuity, 5; pretending, 59; on psychoanalysis, 12; silence, 5, 42, 105, 181; standard samples, 76–77; the unconscious, 102
Wittgenstein Reads Freud (Bouveresse), 11–12, 101, 102
wonder, 29; and doubt, 29
Wood, D., on eternal recurrence, 16

wounds, 18, 51; allure of, 129; history of, 83, 85; original, 51, 60, 113; as philosophical problems, 99; primal, 51, 115, 117

xenophobia, 80

yamas, 21, 142, 147; in ashtanga schema, 162; in childhood, 163; as endogenous, 165–66
yantras. *See* mandalas
YHWH (Yahweh), as endless impermanence, 19, 108, 188
Yogananda, P., and incorruptibility, 174–75

zen calligraphy, 145
zikr, 153